MY TANK IS
FIGHT!

MY TANK IS FIGHT!

ZACK PARSONS

With Artwork by *Mike Doscher* and *Josh Hass*

CITADEL PRESS
Kensington Publishing Corp.
www.kensingtonbooks.com

CITADEL PRESS BOOKS are published by

Kensington Publishing Corp.
850 Third Avenue
New York, NY 10022

All Kensington titles, imprints, and distributed lines are available at special quantity discounts for bulk purchases for sales promotions, premiums, fund-raising, educational, or institutional use. Special book excerpts or customized printings can also be created to fit specific needs. For details, write or phone the office of the Kensington special sales manager: Kensington Publishing Corp., 850 Third Avenue, New York, NY 10022, attn: Special Sales Department; phone 1-800-221-2647.

First printing: October 2006

10 9 8 7 6 5 4 3 2

Printed in the United States of America

Library of Congress Control Number: 2006929661

ISBN 0-8065-2758-7

To Michelle

**The greatest gift a girl could ever hope for is the
dedication in a book about Nazi tanks.**

Contents

Two-Fisted Pulp History

My Tank Is Fight! is my attempt to create something informative, exciting, and not entirely serious. I like to call it "pulp history." There are plenty of books out there on tanks, planes, and even wonder weapons of World War II, but not many of those books try to make their source material exciting. They strip the inventions down to their technical details and forget about just how incredible some of the inventions were. I wanted to create a work that took all the technical details and history, then combined that with action and humor. There is no reason anyone should feel ashamed getting excited about this stuff! These inventions would be right at home in a comic book or an Indiana Jones movie.

When I was initially asked by Kensington Publishing to write a book, I pitched them several ideas. I think "Cyberspace War: The Kung Fu Holocaust" probably played best to my strength of describing elaborate head-kicking sequences in a dystopian future, but they felt that sort of book would be too "niche." That is why they asked me to write a comedic history book about some of the strangest inventions of World War II. They believed that it would have broad appeal and a real shot at making the Oprah Book Club. Did you get that joke I made there? Because they are *broads*, and it would *appeal* to them.

That is precisely the sort of cutting-edge humor you can expect from the rest of this book.

My Tank Is Fight! is based on a series of columns I wrote for the cult humor Web site Something Awful. I shamelessly stole the title from a song by The Darkest of the Hillside Thickets and slapped it over the top of a bunch of mediocre articles I had written about tanks, jets, and various other inventions of World War II. The articles were inexplicably well received, so when the time came for me to transform my Internet rambling into a book, these articles made an obvious choice.

Next to the inventions, my greatest inspiration for this book has been all the old space exploration books aimed at adolescents. I have fond childhood memories of a book about a human mission to Mars, projected to get underway by 1998, that included fabulous domed greenhouses and little adobe habitats. It was as if the authors based the books on a doodle some NASA guy had made on his notebook and decided that was science enough for them. But those books had fantastic color illustrations of rockets leaping into the sky and space conquered by square-jawed astronauts and their dreamy space wives. They told the tales of a future that I could almost believe possible, if I let my cynicism melt away. Real or not, they were inspiring to me.

Most of the inventions included in this book are the same sort of fantastic creations of minds with big ideas and little connection to reality. Some of these inventions were nearly realized during World War II, and others were years away from being possible. Some of these inventions influenced technological development for decades to come, and others were rightfully abandoned by their creators. These were big dreams of powerful weapons and new or strange technologies. I have attempted to tell a tale of a past that you can almost believe possible, if you let your cynicism melt away. I hope it's an exciting vision of a war changed by science gone out of control.

The Nazis

The majority of the inventions covered in this book are German in origin. The desperation of Nazi Germany in the latter years of World War II led to a madcap renaissance of sorts. With Germany nearly beaten, any idea that might shift the odds back in its favor was entertained. Devices and schemes that other nations rejected out of hand would often proceed through several phases of development before termination.

Excellent ideas that were simply too ambitious for a nation being beset on all sides by its enemies were pursued regardless of cost. These inventions often wasted resources and hastened the downfall of Germany.

Japan, the United States, Great Britain, and the Soviet Union all contributed incredible and often preposterous inventions during World War II as well. This book is not intended to make the Germans out to be the only nation creating silly machines; they simply had more of them. Conversely, this book is not intended to romanticize Nazi Germany. National socialism was a horrible ideology made even worse in the hands of a racist psychopath like Adolf Hitler. The Holocaust and the tens of millions of other civilian and military deaths are the greatest human tragedy of all time.

During the fictionalized portions of the book, I decided to focus on one character from the United States, one from the Soviet Union, and two from Nazi Germany. I did my best to portray all four characters as genuinely good and likeable people, as I think most of the people who fought and died in the war—in all wars—are essentially good

SECTION I

LAND

Chapter 1

Panzerkampfwagen VIII Maus

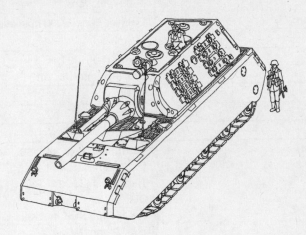

Overview

If you ever find yourself in the mood to develop the world's largest armored fighting vehicle, the Germans would like to recommend that you name it after something really small. Maybe you could go with the "Flea" or the "Amoeba," or maybe even the "Quark." The Germans went with the "Mouse," and look where it got them! On second thought, don't look where it got them, because they spent half a century divided by the nations that defeated them. But hey, no one will forget good old go-getter Germany. They say there is no such thing as bad publicity. I'm looking at you, Holocaust Museum.

The Maus is perhaps the most well known of the superweapons still under development at the end of World War II. A functional prototype was finished, complete with armament, and survives in sort-of-restored condition in a Russian museum. The Maus was enormous. It still dwarfs almost all modern armored vehicles, and adding to the mystique surrounding the Maus are persistent rumors that the completed prototype was in battle against the advancing Soviets. It is unlikely that the Maus saw combat, but it is extremely difficult not to love the Germans' ironic humor in naming their largest tank after a diminutive mammal.

Category:	Superheavy tank
Phase of Development:	Functional prototype
Development Start:	Spring 1942
Development Team:	Krupp and Porsche
Crew:	5
Weight:	188 metric tons
Propulsion:	Daimler-Benz 1,200 hp diesel engine
Speed:	13 kph
Range:	Road: 160–190 km Cross-country: 62 km
Length:	10.09 m
Width:	3.67 m
Height:	3.63 m
Armament:	1 × 128mm KwK 44 L/55 1 × 75mm KwK 44 L/36.5 1 × 7.92mm MG34 OR 1 × 150mm KwK 44 L/38 1 × 7.92mm MG34
Ammunition:	128mm—68 rounds 75mm—200 rounds
Armor (mm/angle):	Turret roof: 40/90 Gun mantlet: 240/round Front turret: 220–240/round Superstructure roof: 50–100/9 Front glacis plate: 200/55 Hull front: 200/35 Belly plate fore: 100/90 Side turret: 200/30 Hull side upper: 180/0 Hull side lower: 100+80/0 Rear turret: 200/15 Hull rear upper: 150/37 Hull rear lower: 150/30 Belly plate aft: 50/90

Development History

The development of the Panzer VIII Maus traces its roots back to 1941, when the German manufacturer Krupp began a comprehensive study of Soviet heavy tanks. It was believed at the time that Soviet tanks of the KV series were precursors to a line of Soviet superheavy tanks. With this mistaken belief came an order from Adolf Hitler to begin design on a tank to succeed the Tiger, which was at the time entering preproduction. The order specified a tank weighing up to 90 tons, armed with either a 105mm or 150mm antitank gun, with a five-man crew, and a maximum speed of 44 kilometers per hour (kph). Krupp submitted plans for two versions (light and heavy) of a tank it nicknamed "Loewe" or "Lion." Hitler put Der Fuhrer's rubberstamp on the project in 1942 and ordered Krupp to ditch the Light Lion in favor of the supersized version.

Along with the order to proceed on the Lion came a number of design tweaks. The Heavy Lion initially included 100 millimeter (mm) of frontal armor protection (the same as the Tiger) that Hitler wanted increased to 140 mm. That's over an inch of mild steel, so that's not exactly an easy adjustment when weight factors in, especially when Hitler's next request was for an increase in the vehicle's speed. The Krupp design for the Heavy Lion topped out at a pitiful 23 kph. Hitler demanded 30 kph of blood be squeezed out of the stone. "Oh, yes, Krupp designers, did we mention that the Fuhrer himself has also asked you to change that 105mm gun to the 150mm gun?" Krupp set to work making revisions while simultaneously hoping for the development of some sort of antigravity metal.

In late March 1942, Hitler pulled the rug out from under the Krupp design team on the Heavy Lion project. He instructed Krupp to join forces with one of his favorite designers, Ferdinand Porsche, in the development of a tank in the 120-ton range. To keep everyone happy, production of the eventual tank was to be split between Krupp and Alkett.

In April 1942, the Mammoth began to take shape on the drawing boards to meet a firm summer of 1943 deadline for the first preproduction model. Because of production delays in the as-yet-unseen 150mm antitank gun, Hitler agreed to a turret mounting both the 128mm KwK 44 L/55 and the 75mm KwK 44 L/36.5. These would be used until such a time as turrets and armament became available for the 150mm model. After more than a year of design and multiple name changes, the Maus emerged in the form of a wooden mockup presented to Hitler in May 1943. This design weighed in at a bridge-bending 188 tons and required a specially designed railway car for transport. Hitler ordered a production run of 150, because he liked big tanks and I cannot lie.

By the time the first turretless prototype chassis from Alkett was undergoing testing at the Porsche Boeblingen facility in December 1943, Hitler had already rescinded his production order. The prototype was dramatically underpowered, and further development continued despite the project's cancellation. By the summer of 1944, Krupp reported that four hulls were nearing completion. Shortly thereafter, all four hulls were ordered scrapped. Even then, work continued on the Maus. In September 1944, the second prototype began testing at the Kummersdorf proving ground. This V2 prototype was equipped with a partially completed turret and dummy armament for testing purposes.

When the Kummersdorf facility was overrun by the Soviets in 1945, the V2 prototype was destroyed. Accounts indicate that it was destroyed by the Germans to prevent its capture, although there is some fanciful speculation that it engaged the Soviets in the defense of Kummersdorf. The V1 prototype and a third hull section were recovered from the facility by the Soviets.

The V1 prototype survives with the repaired V2 turret mounted on it at the Museum of Armored Forces in Kubinka, Russia.

Technical Mumbo Jumbo

The original Maus prototype was powered by a Daimler-Benz aircraft engine and only capable of a top speed of 13 kph. Compared to the Maus, the original Heavy Lion design looked like a drag racer. Attempts to resolve the speed problem by replacing the original aircraft engine with a higher-horsepower diesel engine met with very little success. Because of the ponderous weight and high profile of the Maus, the tracks were extremely wide (1.1 meters each) and featured twelve return rollers on a Skoda volute suspension.

Compounding the speed problem, the Maus was also incapable of crossing almost all bridges because of its 188-ton weight. As a workaround, the Maus was equipped with an electric-drive snorkeling system capable of a fording depth of 8 meters. For those of you not up to speed on your European river depth charts, 8 meters of snorkeling depth would have left the Maus choking on water in a number of major rivers. Adding insult to injury, if a Maus ever suffered a mechanical failure on the battlefield, it was determined that two additional Maus tanks would be required for towing.

The main armament for the Maus was a 128mm KwK 44 L/55, which was virtually identical to the one mounted in the Jagdtiger. This was a very formidable weapon and could engage and destroy all Allied tanks at ranges exceeding 3 kilometers. Secondary armament was coaxial in line with the 128mm gun in the turret and consisted of a 75mm KwK 44 L/36.5. This secondary armament matched that of the early models of the Panzer IV and was intended to fire high-explosive rounds to engage infantry and softer targets. A 7.92mm MG34 machine gun was also mounted coaxially for engaging infantry. The turret was designed to be equipped with a Zeiss rangefinder, and the production model would have likely incorporated German infrared equipment (see chapter 5).

The Maus sported 200 mm-thick front armor well angled at 35 degrees. The turret was even more heavily armored. The sheer sides of the Maus were more lightly armored and vulnerable to superheavy antitank weaponry in the same class as that carried by the Maus. The thinner deck armor was also vulnerable to bombs or rockets launched from the air.

Variants

The primary production variant of the Maus was to be a version mounting the 150mm KwK L/38 in place of the 128mm & 75mm combination platter. A further upgunned version was envisioned with a nonexistent 170mm antitank weapon.

An antiair design dubbed the "Flakzwilling 8.8cm auf Maus" was also tentatively planned. This variant would have mounted two deadly 88mm flak guns in a special turret designed for engaging air targets. This version of the Maus might have actually surpassed the original in terms of all-around effectiveness. The 88mm remained a dangerous weapon throughout the entire war. Though it lacked the punch of the 128mm main gun, this would have been offset by the fact that two of them in a flak turret would have given fighter-bombers in the area something to think twice about.

Analysis

According to Porsche, the final intent of the Maus was to plug gaps in the Atlantic Wall as a (slightly) mobile fortress. A sedentary role like this would have certainly avoided the mobility problems with the Maus, but it seems ridiculous when bunkers and emplaced guns could have been—and were—produced much more rapidly and cheaply than the Maus. For a more believable view of the intended purpose of the Maus, I think it's best to look at when the project was begun. In the spring of 1942, the Germans were concerned about running into Soviet superheavy tanks. They had suffered some setbacks in the Soviet Union during the winter of 1941–42, but spring and summer saw the Germans advancing even farther into Soviet territory than before. This was a victorious Germany still on the "rise" portion of the rise and fall of the Third Reich.

Ultimately, Hitler's decision to cancel official development of the Maus in late 1943 was one of his increasingly rare good ideas. Had the Maus entered service in late 1943 as planned, it might have had a significant psychological impact on the enemy. This effect would have gradually faded as tacticians developed solid ways to take a Maus out of action. Given the pathetic speed and extremely high visible profile of the Maus, I feel this would have happened in a month or less depending on how numerous and vigorously employed the Maus was.

Considered in a vacuum devoid of the realities of war, the Maus was a mighty tank. It was armed and armored so heavily that the sight of one might give pause to an entire company of Allied tanks. Then reality, and infantry, would creep up and throw demolition charges onto it when it inevitably got stuck somewhere, or P-51s would dive from the sky and blast holes in it with rockets and bombs. Maybe a bold tank commander in a Pershing would circumnavigate it and put a plug in its rear armor. Whatever its fate, the Maus was by no means the unobtainable invulnerable tank that Hitler so desperately wanted. Instead, it was a magnificent waste of resources.

Hypothetical Deployment History

Superschweres Panzer Abteilung 400 departed from mustering near Stuttgart on December 6, 1943, under the command of Generalmajor Ferdinand Schuft. Rail bridges in the vicinity of Ulm were incapable of carrying the entrained unit, so the sixteen Maus tanks of the Abteilung were forced to dismount and ford across the Danube. Low waters were found, and the Maus tanks were able to cross without using their snorkels. Despite this, four tanks became inextricably mired in the freezing mud because of their weight and were left behind for engineering teams to recover. The remainder of the unit traveled on by rail to Krakow and was joined in late December by the surviving Maus detachment. By then, a fifth tank had become disabled due to overstressing of the suspension. It was cannibalized for parts and then dynamited by engineers of the sapper platoon. Its turret survived as a gun emplacement.

During their travel, the Maus tanks had attracted a good deal of attention, despite efforts to move in secrecy. Persistent attack by Soviet aircraft forced the tanks into nocturnal travel schedules and resulted in a sixth Maus being lost to a frozen pond concealed by snow in the vicinity of Zhitomir. Superschweres Panzer Abteilung 400 linked up with units of the Seventeenth Corp and formed a defensive line west of Zhitomir in preparation for a counterattack. A Soviet offensive to encircle Zhitomir had begun on Christmas Day and was still underway. On December 26, Schuft detached a platoon of Maus tanks to bolster the defenses within the city. German forces had already retreated into the city itself, and bitter fighting was erupting all along the eastern fringe of Zhitomir. On December 27, the Russians encountered a Maus of the Superschweres Panzer Abteilung. Eleven Soviet tanks, including two heavy tanks, were lost before the Maus was disabled by a hit to the suspension. German forces destroyed the abandoned tank, and over the following days were forced to retreat into the outskirts of the city.

Soviet forces pushed in toward Zhitomir, hammering it with artillery in an effort to close the pincer around the Germans. Generalmajor Schuft, who had been ordered to hold his remaining tanks in reserve, advanced on January 5 against heavy Russian resistance and temporarily smashed the leading edge of the northern arm of the encirclement. Two Maus tanks were disabled, but later repaired, and a third was abandoned and destroyed. Despite urgings by officers in the Zhitomir area, Hitler refused to allow retreat.

Photographs of the Maus began to appear in German and Allied print media. The U.S. and British press enraged Hitler by repeatedly referring to the Maus tanks as "Hitler's only battleships." The Germans released a newsreel showing the abteilung 400 in formation before embarkation at Stuttgart. Joseph Stalin countered soon after with footage of Soviet troops laughing and lounging on the wreckage of a Maus tank.

Encirclement of the Zhitomir area was completed by the first week of January, but tenacious resistance kept the pincer porous. Abteilung 400, by then reduced to only four Maus tanks, affected a breakout to the west through blizzard conditions with survivors from other units in the kessel. During the retreat west, all Maus tanks experienced breakdowns and were abandoned and destroyed. Further production of the Maus was halted, and Superschweres Panzer Abteilung 400 was disbanded. On March 4, Generalmajor Schuft was transferred to the top-secret Landkreuzer Befehl *Phoenix* being formed in Berlin.

What Fight Have Been

11:05 A.M., December 28, 1943
Ukrainian Front, First Ukrainian Front, Special Sniper Detachment
Zhitomir, Ukraine

Avdotya Donetskov settled like a snowflake on the fallen timbers of the second floor of the Zhitomir cinema. She did not make a sound louder than her own heartbeat. She pressed her body flat and slid forward, a centimeter at a time, until she was beneath an incidental lean-to of wood and curling wallpaper. She pulled her cloak over her furry sable *ushanka* and gave the wallpaper above her a gentle tug, so that a thin rivulet of snow powdered her head. The white scarf she wore around her neck and over her mouth directed her exhaled breath back down across her prone body. In moments, the snow falling from the sky had covered her legs and frozen *valenki* boots.

Avdotya waited patiently until she felt completely confident that she was concealed and unseen. She pressed her eyes to the German scope of her Russian rifle. She had earned the scope in one of the most harrowing sniper duels of her life. She had bested the German in the streets of Stalingrad and taken his scope as a trophy. That city had never fully belonged to the Germans, but Zhitomir still did. The majority of the fighting was still to the east, and the Soviet artillery was only just beginning to range the outskirts. Soon it would be falling all around the cinema, but Avdotya would be long gone.

In the heavy snow, Avdotya's ears proved better than her eyes, even with the German scope. She heard the clatter-clack of the tanks' treads resolving beneath the constant thump of artillery landing to the east. They became louder and louder, though the sound did not initially concern her. She had been near many of the fascists' tanks and had put lead through a dozen foolish tank commanders. The cinema was situated at the flattened top of a T intersection. The tanks appeared as ominous shapes in the blowing snow. They moved so slowly that at first she presumed them to be idling, but the sound of their engines grew louder and louder.

They were nearly a block away and already their engines were shaking the structure around her, but at last she could make them out clearly. They were mammoths, the likes of which she had never seen before. German tanks were always ugly, but these were exceptional. They were huge beasts, like slabs of iron with tracks so wide that there seemed little space between them and their boxy turrets, mounted with multiple heavy guns. They were hastily whitewashed, piled up with snow, and she could see none bore the telltale pockmarks of battle. This was something new.

Along with the tanks came the infantry. They were veterans with frozen, snow-caked beards, wearing white smocks and boots stolen from dead Russians. Many had painted their rifles white or wrapped them up in pillowcases. The column of tanks and infantry came to a halt just before the T intersection, and the commander of the lead tank jumped down from the turret. Avdotya watched him carefully through her rifle's scope. He was lean compared to the infantrymen bundled in their multiple layers of clothing. He simply wore a white parka over an insulated coverall. Though he seemed reasonably youthful, his face was heavily lined and scarred, so that the deep cuts of past battles overlapped into his prematurely weathered features.

A German infantryman began an animated conversation with the tanker, gesturing east down the T of the intersection. Avodtya knew from infiltration of Zhitomir the night before that he was pointing to the frontlines being hammered by Soviet artillery. There were hundreds of soldiers there, dug in deep with antitank guns and well-sighted machine gun bunkers. She hoped that the artillery would clear the way for the Russian advance, but it so rarely worked out that way. The Germans could burrow into the ground like root grubs and emerge from the heaviest bombardments practically unharmed.

The tanker had pulled the infantryman aside and was obviously giving the other German a good piece of his mind about what he thought of the plan of attack. The two Germans were several paces away from the tanks and sheltered in the doorway of an abandoned barber's shop. Avdotya had a perfect shot on them, and the loud rumble of the tanks might even cover the noise. She squeezed her left eye shut and took aim at the tanker's chest. At this range, she was reasonably sure of a good head shot, but with the wind and snow she was not going to take any risks. Her finger wrapped around the trigger. Her breathing stilled. Something dark swept past her line of fire.

She immediately opened her other eye and saw that it was a boy, no more than eight, wrapped up in a winter coat and running like a fool toward the column of tanks. He held a German stick grenade in one hand with the pull-pin held in the other, ready to yank it free and hurl the grenade. It was a sad distraction, but the boy's sacrifice would buy her the chance to kill both Germans instead of one. They were moving. They had seen the boy. She tried to get a line of fire, but the tanker had grabbed the boy by the wrists and was struggling with him. The boy screamed and dropped the grenade, but the pull-pin remained wrapped in his fingers. The tanker grabbed it and threw it over a rooftop, but it did not explode.

To Avdotya's amazement, the tanker shoved aside the machine pistol the infantryman had aimed at the boy. He shouted "Go home!" angrily in Russian and slapped the boy on the face. It defied belief. Avdotya would have shot a child trying to blow up her countrymen. The infantryman obviously shared her opinion as he began to yell angrily at the tanker. The German turned away to watch the boy leave by an alleyway running between the cinema and a nearby brick hostel. Something, the scope, a glint from her gun barrel, caught the tanker's eye. He looked right at Avdotya, right through the lens of her scope.

There was a fleeting moment where they were frozen together, apart from the world. Then gunfire erupted in the street below. Wood splinters showered Avdotya's rooftop shooting blind and bullets hissed past her head. With a loud whine, the lead tank's turret began to swivel toward her. It was move or die. She slid back quickly from the shattered facade of the cinema and scrambled for the stairs. She threw herself painfully down the stairs as the world exploded. A second blast tore through the ground floor of the cinema an instant later and flung her through the remnants of the back wall.

Pain shot through her ribcage as something snapped. Avdotya grunted and rolled out into snow. She tasted blood and was half blind with shock. The deadly gravity of unconsciousness dragged at her, but Avdotya resisted. She struggled to her knees and then her feet and ran for her life.

Chapter 2 ─────────────

Landkreuzer P. 1000 Ratte

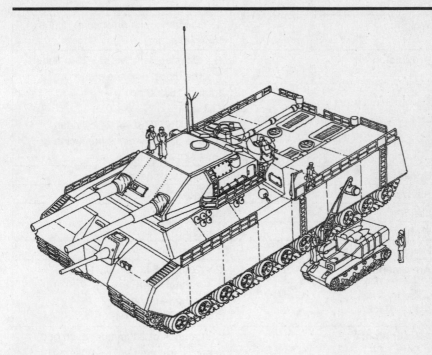

Overview

The world will probably never see an armored land vehicle on the scale of the Ratte. Tellingly, Germans didn't even refer to it as a tank: they called it a "land cruiser." The Ratte was so large that its dimensions had more in common with a naval vessel than a tank. It had the crew compliment of at least four heavy tanks, armament usually seen mounted on heavy cruisers such as the Scharnhorst and Gneisenau, and enough antiaircraft weaponry to ward off waves of attacking fighter-bombers. It was 35 meters long, as tall as some church steeples, and so wide that maneuvering in an urban area would have been either impossible or apocalyptic. The Ratte was so heavy that it would have shattered and churned pavement like a plow through sod and collapsed all but a handful of bridges in Germany.

The Ratte's much smaller cousin, the Maus, turned out to be a ru-

Category:	Ultraheavy land cruiser
Phase of Development:	Preprototype
Development Start:	June 1942
Development Team:	Krupp
Crew:	20+
Weight:	1,000 metric tons (minimum), 2,000+ tons estimated
Propulsion:	8 × Daimler-Benz MB501 20-cylinder marine diesel engines producing a total of 16,000 hp OR 2 × MAN V12Z32/44 24-cylinder marine diesel engines producing a total of 17,000 hp
Speed:	40 kph (supposed)
Range:	Unknown
Length:	35.00 m
Width:	14.00 m
Height:	11.00 m
Armament:	2 × 280mm 54.5 SK C/34 1 × 128mm KwK 44 L/55 8 × 20mm Flak38 2 × 15mm MG 151/15
Ammunition:	100 rounds of 280mm for each gun (estimated) other values unknown
Armor (mm):	(Values estimated) Turret roof: 150 Turret sides: 220 Turret front: 360 Additional armor values unknown

inous waste of resources for very limited applications in combat. Had the Ratte's development progressed even a fraction as far as the Maus, it would have devastated Germany. The Ratte was so large that it would have required naval-scale manufacturing with months of skilled laborers' time involved in the construction of each individual tank. Just building and assembling its components would have required transportation and handling equipment usually relegated to a shipyard.

It is probably to the detriment of the world that the Ratte project was canceled. It would have been cool just to see one of these hideous machines built and, more important, it would have taken the place of perhaps fifty or a hundred more useful tanks like the Panther or Panzer IV. The Ratte would have meant an earlier end to hostilities in Europe, and it would have provided a damn hot ticket at a museum in the United States or the Soviet Union.

Development History

The development history of the Ratte originates with a 1941 strategic study of Soviet heavy tanks conducted by Krupp. This study also gave birth to the Ratte's smaller and more practical relative: the Maus. From the start, the Maus was envisioned as an even larger and more formidable version of a heavy tank, while the Ratte was to be a class of vehicle unto itself.

This 1941 study produced a suggestion from Director of Engineering Grote, who worked for the U-boat arm of the Ministry of Armaments. In June 1942, Grote proposed a 1,000-ton tank that he termed a "Landkreuzer," equipped with naval armament and armored so heavily that only similar naval armament could hope to touch it. To compensate for the immense weight of the vehicle, the Ratte would have sported three 1.2-meter-wide tread-assemblies on each side totaling a tread width of 7.2 meters. This helped with the stability and weight distribution of the Ratte, but its sheer mass would have destroyed pavement and prevented bridge travel. Fortunately, the height of the Ratte and its nearly 2 meters of ground clearance would have allowed it to ford many rivers with ease.

Adolf Hitler became enamored with the idea of a truly supertank and ordered Krupp to set to work developing the Ratte. While development of the Ratte does not seem to have progressed very far, some sources believe that a turret was completed for the Ratte and then used as a fixed gun emplacement in Norway. Despite references in texts about the Ratte, there was no concrete evidence to support the existence of this emplacement. More likely, these authors have mistaken the turrets similar to those of the heavy cruiser Gneisenau for the prototype Ratte turret. The Gneisenau was broken up in 1944, and its turrets were used as emplacements near Rotterdam in Holland. Similar turrets were used near Trondheim in Norway, which was the supposed location of the Ratte turret.

Development of the Ratte was completely canceled in 1943 by the dangerously wise German minister of armaments, Albert Speer. Speer exhibited an uncanny ability to cancel the more moronic and wasteful of Hitler's pet projects and focus German resources on proven weapon systems.

Technical Mumbo Jumbo

There were two proposed power plants for the P. 1000 Ratte. One concept was powered by two MAN V12Z32/44 twenty-four-cylinder diesel engines similar to those used on German submarines. This double-engine design produced a Herculean 17,000 horsepower, and these were consequently the engines used to derive the 44 kph maximum speed of the Ratte by the Germans. The more likely engine was the Daimler-Benz MB501. This twenty-cylinder marine diesel engine was identical to that used on the German fast torpedo boats or S-boats. Linking eight of these engines would have theoretically produced 16,000 horsepower. Given that the MB501 was a more proven, inexpensive, and easier to manage engine, it seems likely this eight-engine design would have appeared in the Ratte prototype.

The primary armament of the Ratte was two 280mm SK C/34 naval guns mounted in a modified naval heavy cruiser turret fitting two of the guns instead of three. The SK C/34 was a devastating piece of artillery capable of penetrating more than 450 mm of armor at its maximum effective direct-fire range of roughly 5 kilometers. The guns could also be elevated up to 40 degrees to achieve a range of 40 kilometers. Armor-piercing and two types of high-explosive shells were available for these weapons. One difficulty facing the 280mm dual battery would have been the Ratte's inability to sufficiently depress its weapons to fire at nearby targets. At a height of 11 meters, and lacking the ability to angle its guns downward significantly, the Ratte would have been unable to fire at targets within a range of 20 to 30 meters. Accompanying vehicles would have likely accomplished this task.

Additional armament was a 128mm antitank gun such as that mounted on the Jagdtiger or Maus, eight 20mm antiaircraft guns (likely with at least four of them as a quad mount), and two 15mm heavy machine guns. The 128mm antitank gun's location on the Ratte is a point of contention among historians. The majority believes it would have been mounted within the primary turret, others believe a smaller secondary turret would have been mounted at the rear of the

Ratte near the engine decking. The rear turret makes more logistical sense, but the surface area of engine decking at the rear of the Ratte might have made this unrealistic. A third option would have been a hull-mounted version of the 128mm gun similar to that seen on the Jagdtiger. This would have at least been able to engage nearer targets than either of the other options.

Additional armament would have been spread on and throughout the Ratte. The heavy machine guns and some of the 20mm guns would have probably been mounted inside ball mounts in the hull of the Ratte. A quad 20mm flak gun could have been mounted on the extremely large top surface of the turret and additional 20mm guns mounted on the top hull at the rear of the Ratte. If they were willing to put up with the exhaust fumes, an entire platoon of panzergrenadiers could have sat atop the rear hull of the Maus.

While the Ratte was supposedly a 1,000-ton vehicle, this number was an almost mystically optimistic figure, much like the 100-ton weight intended for the Maus. The turret alone for the Ratte would have weighed more than 600 metric tons. The actual combat-loaded weight of the Ratte would have been closer to 1,800 tons. The speed, range, and longevity of the engines and transmission would have suffered accordingly.

Variants

The Ratte was a paper panzer; as such, the only real variants were the two choices of engines.

Analysis

The Ratte was a very problematic vehicle, and its size was responsible for most of the issues it would have encountered on a hypothetical battlefield. A Ratte on the move would have been relegated to fields and countryside, because of its road-destroying weight. Without bridges as a river-crossing option, the Ratte would have been unable to cross flooded or deep rivers, and scouting parties might have wasted lengthy periods and squandered lives finding a crossing point.

Gunners on a Ratte would have found it awkward to engage targets from close or medium range with even a hull-mounted 128mm gun. Concealing the Ratte from aircraft would have required a blimp hangar or some sort of bizarre camouflage that would make it resemble a building. Such camouflage is feasible, if comical, but would have been useless the first time ground units spotted the Ratte. From that point on, the Ratte would have been constantly harassed by fighter-bombers. Even if the Ratte's 20mm antiaircraft guns had managed to drive these off, it was such an enormous target that high-altitude bombers could have been employed to attack it.

Not everything was bad about the Ratte. Infantry would have been less of a risk than with the Maus, because of the number of point defense weapons and the space for infantry to ride on the vehicle's hull. The Ratte would have likely served as the cornerstone of a unit of more normal military vehicles, and these would have assisted in defending it from enemy tanks and aircraft. Enemy *armor* posed almost no conceivable threat to the Ratte. They might have destroyed things like the antiaircraft gun on the turret or damaged radio antennas or weapon optics, but beyond minor damage, enemy tanks were toys next to this mammoth vehicle. Enemy artillery was slightly more threatening and became downright dangerous if the Ratte made the mistake of straying within range of a naval bombardment.

The greatest strength of the Ratte would have been its ability to single-handedly halt a major enemy offensive. It would have been slow and poor on the attack, but the sight of a Ratte looming out of fog on a battlefield would have almost immediately scattered enemy ground forces. If they didn't flee right away, they would once they realized their weapons were nearly useless against it.

Make no mistake, the astronomical cost of building a Ratte would not have been offset by its strengths. Once deployed and used in combat, it was just a matter of time before enemy aircraft destroyed it. With its poor speed and the limitations of the terrain, the Ratte would not have enjoyed the same advantages of a wide open sea as its naval counterparts. The Ratte could have turned the tide of a single battle at the cost of a campaign.

Hypothetical Deployment History

Construction began on three Landkreuzer Rattes in July 1943 at modified shipyards in Hamburg. Bombing and attacks throughout the year delayed the construction significantly. The first Ratte was completed in March 1944, and the Ratte was moved with difficulty to a staging area east of Berlin. Training began for the crews of Landkreuzer Befehl

Phoenix as the unit awaited the arrival of its remaining two vehicles. In the meantime, a force of panzers and panzergrenadiers were formed into three kampfgruppen with a Ratte as the centerpiece of each. The second Ratte arrived in late April 1944. The third Ratte was bombed and damaged beyond repair while still under construction. The Allies believed that they destroyed an unusual light cruiser design.

On August 15, 1944, former Maus commander Generalmajor Ferdinand Schuft took charge of Landkreuzergruppe 216 consisting of one Ratte *Midgardschlange*, some thirty panzers, dozens of lighter vehicles, and almost a thousand infantrymen. The unit was to be deployed to engage Soviet forces approaching the German border through Poland, and on August 26, lead elements engaged in a moving skirmish with the Soviet tank armies. Generalmajor Schuft ordered his troops into ambush position from his command Ratte and moved his own vehicle into relative concealment inside a primeval forest. Radio aerials extending well past the treetops were camouflaged with bark and leaves.

On August 28, the tip of the Soviet advance was engaged in force and turned back without the direct involvement of the lurking Ratte. The following day the Soviets withdrew to assess the German force's disposition. On the night of August 29, the panzers and light vehicles rumbled out of the forest with the *Midgardschlange* lumbering behind them. Scouts reached the Soviet lines in the gloomy light of predawn, and the Ratte immediately began a devastating bombardment of Soviet rear echelons. The panzers and infantry advanced into the Soviet lines, and the battle grew intense.

Wondering where the heavy artillery was situated, Soviet commanders dispatched several scout aircraft. One happened upon the Ratte as it continued to move toward Soviet lines, but was shot down by antiaircraft fire before it could notify ground forces. By noon, the Ratte was visible as an ominous shape in the distance. At 12:30, the badly mauled panzers and infantry fell back with the Soviets in hot pursuit. As they pulled away, the Ratte began to open fire with its 280mm guns in the direct-fire role. Soviet tank forces were pummeled and smashed. Those vehicles that got close enough to fire on the Ratte quickly realized their folly.

Soviet tanks withdrew, and Soviet artillery batteries exchanged fire with the Ratte. The Ratte got the better of them but also began sustaining damage from the volume of fire being directed at it. By the late afternoon, most of the Ratte's antiaircraft guns had been knocked out and the 280mm guns were down to their last fifteen shells. With dusk gathering, Soviet fighter-bombers attacked in force, screaming down on the nearly defenseless Ratte. At 6:23, a 500-pound bomb penetrated the engine deck and destroyed all but two of the engines. The Ratte was incapable of doing anything more than turning slowly and rotating its turret.

Generalmajor Schuft ordered the Ratte to be evacuated and demolished, but at 6:29, a second 500-pound bomb penetrated the top armor of the turret and struck the remaining shells in the Ratte's magazine. With a roar and flash of fire, the mighty *Midgardschlange* was decapitated. Generalmajor Schuft and all but a few lucky crewmen were killed by the explosion and the ensuing fires that raged through the scarred hull.

The remaining Ratte was rushed to engage the Soviets but was destroyed by American long-range bombers long before it reached the enemy lines.

What Fight Have Been

12:28 P.M., August 29, 1944
Eastern Front, Army Group North Ukraine
8 Kilometers East of Sandomierz

Viktor Fleischer cursed and dropped down into the turret of the Panther. The hatch slammed shut behind him.

"Oberst!" Willi Bayer called from the radio operator's position.

"I am aware of your situation." Viktor yelled back over the din of the engine and yanked a long sliver of one of the radio antennas from his forearm.

Viktor glanced over at Heinrich Schöpke, who was pressed to the gun sight and had blood from metal flaking speckling his cheek.

"Armor-piercing up!" shouted Gunther Koch, who was the loader.

"Heinrich, pick your target. Try to ease things up a bit for the grenadiers." Viktor turned his head to shout down to his long-time driver Jacques "Franky" Meijer. "Franky, give him a shot and then I want you to veer northwest."

The stench of burning gasoline and propellant was nearly overpowering in the enclosed turret. Viktor surveyed the battlefield as best he could through the cupola viewing blocks.

Panzer Detachment 216, supposedly of battalion strength, was attempting to disengage from the Soviet forces of the First Ukrainian Front. They had slammed headlong into the Soviet lines and rolled them back several kilometers. Years ago, that might have been the end of things, but Marshal Ivan Konev or one of his subordinates had learned that a tank penetration did not mean defeat. Soviet Guards tanks, the more dangerous up-gunned T-34s, had come boiling out of a wooded area to the northeast. Dismounted tank infantry teams were in a hell of a bloody grapple with the panzergrenadiers on loan from Seventeenth Panzer.

Detachment 216's retreat was all part of some elaborate scheme cooked up by Generalmajor Schuft to entrap the Soviet counterattack in the *Midgardschlange*'s ranged artillery zone. Making things more difficult was the fact that whatever panzers made it out would have to navigate the immense craters left in the wake of Schuft's previous bombardment a kilometer or so to the west. Although Viktor hated the wasteful metal beast the staff officers fawned over, he was forced to admit its barrage in support of the initial assault had been quite impressive. He just hoped he would live to see it happen again when Schuft's trap was sprung.

"Tank to rear, seven hundred meters!" Heinrich called his target.

Viktor spotted it, a T-34 spinning its treads over one of the former Soviet trenches as it tried to crush the German grenadiers who had taken them.

"Fire!"

The percussion of the 75mm gun crazed Viktor's vision and jarred his bones. A tongue of flame lanced out from the long barrel, and a moment later the Soviet tank slewed sideways and spit fire from its hatches. A crewman toppled out of a hull hatch, his legs ablaze, and tumbled into the trench where he was no doubt dealt with impolitely by the panzergrenadiers.

"Good kill," Viktor said through clenched teeth. "Load me a high explosive on the next one. Heinrich, give me an infantry target."

The tank rocked as Franky rotated it to the bearing Viktor had ordered. The turret traversed at minimum speed with an electric whine and Heinrich called out a new target. Viktor peered at the mass of infantry Heinrich had spotted advancing from the woods in staggered lines. Gunther announced ready.

"Fire!"

Viktor kept his eye on the infantry despite the blast from the gun and could almost make out the wraithlike shape of the explosive round as it sailed into the tree line. The sound of the explosion was all but lost amid the din of battle, but he smiled grimly as dozens of Russians toppled over. Their advance faltered.

"Load antiarmor!" Viktor cried.

The T-34s were faster than the Major Michael Baum's Tigers driving in reverse, and the enemy was already moving to encircle the retreating grenadiers. Trap though it might be, the situation was turning into a rout. Viktor could see no more than three other tanks not counting Baum's stalwart Tigers, and most of the grenadier's half-tracks were burning. Viktor's view of the battle was already restricted by buttoning up the turret and was growing worse by the second as they passed still-burning Soviet tanks and a few killed panzers facing east. He swore and threw open the hatch again to stand in the cupola.

"Armor-piercing up!"

"Damn it all, give me a target!" Heinrich cursed.

"Ten degrees right!" Viktor shouted back. "Make it quick and you can get a rear shot!"

A low rumbling grew at Viktor's back. It was so powerful and nearly subsonic that it was more a presence than a sound, and he had to resist the urge to turn and look.

"Got him!" Heinrich replied.

"Uh, Viktor, I—" Franky called over the intercom.

"Fire!"

Heinrich did not hesitate. Heat and dust thrown up by the gun walloped Viktor in the face. It hurt a bit, but any pain was overcome by the sight of the beautiful magazine hit Heinrich had scored. The force of the explosion split the T-34 into halves that were thrown in the air like cast dice. Its severed turret spun higher and farther away from its sundered bulk, trailing metal and shredded men in its incendiary tail.

The rumble had become more overbearing. Things not firmly secured to the tank and not already vibrating from the Panther's motion began to move about. Even the burned out hulks of tanks nearby were shaking and shedding blackened plates of steel. Submerged within this sonic wave was a constant crackle and snap that seemed almost electrical. Viktor could resist no longer, he turned and faced into the noise.

Midgardschlange's arrival was preceded by the mad flight of deer and rabbits from the distant woods. The tall spruce trees began to shake as though caught by cyclones and then they splintered and toppled to be ground beneath the churning treads of the Ratte. Viktor had traveled with it in convoy for weeks and knew the vehicle to be quite slow, but as it moved at maximum speed from the woods, it seemed a charging bull with its horns the depressed barrels of the 280mm naval guns. Behind the Ratte was a swath of felled and pulped trees extending deep into the woods. No sappers followed in its wake to brace the trees upright and conceal the vehicle's passing.

When the guns spoke, all else was lost for a moment. Two explosions as large as houses blossomed at the ends of the barrels, and a split-second later Viktor rocked back in the cupola as the noise of their report rippled over him. Their shots whistled directly overhead and Viktor turned—too slow—to see the volcanic eruptions of fire, dirt, and debris they created in the mass of Soviet tanks. To their credit, or perhaps not, the Soviets did not hesitate in their advance. Viktor's jubilation at the sight of the colossal tank was tempered quickly as Major Baum's Tiger disintegrated under the heavy guns of Soviet tank-killers joining the battle.

Midgardschlange's guns devastated the advancing waves of Soviet armor, but even as the casualties mounted, Viktor knew that it would not be enough. If Konev was willing to throw an entire division in to stop the German counterattack, then aircraft would not be far behind. Soviet tanks might not be able to penetrate the immense hide of that rolling fortress, but the bombs and rockets fired from airplanes surely would.

"Get us to hull down," Viktor instructed over the intercom. "We'll cover the retreat as long as we can and then pull back behind the Landkreuzer."

Viktor's standing orders called for a complete withdrawal. He did not plan on throwing his life and his men's lives away because Schuft wanted to impress Konev with his gigantic toy. The ground heaved again, and two more shells whistled overhead. The 20mm guns on the Ratte began to spit streams of tracers, and the last dismounted reserves of German infantry opened fire from within the concealment of the forest on either side of the Ratte. Viktor shook his head and began searching out another target for Heinrich.

Chapter 3 ————————————

V-3 Hochdruckpumpe

———————————————

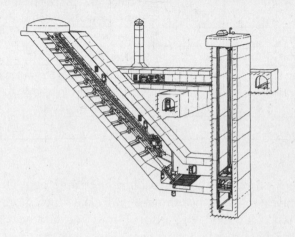

Overview

By 1944, the Allied bombings of German cities and military facilities were proving to be a public relations disaster for the Nazis. It's pretty hard to talk about how awesome the Reich is and how you are beating everyone so badly when the British and Americans are raining fire on you almost nightly. Fortunately for the Nazis, there were three wonder weapons almost ready to be unleashed on the unsuspecting Allies. In June 1944, the Germans began their exceedingly expensive bombardment of greater London using their V-1 flying bombs. Imagine a really crappy and inaccurate cruise missile that made a scary noise, and that was pretty much what the V-1s were. They were followed in September 1944 by the V-2 rockets developed by Wernher von Braun. The V-2s were a little scarier because they carried more explosives and could not be shot down.

The V designation came from the German word *Vergeltungswaffe*, meaning "vengeance weapon" or "reprisal weapon." The Nazi's suave PR cripple-footed Joseph Goebbels put the term to good use in radio broadcasts describing the horror the Nazis were unleashing on the

Category:	Extremely long-range artillery emplacement
Phase of Development:	Initial production
Development Start:	1941
Development Team:	August Coenders and Saar Roechling
Projectile:	150mm fin-stabilized projectile with 140 kg explosive charge
Barrel Length:	140 m
Muzzle Velocity:	1,500 m/sec
Rate of Fire:	1 round for every 5 minutes per gun, 1 round per every minute for the Mimoyecques battery
Range:	165 km

British as repayment for the Allied bombing campaign. Despite Nazi histrionics, neither the V-1 nor the V-2 really did much more than scare the population of London. But Adolf Hitler had another trick up his sleeve: the V-3 battery being constructed by slave labor underground at Mimoyecques, France. Unlike the V-1 and V-2, the V-3 was basically a set of five giant artillery pieces permanently aimed at London. These unusual guns used a series of explosive side chambers to accelerate a 140-kilogram shell to 1,500 meters per second and send it across the Channel and into London.

The explosive potential of a 140-kilogram charge was not that significant, but with several five-gun batteries, the Germans believed they could fire a projectile at London once every 12 seconds. Since the projectiles were not actually rockets, they could be produced relatively cheaply. As long as the underground bunker containing the V-3 guns survived and ammunition was available, the Germans could maintain a devastating barrage on England's capital. Hitler's plans for the V-3 came to a dramatic end before the first V-2 rockets began to rain down on London. With the battery nearing completion in July 1944, the British managed to drop three huge Tallboy bombs down the uncovered shafts of the V-3 guns. The bunker was heavily damaged. Before it could be repaired, the Germans abandoned the bunker in the face of the advancing Allied land invasion.

Development History

In 1941, August Coenders, an engineer at the Saar Roechling Steelworks, came up with the idea of using electrically activated charges in angled side chambers to accelerate a cannon-fired projectile beyond the maximum velocity attainable through normal means. His idea was not completely original. During the U.S. Civil War, two inventors had tried and failed to construct a similar gun and managed only to blow up their prototype. Nevertheless, Coenders convinced his bosses that his proposal was worth exploring, and they took it to the German High Command. Approval and funding was granted for a subscale prototype of the gun to demonstrate the principles behind its operation.

Construction of a functional prototype was completed in 1943. Testing commenced in May of that year in Poland under the supervision of SS General and V-projects diva Hans Kammler. The 60-meter-long miniature V-3 was successful in launching a specially designed discarding sabot round over 15 kilometers. The discarding sabot round was a dart-like submunition. Once it exited the barrel of the V-3, the case or sabot surrounding the dart would fall away, thereby allowing fins on the shell to stabilize its flight path. Those who witnessed the tests of the scaled-down V-3 were very impressed, and Hitler's love for artillery inspired him to place a preposterous order for 150 full-sized V-3 guns.

The order of 150 V-3 guns was divided into five-gun batteries. Mimoyecques, France, in the Calais region was selected as the first site for the V-3 batteries. Five of these five-gun batteries were to be constructed, theoretically allowing the Germans to fire 300 shells an hour at London from Mimoyecques. Construction began on the first of these batteries in September 1943.

Each V-3 gun consisted of interlocking 5-meter lengths of barrel with two attached side chambers where the explosive charges were placed. When connected, these interlocking tubes created a total barrel length of 150 meters all sunken into an angled shaft dug into the ground. The mouths of these gun tunnels were capped with 5-meter-thick slabs of concrete that could be slowly rotated out of the way so that the guns could fire. Surrounding the gun battery was an elaborate bunker complex with space for ammunition storage, command and control, and even sleeping quarters and a dining area. This vast complex took hundreds of slave laborers nearly a full year to prepare.

Meanwhile, the French Resistance notified the Allies of the location of the underground bunker, and in November 1944 the Allied bombing raids began. For months, these bombings did little to disrupt the construction of the bunker. Even the 5,400-kilogram bunker-busting Tallboy bombs used by the British proved insufficient to penetrate the incredibly thick concrete walls of the bunker.

The spinal columns of the V-3 guns were very unusual looking and developed several nicknames. Official German documents refer to the V-3 as a "Hochdruckpumpe" (High-pressure pump) partially as a means of concealing the weapon's true identity. The guns also developed the whimsical nicknames "Tausendfüßler" (Millipede) and "Fleißiges Lieschen" (Busy Lizzie).

In July 1944, the bunker was nearly completed, and the Germans began to prepare the V-3 battery for test firing. On July 6, an Allied bombing raid struck when the concrete domes covering the gun shafts were open. Unbeknown to the Allies, three of their Tallboy bombs dropped directly down the gun shafts and exploded inside. Dozens of unfortunate slave laborers were killed, and the bunker suffered extensive damage. Not realizing the damage they had inflicted, the Allies continued to bomb the bunker and develop new techniques in the hopes of destroying the V-3 site.

One such technique was dubbed Project Aphrodite. In a daring maneuver, a two-man crew would fly a B-17 crammed full with 10-tons of explosives toward the target. When they neared the target, the crew would bail out and a second B-17 would use a radio control stick and a crude TV system to guide the bomber into the bunker. This method was attempted several times and failed miserably, either missing the bunker entirely or inflicting no more damage than the Tallboys. Joseph Kennedy Jr., the brother of the late President John F. Kennedy, was actually killed on one of these missions when he bailed out of his bomber. Project Aphrodite was abandoned in August 1944.

By the end of August, it was clear to the Germans that the V-3 battery could not be made operational in time to fire in the face of the advancing Allied invasion force. It was abandoned by the Germans and captured by the British. On May 9, 1945, the guns were dynamited and the bunker rendered unusable by the British as a precaution to prevent the French from having a premade "London gun." Portions of the Mimoyecques V-3 complex were open to the public as of 2006.

Two additional scaled-down V-3 guns were constructed in the hopes that they could be used during the Ardennes offensive. These guns were not ready in time to bulge any battles, but in January 1945 they were used to bombard Antwerp and Luxembourg. Both guns exploded after firing only a few projectiles.

Technical Mumbo Jumbo

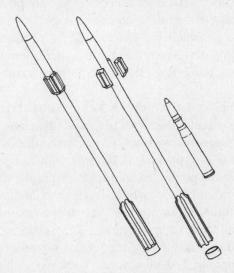

The V-3's 150mm projectiles (left) and a conventional artillery round.

The easiest way to visualize the V-3 is to picture exceptionally long 150mm cannons with short 150mm cannons attached to the barrels in pairs. A projectile is launched by the central cannon, and as the projectile travels up the barrel, these short cannons fire sequentially as the projectile passes. The short cannons are angled at 30 degrees to further enhance the velocity of the projectile with the pressure they create. By the time the projectile exits the barrel, it is traveling at 1,500 meters per second and has been given boosts by twenty-eight little cannons.

These little cannons were actually short reinforced pressure chambers packed with explosives. The exact type and size of explosive charge used is a source of some confusion. Some believe simple explosive charges were used, while others believe that the pressure chambers contained rocket motors. The charges were activated by an electric trigger, and I believe that an explosive charge rather than a rocket motor was used. The Germans wanted to cram as much force as possible behind the projectile before it exited the barrel. A rocket motor did not activate as predictably as an explosive charge, and it would have produced a constant stream rather than a burst of pressure. I believe this theory is reinforced by the damage sustained to the two V-3 guns fired at Antwerp and Luxembourg.

The gun itself was constructed from connected 5-meter-long sections of barrel ending in a pair of pressure chambers. It was the hope of the Germans that as the barrel sustained damage from the explosive forces at work inside, a failed section could simply be removed and replaced. By reducing the gun to component parts, it also greatly increased the speed at which V-3 guns could be produced. It was a lot easier for Roechling and Krupp to create 5-meter lengths of tube with pressure chambers than it would have been to create a single 150-meter-long gun.

After being emplaced, the aim of a V-3 gun could be adjusted somewhat by adding or removing wooden planks beneath the gun barrel. The guns at Mimoyecques were preaimed at London, and it can be assumed that after a day or several days of bombardment, the crews would have painstakingly added hundreds of planks to adjust the aim a degree. In this manner, a slowly creeping barrage could be created, although it was limited to only a few increments of aiming by the construction and emplacement of the guns.

The shells fired by the V-3 were unique 2.4-meter-long arrow-shaped submunitions weighing 140 kilograms. These fin-stabilized projectiles were exceptionally accurate and quite potent by artillery standards. Keep in mind that their weight of 140 kilograms represents only the casing and the explosive charge. No propellant was integrated into these shells.

Variants

Two variants—the V-1 & V-2 rockets—have already been discussed in this chapter. Many other superguns have followed in the V-3's footsteps, including the famous HARP gun used by the Canadians for launching atmospheric probes. The HARP gun propelled sensors and experiments reliably and cheaply to the edge of space in a launch vehicle very similar to the shells used by the V-3. The project was abruptly canceled in 1967 on the cusp of the first efforts to launch an orbital payload.

Analysis

Had the V-3 become operational, it would have certainly been capable of at least living up to its promise of shelling London. However, a 25-

gun battery at its most optimistically effective rate of 300 shells an hour would have taken weeks to pummel London severely. Given the failure rate of the scaled-down V3s, such a prolonged bombardment capability seems unlikely. Even if the V-3 batteries had reduced London to rubble over the course of several months, would doing so have ultimately benefited Nazi Germany? Despite their modular nature, the V-3 guns were not cheap and the bunkers that housed and served them were elaborate and expensive. When Mimoyecques was encircled by the British, the Germans did not even attempt to use these bunkers as a strong point. They were not designed to protect anything other than the V-3 guns.

Ultimately, the V-3 emplacements could have provided a potentially superior alternative to the even more wasteful V-1 and V-2 projects. That's sort of like saying a fatal heart attack is a good alternative to being thrown into the magma-filled caldera of an active volcano. You're just trading one bad idea for another. Furthermore, the V-3 guns really didn't even look very cool. They resembled the sort of thing you might see a coal cart trundling up at a working bauxite vein. Not the kind of thing you can put on a propaganda poster to strike fear into the hearts of your enemies.

Hypothetical Deployment History

Construction began simultaneously on five V-3 bunkers at Mimoyecques in July 1943. Allied efforts to bomb the bunkers met with repeated failures and barely slowed the subterranean slave labor construction. In July 1944, with the bunkers nearing operational readiness, a lucky bombing raid by the Allies knocked one of the batteries out of action. On July 27, the other four batteries began operating. It quickly became apparent that the batteries could only operate for a very limited amount of time as the Allies had a bad habit of sending planes to bomb the bunkers once shells began to hit London. After several days of bombardment and hundreds of Londoners dead, the British began to send routine aerial patrols to the vicinity of the bunkers.

On August 2 during a brief daytime bombardment period, the Allies managed to knock out two more bunkers with lucky bomb strikes, though they lost two B-17s when they collided with shells from the V-3 batteries. Allied plans called for the entire Calais region, including the V-3 site, to be bypassed in favor of a rapid advance on

Holland. However, consistent shelling from the area and the increasingly apparent failures of Operation Market Garden led Allied planners to reconsider.

In late August 1944, Canadian, British, and Czech forces began a clearing of the Calais ports. The Germans abandoned the V-3 bunkers in early September, leaving behind only a small garrison that surrendered after a short but bloody fight. The bunkers became a command post for the Canadians soon afterward. British and American intelligence experts visited the site, marveled at the size of the facilities, and joked about the pointlessness of the German endeavor. Winston Churchill even referred derisively to the artillery pieces as "Hitler's broken ladders" after announcing that the guns had been silenced in a radio broadcast.

What Fight Have Been

1:04 P.M., September 6, 1944
Operation Wellhit, HQ Seventh Canadian Infantry Brigade
Mimoyecques, France

R. E. Lincoln and his hapless army photographer, Lieutenant Louis Spacer, spent most of the day driving. They drove past field hospitals packed with wounded, past long and winding columns of German prisoners, and past more than one "point of no return." R.E. usually wasn't all that interested in returning. He would wait for the damned invasion to catch up with him if he had to. He just kept following the distant rumble of artillery like a bloodhound on the trail of a fox.

At Leubringhen, a group of Canadian MPs warned him not to drive east, so he drove east. Near Landrethun Le Nord, he caught up with a team of engineers blowing long-range batteries with dynamite. Their officer yelled at him to turn around, so he drove east. R.E. was chasing a rumor east. It was a highly classified and unofficial rumor that the bunkers that housed the guns being used to shell London daily had been overrun by the Canadians. At last, Lieutenant Spacer chauffeured him to those fabled bunkers of Mimoyecques.

"By God," R.E. cheered, "we'll beat those eggheads from the Office of Strategic Services to the prize."

Before gaining entrance to the bunker complex, they had to pass a sandbagged and heavily armed checkpoint. They were introduced to the checkpoint when a machine gun being manned by jumpy members of the Seventh Canadian Infantry's HQ detachment opened fire. R.E. got one good look at the yawning tunnel mouth disappearing into the hillside and then tracers zipped all around the jeep. The right front tire popped and the little vehicle slewed off the road into a ditch. The front end of the jeep slammed into the back end of an abandoned German half-track. Lieutenant Spacer gave himself a good crack on the jeep's steering wheel and R.E. cried out with dismay as two dozen sheets of notes and sketches flew from his knapsack.

"United States Army!" R.E. shouted as he scrambled to reach his papers before the wind took them away. "Damn it all, we're United States Army!"

A quartet of Canadians skidded to a halt in their own jeep just as R.E. finished collecting his papers. Two corporals and two privates practically tripped each other up in an effort to simultaneously apologize and make sure no one was severely injured. Two minutes of this and then a sergeant arrived and the yelling began. The noncommissioned officer (NCO) berated the men from the checkpoint, then amplified his anger and directed it at Lieutenant Spacer. He demanded a litany of signed passes, orders, and countersigned orders from Spacer. When Spacer just shrugged sheepishly, the red-faced sergeant turned on R.E. and launched another salvo of bureaucratic vitriol.

R.E. let the NCO rant for a few moments and then held up his hand. He made a show of extracting a notepad from his knapsack and flipping to a page.

"Let the Canadians prove their mettle after their past failures," R.E. pretended to read aloud from the blank notebook. "Let us see if they have in them the iron to silence the guns that fall on London. I sincerely doubt it."

When R.E.'s gaze returned to the sergeant, he was satisfied to see the man preparing to punch him in the face.

"Lord Louis Mountbatten, Supreme Allied Commander, Southeast Asia," R.E. said while he flipped the notepad closed. "I'm here to prove that no-good son of a bitch wrong, Sergeant. If you don't let me in, if you insist on holding myself and the good Lieutenant Spacer, then I will be forced to file a report with my newspaper that omits the details of your triumph."

Twenty minutes later, Captain Harold Pearlman was escorting R.E. and Lieutenant Spacer deep into the bowels of the Mimoyecques battery. Signs of the recent fight were evident within the main shaft and around the rail cars that were still laden with shells and explosive charges. Bloodstains and bullet holes marked the tide of battle on the whitewashed walls of the tunnel. Four gun shafts branched off from the main rail line into the tunnel, each serviced by an elevator and a secondary magazine. Two of the gun shafts were accessible. One of those showed signs of heavy damage from a bombing raid. The other two shafts were littered with fallen debris, partially collapsed, and totally off limits. R.E. distracted Pearlman long enough for the ever reluctant Lieutenant Spacer to surreptitiously snap photographs of these areas.

The entire compound stank of cordite and death. The smell of powder could be easily traced to the guns. The source of the stench of decay was revealed when Captain Pearlman explained that bombing raids had buried dozens of slave laborers in the gun shafts and the Germans had put no effort into excavating those trapped within. Pearlman went on to explain that the surviving laborers, numbering into the hundreds, had been shipped out like livestock by rail a few days before Mimoyecques was taken. R.E. lit his pipe to cover the smell and Pearlman nearly had a seizure.

"We're sitting on around three hundred tons of explosives!" Pearlman grabbed for the pipe.

"I'm carrying around a dozen pinches of Gold Block," R.E. said as he held the pipe away. "I do not ignite this lightly."

Hours later, with two full notepads and dozens of photographs, R.E. and Lieutenant Spacer departed in their repaired jeep. They headed west so that R.E. could file his report back to the *New York Record*. On their way, they passed a convoy of Americans in trucks and jeeps bound for Mimoyecques. Scads of officers in starched uniforms were packed like eggs into the jeeps. R.E. tipped his imaginary hat in the direction of his defeated opponents from the OSS and grinned in the face of their withering glares.

Chapter 4

Panzerabwehrrakete X-7 Rotkäppchen

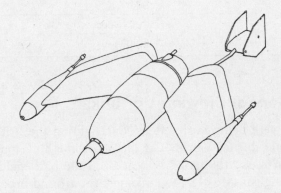

Overview

The world's most ubiquitous antitank weapon these days is the RPG-7 manufactured originally by the Soviets and now by several other nations. This weapon is a lineal descendant of Germany's World War II–era panzerfaust. What many may not know is that the advanced-guided antitank missiles used by the United States in present conflicts are also very similar to one of Germany's World War II creations.

The X-7 rotkäppchen (Little Red Riding Hood) was the world's first wire-guided antitank missile. Developed beginning in 1943 by Max Kramer, the weapon was a greatly scaled-down version of Kramer's X-4 wire-guided air-to-air missile. Capable of being carried and operated by a single man, the missile utilized principles such as wire-linked Manual Command Line of Site that remain in use with modern antitank weapons. Kramer even experimented with various types of semiautonomous infrared and optical guidance systems for the weapon.

Category:	Wire-guided antitank rocket
Phase of Development:	Trial production run
Development Start:	1943
Development Team:	Max Kramer and Ruhrstahl AG
Projectile:	2-stage wire-guided antitank rocket with a 2.5 kg hollow-charge warhead
Length:	95 cm
Wingspan:	60 cm
Weight:	9 kg
Velocity:	100 m/sec
Range:	1,200 m

A Brief History of Blowing Up Tanks

The Germans were being fairly effective in fighting the British into a bloody stalemate during World War I. Then something that military historians refer to as "the tank" appeared on the battlefield courtesy of the King's English. Mostly, the tanks just sat around broken down, but when they were working, the British gave the Germans quite a fright. The sight of those slow-moving early tanks crawling across the moonscape of a battlefield was probably much like the Aztecs catching their first face full of conquistador musket. Unlike the Aztecs, the Germans had more to fall back on than chucking a couple sacrifices down the old Tenochtitlán prayer pit. They turned their ingenuity to constructing a means to overcome the armored hides of the British vehicles.

Specialty bullets worked as a stopgap measure, but in 1918 Mauser began to mass-produce a 13.2mm antitank rifle. It was bulky and fairly difficult to operate, but it worked. The real arms race between the tank and man-portable antitank weaponry had begun.

Tanks on all sides operating during World War II were generally more heavily armored than the scant centimeter-thick hides of their World War I predecessors. All sides also fielded antitank rifles at the outbreak of hostilities, though they were only capable of penetrating the most lightly armored tanks. It was not until 1942 that the first really effective man-portable antitank solution appeared on the battlefield. The American bazooka was an electrically activated rocket grenade launcher. The bazooka was an effective weapon against the side and rear armor on nearly all German tanks, but it was by no means the best antitank weapon produced during the war.

The British-developed PIAT (Projector, Infantry, Anti-Tank) launched a heavier charge using what amounted to a big spring. Its chief advantages were that it could be fired from inside structures and it did not produce any exhaust gas that could reveal the position of the gunner. The PIAT was heavy, inaccurate, it took a long time to reload, and shells sometimes failed to detonate. Though it is widely regarded as a fairly poor weapon, it was used to great effect by some particularly courageous British soldiers.

The Germans developed two notable infantry antitank rocket launchers. Their own original design was a disposable and lightweight one-shot rocket launcher called panzerfaust (tank fist). The size of the launcher and the charge, known as a paustpatrone, escalated dramatically throughout the war. It was an effective weapon and easy to handle, though with very poor range. What made it remarkable was that it was simple and cheap to produce. Nearly every squad of infantry could be equipped with at least one panzerfaust.

The panzerschreck (tank terror) was a reengineering of captured American bazookas. The panzerschreck fired an 88mm rocket that was superior to the projectile launched from the bazooka. Unfortunately for the soldier firing the weapon, this rocket continued to expel superheated exhaust for the first few meters of its flight. The Germans had not yet developed a human face capable of enduring the exhaust from their rocket without injury. In lieu of tougher faces, a fireproof shield with a mica view port was added to the panzerschreck. This addition placed the shield in the direct path of the exhaust and turned the recoilless weapon into a weapon with a tendency to recoil its shield directly into the face of the gunner. Despite this unpleasantness, the reusable panzerschreck was extremely effective and was issued to specialist tank hunter detachments, presumably along with bandages for their repeatedly broken noses.

None of these man-portable weapons came close to matching the range of an antitank rifle, let alone antitank artillery. Their limitations forced infantry to either wait for a tank to approach to within 100 to 150 meters or charge out and assault a tank. Even if they were hiding in ambush, infantry usually only had one shot at the enemy since, other than the PIAT, the smoke and fire produced by the rocket gave away their position. Antitank rifles had the range to allow infantry to (somewhat) safely engage tanks, but they could not fire shells large enough to harm most tanks. A better solution was needed and the Germans found it in a somewhat unlikely source.

Development History

The development history of the X-7 antitank rocket began with the development of its airborne predecessor, the X-4. Max Kramer of Ruhrstahl AG began work on the X-4 guided air-to-air missile in 1943 and received a development order in the summer of that year. The X-4 was roughly 2 meters in length and consisted of four swept-back stabilizer wings, two of which spooled out guidance wire from pods on the wingtips, and four smaller tail stabilizers. The X-4 was nearly supersonic and featured a 20-kilogram warhead capable of reducing virtually any aircraft into a puff of debris. The flight of the X-4 was controlled from the cockpit or bombardier's position of the launching aircraft using two joysticks. Flares in the wingtips of the missile made the X-4 easier to visually track and guide.

Tests conducted throughout 1944 demonstrated the X-4's excellent accuracy and plans were made for the weapon to enter mass production. In 1945, thousands of production bodies for the X-4 had been completed, but the usual delays in engine production caused by Allied bombings precluded the completion and operational deployment of the missile.

Long before the war ended and the X-4 project came to an end, Kramer had moved on to smaller and more terrestrial things. Demands for a more accurate and longer-range infantry antitank weapon inspired him to adapt his air-to-air missile for ground launching. This was made even easier by the fact that Kramer had already developed a version of X-4 for the air-to-ground role.

The X-7 project began in 1944 with the goal of producing a light antitank missile capable of being carried and operated by one or two men. The X-7 was functionally very similar to the X-4. It consisted of two rather than four larger stabilizer wings and had a boom-mounted tail elevator for flight path adjustments. Like the X-4, the X-7 would rotate while in flight to increase the stability of its trajectory. The X-7 was much smaller than the X-4. It was less than half as long and much lighter in weight, partially due to a reduced fuel load.

The first test of the X-7 was conducted only months after the project began. On September 21, 1944, the first live firing of seven missiles was conducted. A target tank was placed at a range of 500 meters from the launch position. The first four missiles made contact with the ground during their flight and broke apart or exploded. The next two missiles experienced engine failures—the kind where the engine explodes. The seventh and final missile zipped from the rails and burned through its two-stage rocket motor. A little over five seconds after it left the rails the X-7 struck the tank and completely destroyed it.

Incredibly, this inauspicious test run was sufficient for the needs of the German army. An order was issued for a trial production run and a few hundred X-7 rockets were completed. Many were expended in further tests and training, but it is rumored that an unknown number were used on the eastern front in the closing days of the war. A large number of completed X-7s were captured as the Allies advanced and captured Ruhrstahl AG production facilities in Neubrandenburg and Brackwede.

Technical Mumbo Jumbo

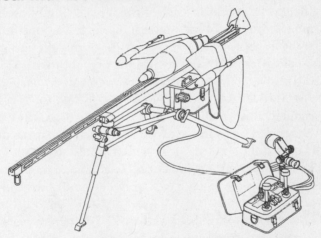

The X-7 rocket, controls, launch rail, and sighting device.

The heart of the X-7 rocket was a 46-centimeter-long fuselage containing the WASAG 109–506 two-stage rocket motor. An angled framework boom extended from the underside of the fuselage adding approximately 40 centimeters to the rocket's overall length. This boom terminated in a single elevator that served as both a horizontal and vertical control surface as the rocket rotated in flight. The 2.5-kilogram hollow-charge antitank warhead was mounted in the nose of the rocket and was detonated by a 10-centimeter-long detonator cap protruding from the rocket's nose. Two stabilizer wings with a span of 60 centimeters protruded from the rocket's fuselage and terminated in nacelles containing the spools of guide wires that doubled as gas vents.

The X-7 was launched from a 1.5-meter-long horizontal rail stabilized on top of a tripod. The rail would be rotated to aim directly at a target and the gunner would optimally be positioned in a trench or bunker as near as possible to the firing location. At launch, a 300-volt battery triggered a small gunpowder charge to propel the X-7 from its launch rail. The gas from this explosion would also be vented through the nacelles to begin the rocket's gyroscopic rotation during flight. It would rotate roughly twice per second. A fraction of a second after leaving the rail, the first stage of the WASAG rocket would activate. This would burn for 2.5 seconds and bring the rocket to its full flight speed of 100 meters per second. The second stage of the rocket burned for 8 seconds but provided much less thrust, just enough to maintain its velocity. The rocket had a maximum range of 1,200 meters or roughly 12 seconds of flight.

During flight, the operator tracked the missile by a phosphorescent tracer burning in the rear of the rocket's fuselage. The operator simply had to keep the tracer visually over the target during the rocket's flight, a technique called Manual Command Line of Sight that is still used in wire-guided missiles. Course corrections were made using two joysticks, one for vertical and one for horizontal. Response to corrections was not instantaneous because of the rocket's single control surface in the tail. If the rocket's elevator was vertical when the operator made a horizontal correction, a mechanical switch would delay the input until the rocket had rotated into position. This unique method gave the X-7 a steep learning curve and probably accounted for most of the ground contact accidents.

The X-7 detonated on impact and the 2.5-kilogram warhead was sufficient to penetrate approximately 200 mm of steel. Different fusing methods and warheads had been developed for the X-4 air-to-air missile and could likely be duplicated to provide more versatility in an X-7 battery. The entire package of launch rail, tripod, missile, and control box weighed less than 30 kilograms.

Variants

Several variants were considered for production or limited production of the X-7. These all centered on changes to the rocket's guidance system. The Steinbock (Ibex) system replaced the spools of guide wires with an infrared system for transmitting course corrections. It was basically the world's first wireless videogame controller. Another method referred to as the Pfeifenkopf (Pipe Bowl) used two sighting mechanisms for early computational guidance. One sight would be aimed at the target and the other would be used to follow the missile. Differences in angle would be calculated and used to adjust the missile's course.

There was also a TV-guided version of the X-7 under development. This version utilized an early video camera known as an Ikonoskop, mounted in the rocket itself, to acquire the target and allow the pilot to guide the missile during flight. If this design had been implemented in a manner that did not degrade the performance of the X-7, it would have been an incredible advance in the effectiveness of the missile. It would have allowed soldiers to fire the weapon from locations safely away from the launcher. Unfortunately for the Germans, it is unlikely the Ikonoskop-equipped X-7 was ever near deployment. It would have increased the overall weight and complexity of the unit by a large margin. Strapping a video camera to the missile would have also negatively impacted the flight characteristics of a projectile that was already difficult to control.

Analysis

The X-7 was a groundbreaking weapon system. Though it was not the first missile to incorporate wire guidance, it was the pioneer among ground-launched antitank missiles. The unfortunate debut of the X-7 cannot be ignored, but it should also not be overemphasized. No other German infantry antitank rocket could even hit a tank at a range of 500 meters. Adequate training of the X-7 operators would have reduced the failure rate caused by their unconventional steering methods whether or not there were any refinements made in the design. Had the X-7 reached the front in large numbers, it might have equalized the battle between armor and infantry to some degree. It was not as flexible as simple weapon systems like the panzerfaust, but its long-range theoretical accuracy and relatively heavy warhead would have made it a real threat.

Hypothetical Deployment History

The first major allotment of production models of the X-7 reached tank hunter detachments with Army Group Center located along the Neisse River on April 14, 1945. Ferdinand Schoerner's ravaged Army Group was facing off against the First Ukrainian Front and more than 2 million men under Marshal Konev. The Germans had dug in deep along the Neisse. It was one of the last barriers in the sector between Konev and a swing north to Berlin. Concrete bunkers, trenches, and other prepared positions seemed substantial, but were about to be crushed beneath unrelenting aerial and artillery bombardment. The tank hunter units were constantly in action, skirmishing with Soviet probes for an upcoming final offensive to complete the encirclement of Berlin. On the night of April 15, by the spectral infrared light provided by an Uhu searchlight (see chapter 5), a battery of four X-7 rockets ambushed a Guards Tank Company at a range of 340 meters. One rocket exploded only a few dozen meters from the launch trench, lightly wounding a crew. A second X-7 lost control and detonated on the ground. The remaining two rockets found their targets and completely killed two Soviet T-34/85s.

The celebrations were short lived. The tank hunters fled from the charging tanks and let teams equipped with the panzerschreck and panzerfaust handle the remainder of the battle. The position on the eastern bank of the Neisse could not be held and German forces retreated west as the Soviets began to take and establish crossing points. All the X-7s available were pressed into action, with quite good results. One detachment, equipped with five X-7 launch systems and seven of the missiles, managed to kill six enemy tanks that morning. Casualties among tank hunters were terrible, however, as many were forced to engage tanks from shorter ranges and suffer the consequences of remaining stationary during the missile's flight.

Schoerner's men held the front with nothing but tenacity. Schoerner refused to commit his tank reserves to the fight and the Soviets poured through a gap. The beleaguered tank hunters on Schoerner's southern flank had no shortage of targets. They fired X-7 rockets at the Soviet tanks from long range and then used panzerschreck rockets as the enemy charged closer. The German teams were wiped out, and only a few escaped from their trenches into the denuded forests or the city. The X-7 did its job, it held part of the line for one more day, but

Schoerner's sector was reeling under blows from Konev's forces and the Seelow Heights would soon be lost as well.

What Fight Have Been

5:08 A.M., April 16, 1945
First Ukrainian Front, Special Sniper Detachment
Berlin Approach, South of the Seelow Heights

Frost glistened on the burned hulks of a dozen tanks and hundreds of corpses. A few of the wrecks smoldered silently. The robins were out, hopping across the cratered moonscape searching for a bounty of worms that had been churned up by the relentless artillery barrage of the previous day. To the east of this fractured pastoral setting lay the bulk of the First Ukrainian Front, bloodied but eager to reenter the battle. To the west, in the splintered timbers and ashes of a burned out forest, were the remaining stalwarts of a force of German infantry.

Konev's probing attacks across the Neisse had run into the tank hunters and infantry serving as the rearguard for the withdrawing Germans. The fascists were using some new rocket to destroy tanks, and it had blunted the armored probe. When infantry had been used to screen the tanks, they had suffered terrible casualties at the hands of concealed machine guns. Konev had no intention of being slowed in his advance. He called up the snipers and sent them in to eliminate the rocket launchers. A massive barrage of artillery and aircraft would commence at 6:00 A.M. whether or not the snipers had succeeded. Then the main assault would begin.

To Avdotya Donetskov, it was the worst sort of task she could be given. She did not resent it, because it was her duty as a sniper, but she would rather be deep behind enemy lines than trapped between the enemy and the indiscriminant destruction of a creeping barrage.

"Pssssh," hissed Elana Itsaia, "bird caught a big worm."

Avdotya lifted her eye from her scope and looked over to where her latest partner was pointing. The woman had spotted a robin struggling to pick up a fat grub worm too large for its beak. With a mild wave of revulsion she realized it was a human finger.

"Ahhh, little Dunya," Elana patted a gloved hand across Avdotya's backside. "You are too sensitive."

"Quiet," Avdotya whispered. "Look at the Germans, not what the birds are doing to our comrades."

It was amazing that any of the fascists had survived the firestorm the artillery had sparked in the woods. The entire area was blackened and pocked with craters. The Germans, soot covered, were still there. Some had reinforced their trenches and foxholes with fallen timbers, but most had simply used the ruin to further conceal themselves inside the wood. The Germans were obviously exhausted. Their features were pinched with strain or slack with shock. Still, they toiled and looked out at the kill zone with readiness. Some appeared fearful, but to Avdotya most of them seemed resigned to fight and die on the spot.

Now you know how it feels to fight for your homes, Avdotya thought. *I have no pity for you.*

She pitied them anyway.

"There." Elana pointed again, a measured gesture using only her fingertip.

Avdotya peered through the scope on her rifle and found the group of Germans Elana had spotted. There were three of them in a single slit trench. They were standing and fiddling with what looked like a painter's easel made from metal and bent to be horizontal. Only the top of the contraption and their helmeted heads were visible above the mouth of the trench. What had caught Elana's attention was the fourth soldier who had crawled to them dragging some sort of sledge behind him. This man pushed the sledge up to the westward lip of the trench and then half fell into the trench with the others. Avdotya could make out four canvas-wrapped parcels, each a bit more than a meter in length, lashed to the sledge with telephone wire.

They waited on the Germans. In the half-light of dawn, the fascists dragged the bundles one by one down into the trench. They disappeared for several minutes and Avdotya imagined them opening the parcels to find cakes, letters, and baubles from home. Her belly grumbled at the thought of little Tolya's last birthday pastry, then she put the thought from her mind before the sadness could return. Two of the Germans appeared above the trench holding what was undoubtedly one of their tank-killing rockets. It had two wings and a strange tail that locked over the easel that was apparently the framework of a launching device. Another one of the Germans reappeared a few meters away at the far edge of the trench. He began securing a periscope-like device to the earthen wall.

"Take left," Avdotya whispered, "I have right."

"That's only one for me and two for—" a third man appeared at the launcher, "three for you."

"Take left."

Avdotya inhaled deeply and slid her finger into the trigger guard of her Mosin-Nagant. A robin chirped nearby. Elana fired first, her rifle a jarring annoyance to Avdotya as she lined up her own shot.

Avdotya squeezed the trigger and fired. She hit the first German just below his left eye. She threw the bolt and resighted. Avdotya squeezed the trigger and fired. She hit the second German in the throat. She threw the bolt and resighted. Avdotya squeezed the trigger and fired. She hit the third German in the collarbone. She threw the bolt and resighted. Avdotya squeezed the trigger and fired. The third German disappeared into the trench. She twisted around to escape.

Elana was already running, standing upright almost completely in the open. The machine guns took to her like kestrels on a steppe mouse. They lifted her up an inch into the air and dropped her in a heap. The Germans kept firing into the dead body. Avdotya worked her body down deeper into her shooting spot. The Germans had not seen her, but they would be watching now. She could do little more than wait for the storm of artillery to begin and hope that it landed on the Germans rather than on her.

Chapter 5

Nachtsichtgeraten—German Night-Vision Devices

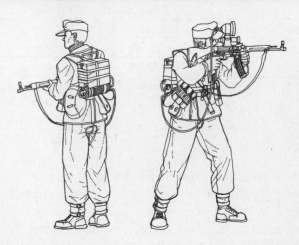

Overview

In daylight, primitive man was king of all he surveyed. After nightfall, mankind huddled in small groups afraid of the terrifying predators of the impenetrable dark. Nocturnal hunters stalked our ancestors with impunity. Predatory cats with excellent night vision prowled beyond ancient man's pitiful natural ability to overcome darkness. Giant Cenozoic owls the size of churches swooped up entire families of soft-skinned humans to feed to their wretchedly hooting offspring. The hated Night Elephants descended from their mountaintop aeries to impale humans on their hollow tusks and drink their blood. Then, by hook or crook, mankind discovered fire and gave darkness a modest shove back.

In the scheme of natural history, it was a short jump from those cavemen in animal skins huddled around a cook fire to the first electric lights. Mankind was suddenly able to live and operate, almost unimpeded, throughout the day and night. The one remaining exception to this rule was military operations. Using artificial light meant giving away your position to rule the enemy. You could send a bunch

	FG 1250	ZG 1229 Vampir
Category:	Vehicle-mounted active IR sighting device	Rifle-mounted R sighting device
Stage of Development:	Limited production	Limited production
Development Start:	1941	1943
Development Team:	Ing Gaertner of Zeiss(Leitz)	Ing Gaertner of Zeiss (Leitz)
Field of View:	30 degrees	2 degrees
Active Range:	400 m	100 m
Passive Range:	8,000 m	Unknown
Weight:	Unknown	2.5 kg for optics, 15 kg (approximate) for power supply

of soldiers out to attack with flashlights, but then the guys with no flashlights would just shoot the people coming toward them. Darkness could be used by elite forces of commandos to conceal their movements or by generals to cover a realignment of forces in the relative safety behind the front lines, but mounting an attack at night remained a dangerous prospect.

During World War I; flares, flashes of artillery, or the moon seen filtered through some mustard gas were the only night lights available to soldiers. Something had to be done about all that damned darkness! In the years leading up to World War II, Ing Gaertner of the German optics firm Zeiss began to experiment with means for sensing long-wavelength nonvisible light. At the time, it was referred to as Ultrarotstrahlung (infrared radiation). These days we just call it infrared (IR). Competitors at the engineering firm of AG (AEG) also began to develop similar sensing devices, and by the middle of the war, Zeiss, AG, and others were producing a wide variety of designs. For the purposes of this chapter, I focus primarily on the two most successful: the FG 1250 vehicle IR solution and the sinisterly named ZG 1229 Vampir infantry night sight.

With these devices, military commanders finally had the ability to pursue targets in darkest night, seeing but unseen. Too bad they were all clunky, prone to failure, difficult to use, and hard to produce.

The Mole Men of Infrared

Think of your eyes as a castle and normal light radiation as goblins that run around outside in a mad pack and then assault the castle. The rampaging horde of goblins overcomes your castle's defenses and sacks the place, and then they burn it to the ground. When they burn your castle, that's how you see! IR radiation is more like the treacherous mole men who burrow beneath the moat and erupt in your throne room. They sack the place and kill everyone just like the goblins, but they leave the castle intact so you never actually see anything. Actually, that was more confusing than not knowing about infrared. Let's try again.

Red is the color of visible light, with the longest wavelength. When the wavelength increases, the color red becomes the color invisible and that's where you'll find "near infrared" electromagnetic radiation. It's still actually red, but we can't see it and there's a lot of it out there. When the wavelength becomes longer, but before it reaches microwave radiation sizes, it is known as "far infrared" or "thermal radiation." The easiest way to think of near and far IR is that near IR is light that we can't see and far IR is heat energy. Robocop, the Predator, and many aircraft-mounted IR sights can see far IR radiation, whereas most modern IR night-vision equipment views near IR.

Generation 0 night-vision devices, including the German devices covered in this chapter and the devices used by the Americans such as the Snooperscope, were all designed to view near IR. There are two different ways these devices accomplished their task. In passive mode, the devices would simply amplify ambient IR light and allow the user to see further and better than a normal person at night. You will notice in the statistics box for the FG 1250 that it had a much greater passive viewing range than in active mode. This is simply the maximum range at which the device could amplify any IR light. These early devices were very poor at passive viewing and produced blurry and sometimes confusing images. If a person using normal vision to see at night is completely blind, then a person with an early IR scope in passive mode is a person with severe cataracts.

These early night-vision devices were much more effective in active mode when their ability to amplify IR light was coupled with various sizes of IR illuminators. Active IR night-vision equipment projects a beam of IR light that is invisible to the naked eye but illuminates an area clearly for anyone with near IR amplification. Most modern low-light video cameras use this technique and those creepy eyeballs Paris Hilton gets in her famous video are the result of the really bright IR light on the camera being reflected in her eyes. If you have one of these cameras, you might be interested to look at the end of your TV remote control some time. The remote uses a near IR LED to send signals to the television and actually emits extremely bright IR light.

Both the FG 1250 and ZG 1229 incorporated IR searchlights into their design and these provided very clear night vision (for the time) out to a range of 400 meters and 100 meters, respectively. Modern active IR equipment offers much greater image clarity and is limited in range only by the intensity and size of the spotlight equipment. The down side to active IR (and why it is rarely used in war) is that most modern militaries have at least some IR equipment and the spotlights will show up as brightly as one visible to the naked eye for the enemy. Neither the Germans nor the Americans had to deal with this particular disadvantage during the course of World War II because the Germans only deployed their IR equipment on the eastern front.

Development History

Before World War II, scientists in a number of countries, including the United States, England, and Germany, were experimenting with IR radiation detection. The first military application of IR-sensing equipment was the German Spanner I developed by AG and Mayer with assistance from Gaertner and Zeiss. It was a passive IR detector coupled with a 300-watt IR illuminator designed to be used as a night sight for fixed or towed artillery.

The next installment of the Spanner series (the Spanner II) was a similar passive IR design to the Spanner I. In 1941, it was fitted to the Bf 110 night fighter for testing as an aid to aerial combat, but it proved inadequate for the job and was later mass-produced for use as a night sight for flak batteries. The Spanner series also resulted in versions III and IV in 1942 and 1943, respectively, though neither ever entered mass production. The Spanner III was tested and ultimately abandoned, while the Spanner IV was intended for night-fighter duty on the Do 217.

The FG 1223 from AG and Zeiss was developed and tested in 1942 as a night-vision optic for the PAK 40 75mm antitank gun. It entered production in the same year and was the first mass-produced German IR scope, beating the Spanner II to mass production. The FG 1223 was the real precursor to the FG 1250, and Gaertner led the way as the 1223 evolved into the 1250.

Later versions of the FG 1223 and then the FG 1250 were designed as IR optics for use by tank commanders. The FG 1250 was a flexible platform for night fighting and could be attached to a machine gun or directly to a vehicle's hull for use by the driver at night. The latter configuration was of dubious use in combat, especially since it required the driver to leave the vehicle hatch open, but it was adequate for maneuvering slowly or on roadways.

As the practicality of the FG 1250 as a night-fighting solution became increasingly clear, it was realized that accompanying infantry would need to be similarly equipped. The ZG 1229 Vampir scope and IR lamp combination were developed for use in conjunction with the Sturmgewehr 44 assault rifle. This potent weapon was the world's first true assault rifle and the Vampir system, though unwieldy, gave the infantry utilizing the combination of the two the ability to function at night.

Both the ZG 1229 and the FG 1250 were mass-produced, and the Vampir is believed to have seen combat beginning in February or March 1945. Other systems, including the FG 1251 Uhu (Owl) developed from the Kriegsmarine's JIIb Gerät Mosel shore surveillance system, were designed to work in conjunction with the tanks and infantry outfitted for night fighting. The Uhu was a redesign of the common SdKfz 251 half-track that incorporated a 6,000-watt illuminator used to extend the range of any passive IR equipment in the vicinity of its beam. This was particularly useful for Panther teams equipped with the FG 1250 that could fire and move while the Uhu followed or lurked nearby.

By the time any of this equipment was deployed in modest quantities, the war of numbers had already been lost by the Germans. Fat lot of good seeing in the dark is going to do you when all you can see is that there are more enemy tanks than you have antitank rounds.

Technical Mumbo Jumbo

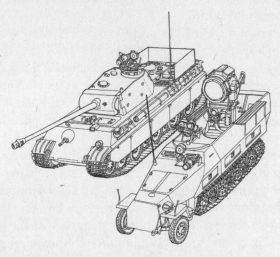

A Panther tank (left) outfitted with solution A and
an Uhu equipped with solution B.

The FG 1250 produced by AG and Zeiss consisted of a passive IR viewer with a 30-degree field of view and a 200-watt IR illuminator for use in active mode. The FG 1250 possessed an 8,000-meter passive range and a 400-meter active range. In passive mode, the device produced insufficient image fidelity for target acquisition. A panzer utilizing the FG 1250 could be assisted by an Uhu and its more powerful illuminator to extend its active range to approximately 1.5 kilometers.

The FG 1250 could be fitted to the Panther Ausf. G medium tank or the SdKfz 251 Falke (Falcon). The most common fitting for the Panther was a single FG 1250 sight and illuminator bolted to the commander's cupola turret ring. The commander's set could be linked to the internal elevation indicator for the main gun to allow the commander to assist the gunner in night sighting of targets. This configuration was referred to as "solution A."

"Solution B" could be used on the Panther as well, though it originated from the Falke night-fighting half-track. This configuration involved adding a machine-gun to the commander's set and incorporating an additional FG 1250 and illuminator for the driver. The driver had to remain exposed while using his set for the Panther version of the solution B and it was therefore likely to be of little practical value in combat. It should be noted that there is no concrete evidence that the solution B was ever used in a combat Panther.

Infantry accompanying night-fighting vehicles and the crews of the vehicles themselves were equipped with the ZG 1229 Vampir individual IR sight. This device was essentially the FG 1250 scaled down to fit (awkwardly) atop a Sturmgewehr 44 assault rifle. The scope and the 36-watt illuminator weighed in at about 2.5 kilograms and attached to special factory-modified fittings on the top of the rifle. The Vampir's illuminator drew power from a 12.5-kilogram battery mounted inside a wooden box attached to a backpack frame. Not exactly the sort of thing you'd want to carry along with all your usual gear. Beneath the bulky battery was a second battery contained inside a cylindrical gas-mask case that provided power for the Vampir scope. The Vampir illuminator was only effective out to roughly 100 meters.

Variants

There was a wide array of experimental and early-production night-fighting equipment in use by the German military at the end of World War II. The Kriegsmarine, in particular, had a greater ability to deploy very large IR illuminators for use on ships and in coastal defense. The Luftwaffe also found a variety of uses for IR-sensing equipment, including using it to detect IR guidance beams and to aid in target acquisition during night engagements.

Analysis

The FG 1250 transformed the Panther into a nocturnal predator unparalleled at the time. It was able to engage targets on its own terms and strike without allowing the enemy to effectively retaliate. Night-fighting equipment has since become an integral part of modern strategic planning. Even third world nations are able to field a large quantity of semiobsolescent IR equipment. The Vampir, though less immediately useful than the FG 1250, was a stepping stone to similar innovations in warfare.

Unfortunately for the Germans, mobility was distinctly hampered by all the bombs and artillery shells falling on their heads by the time significant deployments of night-fighting equipment became possible. Although the equipment was no doubt appreciated by units equipped with it, the limited amount available to the insufficient reserves of forces did not really impact the course of the war.

Hypothetical Deployment History

The Vampir or its experimental predecessors were seeing combat by late 1944 and by early 1945 the FG 1250 was beginning to reach units in limited numbers. Exact figures of available equipment and the specifics of engagements in which the gear was used remain shrouded in mystery.

What Fight Have Been

9:53 P.M., April 28, 1945
"Fortress Berlin," Army Group Vistula, Fifty-sixth Panzer Corps Remnants
Four Blocks Northeast of the Flakturm II in Friedrichshain District

Berlin was burning so brightly that it seemed the sun had paused on the horizon at dusk and never fully set. It was an unnatural living light that would brightly illuminate the rubble-strewn streets and then shift on the winds and cast everything into shadow. Artillery and rockets were constantly hammering all parts of Berlin that were not already under Soviet control.

Unit cohesion had collapsed to the point that a lone Panther tank, situated facing a broad open plaza, was the lynchpin of a feeble defensive line that stretched for several blocks. Crude barricades and rubble provided cover for the terrified conscript militias of Volkssturm that Germany's remaining leaders hoped would slow the Russians. The last scraps of real military units were interspersed almost randomly. A dead horse had been partially butchered for its meat and lay with its head in the rancid fountain in the center of the plaza.

Beneath the pall of the convection currents, Viktor Fleischer wiped sweat from his brow and pressed his eye once again to the rubber rim of the IR optic. Through the green light of the scope he could see clearly. The coming and going of illumination from the fires was just a phantom tracing back and forth across his field of view like white summer clouds passing overhead.

The powerful IR searchlight on the Panther caught the blobby shapes of men in civilian clothes moving between ruined buildings and out into the open street. If there were any Russians waiting down the road, the idiots were dead meat.

"They're back," Viktor informed his radio operator. "Make sure the Volkssturm hold their fire this time."

The civilians came in a disorganized single file with a few grouped together to carry heavy objects. Everything was draped in canvas, but Viktor knew from the incident two hours earlier that they were moving the priceless art and artifacts of Berlin to the concrete redoubt of the Flakturm. Even Viktor had to admit that the sight was rather demoralizing. It was a practical admission that all of Berlin was to be leveled or consumed by fire.

Willi Bayer popped the driver's hatch on the hull of the Panther and shouted out to the Volkssturm that civilians were approaching. Viktor knew that when the Russians finally attacked the only Volkssturm who might survive would be the ones who ran or surrendered at the very beginning. They were a scratch militia, barely better than straw men soaked in gasoline. Half of them did not even have rifles and only a few infirm veterans of the Great War knew how to handle the weapons. Viktor had been there when more than one of their pitiful positions had been smashed aside in seconds by a Soviet tank.

Viktor lifted his eye from the IR scope when the civilians drew closer and he watched them file past the panzer. A slim few smiled, waved, or shouted "Good luck!" hoarsely. Most of them just stared ahead, as broken and resigned to death as the Volkssturm huddling behind the barricades. He was still thinking about the somber procession when the Russians finally arrived to put a stop to the waiting.

Their presence was announced by a rattle of treads on stone, perhaps three blocks to the north. Through the spectral green glare of the IR scope Viktor watched them come. Two columns of Guards tanks approached the ill-defended plaza along two parallel streets from the north. Viktor knew that the plaza was a terrible position to try to hold, but with orders from Adolf Hitler there was little latitude for maneuver.

The first move was left to Viktor and his night vision. The Panther claimed the first vehicle of each column and for a moment the Soviet advance stalled. Then, with revving engines and gusts of diesel smoke, the columns rammed the burning T-34s out of the way and continued the advance. By then, the Russians were firing madly into the plaza. Machine guns ripped through the flimsy barricades and slaughtered the Volkssturm. Cannons flashed and bursts of fire and brick erupted all around the plaza. One of the poor fools fired off a panzerfaust at the Russians and the rocket streaked over the derelict fountain in the center of the plaza and crashed uselessly into the ruins of a church. A single Russian high-explosive round answered the futile gesture and put a stop to a second attempt.

The Panther fired again and again, spent casings clattering loudly on the deck. Viktor was proud of his crew. They had been through a lot together and he believed them the best on the whole eastern front. For a wonderful few seconds he watched the ruin their tank had put to the confined Russians and he thought they might just single-handedly halt the advance. Then he spotted the Russians flanking from the east and west down the wider boulevards. He did not even have time to order Jacques "Franky" Meijer to throw the Panther into reverse. The Panther filled with a roar, smoke, and fire. Viktor fell down onto the deck and then scrambled blindly for the hatch. Heat and bodies pressed in around him and the thick smoke stifled his breath.

Viktor emerged with a gasp. He was stone deaf and oblivious to the bullets hissing through the air around him as he forced himself from the turret hatch. Everything seemed to swim and then spin upside down, but he realized he was falling headfirst down the side of the panzer. He brought his arm up to shield his face as he landed on the street and then flopped onto his back. For a moment the wind carried the smoke and fires away and he had a fleeting glimpse of the night sky, velvet and speckled with shimmering stars.

Beautiful, he thought, *I hope Konrad is there and never has to come back*. Viktor felt himself being dragged away from the burning Panther and then he felt nothing at all.

Viktor came to in a bakery's kitchen many minutes later. He sat up suddenly and gasped for air, inhaling deep drafts of brick dust that sent him into fits of coughing. Streams of mortar were falling from the stone arches holding up the ceiling as artillery pounded a nearby block. The aroma of fresh bread had long since been chased out by the thick stink of smoke, gasoline, and the dead. Franky slumped with his back to a chipped counter. Blood darkened the chest of his coverall and in the flares of light from outside Viktor could see more trickling from a terrible wound in his neck.

"He's dead, sir." Half dazed still, Viktor turned toward the voice and saw Willi crouched beside him. "It was quick, anyway. Shot in the back."

"What . . . Gunther?" Viktor choked out.

"Here, sir!" Gunther Koch called from across the room where he sheltered beside an empty window frame watching the street outside.

"I couldn't get your walking cane, sir," Heinrich Schöpke spoke up from Viktor's other side, "but I did grab this."

Heinrich slid the heavy bundle of Viktor's nachtjaeger frame across the floor. Viktor looked back up at Gunther and saw now that he was watching the street through the scope of his Vampir sight.

"You should have left it," Viktor said while he stood and began to shrug into the pack.

Willi helped him secure the heavy batteries around his shoulders and waist. They all wore their equipment, even Franky, and with their black panzer uniforms and their bare skin streaked with smoke and grime they looked the part of commandos.

"Like the SS boys we saw off last night," Willi remarked with a crooked smile as he looked Viktor over.

"Yeah, only they're all dead," Gunther added. "We've got a bit of life left in us."

Viktor switched on the Vampir and sighted through the scope out into the street once to make sure the temperamental and heavy equipment still worked. The shadows outside vanished in an eerie ring of green light through the monochrome view of the scope.

"Can we make it back to the Flakturm?" Viktor asked, switching it back off.

"Don't think so, sir. Tanks have already cut us off in that direction," Gunther gestured out the window, "and the back way is covered by a sniper."

"That's who got Franky," added Willi.

"Where?" Viktor asked.

"Through the back of the neck, you can—" Gunther began.

"No. Where is the way out through the back?" Viktor cut him off.

Willi showed him to the back door of the bakery. Viktor lowered himself unsteadily to the floor, his bad knee sending sparks of pain up his thigh as it made contact with the cracked tiles on the floor. He lowered all the way down to his belly and crawled to the door. He opened it just wide enough to press his rifle outside and use the Vampir to see what lay beyond.

The back area was fenced on the left and hemmed in by a ruined building straight ahead, but it veered into an alleyway to the right. Where the corner turned Viktor could see the glistening dark stain of blood that marked Franky's demise. It trailed back around and toward the bakery's rear entrance. Viktor awkwardly panned the rifle and scope to see the building the shot had come from. It was at the edge of the IR lamp's power, a quarter-block away, a four-story luxury apartment reduced to crumbling exterior walls and crazily tilted floors.

"Do you see him?" Willi whispered.

"I see where he was," Viktor replied. "Now to see where he is."

Viktor panned the rifle around methodically, watching through its narrow field of view for the best sniping spot. If the sniper was decent, he doubted that he would actually see him, but if the sniper was that good, he would pick the best possible fallback. Viktor just hoped he had a good enough eye for that sort of thing himself, or he would never spot it.

"There," Viktor said at last.

The IR beam reflected from something and with a moment to focus Viktor realized it was the barrel of the sniper's rifle. The spot was nearly perfect. He couldn't actually see the sniper, but if he had been standing at the door the sniper would have already shot him. The sniper was on the third floor of the building directly opposite the door, buried somewhere in a tangle of fallen pipes and bricks in the gutted remains of the structure.

"What do we do now?" Willi asked.

"We introduce ourselves."

"I can see infantry coming this way, so we need to move quickly," Gunther added with urgency.

"Heinrich, Gunther, I want you to stay here. Lay low and keep quiet. If the Russians decide to stop off for a loaf of bread, try to handle things without drawing any attention."

Viktor turned to Willi.

"Willi, you are with me. We crawl on our bellies like snakes and find that sniper's nest."

Getting out the back took longer than Viktor had hoped. They could not open the door very far or else they would betray their intentions. That meant unbuckling all the bulky IR equipment and sliding it out through the doorway a piece at a time. When they finally went out they did so awkwardly, on their sides, wriggling through the cracked doorway and waiting each second for the sniper to send a bullet into their head. Gunther and Heinrich stayed out of sight inside the bakery, listening over the thump of artillery to the growing clatter of approaching infantry and terse orders barked in Russian.

Climbing up to the sniper's spot was not an easy task either. Each step within the ruined building required caution on the collapsing floors. They were clumsy in the nachtjaeger frames with their heavy backpacks and Viktor's lame leg plagued him with each step, but their footfalls were drowned out in the ceaseless barrage of artillery falling on Berlin. They were ascending a tilting staircase to the level on which the sniper was perched when a Russian tank rumbled past the bakery. Viktor watched through the ruined wall as its turret slowly rotated. *Get out, get out*, Viktor willed Heinrich and Gunther, but there was nowhere for them to go.

The sagging roof of the bakery lifted up and then fell inward. Dust, fire, and masonry blew out in all directions and pieces of brick clattered around Viktor. Clear as day, Viktor could see the Russian soldiers waiting dispassionately for anyone who might emerge. After a moment, Heinrich staggered out, covered in dust and streaked with blood. He held his hands up in surrender, though one hand was shredded and dangled uselessly from his wrist. Viktor closed his eyes and listened to the Russians gun poor Heinrich down.

With Stalin Organs moaning in the distance and fire crashing all around him, Viktor stomped up the last of the staircase with Willi at his heels. It was no surprise to find a pair of Russians rather than a lone sniper. A boy no more than fifteen in a dun-colored padded jacket crouched behind an overturned desk. The sniper lay prone at his side, still facing the bakery.

"Hey, Russ!" Viktor felt drunk.

The boy turned first, his eyes wide with fear. Viktor squeezed the trigger of his rifle and the gun chattered. Puffs of down sprayed from the boy's jacket. He cried out and fell over the back of the desk, his arms still flailing as he dropped off the open side of the building. The sniper turned with a pistol in her hand.

"You!" Viktor exclaimed.

It was the sniper from Zhitomir, the one who had let him live. Her pistol was aimed at his chest. For a moment they remained transfixed by recognition, anger, and confusion.

Then Willi stormed to the top of the staircase and the spell was broken. Viktor threw out his arm and batted away Willi's rifle just as it began to fire. With a cry of surprise and a crack of strained timbers the floor suddenly gave way and Willi fell down to the lower level. The sniper fired her pistol twice and Viktor felt the bullets dimly, as though she had flicked him hard with her finger. Then he was on his back, staring up at the ceiling, his pulse loud and erratic in his ears.

The drum of his heart slowed and the sniper's face filled his vision.

Her expression was not kind exactly, but sad. The drum grew silent. Her face became Anna's.

"That's all, then?" Viktor asked.

Avdotya Donetskov lingered for a moment, looking down at Viktor's lifeless features. She closed his eyes with a brush of her fingertips and fled into the dying city before the other German could regain consciousness.

Chapter 6

Landkreuzer P. 1500 Monster

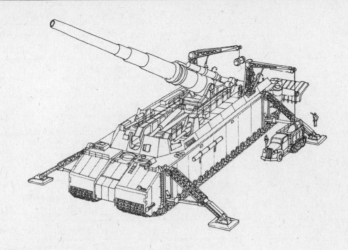

Overview

Developed as an offshoot of Krupp's previous work with large self-propelled artillery and its experience with the brief Ratte program, the P. 1500 Monster was an effort to wed an ultraheavy Landkreuzer chassis with the largest artillery piece ever built. The 800mm Dora E was an incredibly powerful weapon capable of penetrating a meter of armor or reinforced concrete. You may have seen one of roughly 250,000 different documentaries about this railway gun. Hampered by its confinement to railways, Krupp hoped to set it free like a beautiful butterfly by replacing an entire rail convoy with a huge supertank.

Built around the over 1,300-ton (including railway carriage) Dora gun, the Monster would have possessed dimensions even larger than the Ratte, with allowances for armored magazines (each high-explosive shell weighed nearly 5 metric tons), reloading cranes, defensive armament, and two 150mm howitzers. Such a massive undertaking would require elaborate engineering feats and the resources of much of Krupp's vast industrial empire. A girl can dream.

Category:	Ultraheavy self-propelled artillery
Phase of Development:	Preprototype
Development Start:	December 1942
Development Team:	Krupp
Crew:	100+
Weight:	2,500 metric tons (estimated)
Propulsion:	4 × 2,200 hp MAN M9V, 40/46 U-boat diesel engines
Speed:	15 kph (estimated)
Range:	Unknown
Length:	42.00 m
Width:	18.00 m
Height:	7.00 m (not including gun)
Armament:	1 × 800mm Dora/Gustav K (E) railway gun 2 × 150mm sFH 18/1 L/30 howitzers Multiple 15mm MG 151/15
Ammunition:	30 × 800mm HE rounds (estimated)
	12 × 800mm AP rounds (estimated)
	100 × 150mm HE rounds
Armor (mm):	Hull front: 250 Additional armor values unknown

Development History

One fine November morning, Adolf Hitler awoke from his dreams of conquest, leapt from his bed in naught but his bare bodkin, and cried out across the sleepy town of Obersalzberg, "Let them build a tracked artillery carriage as high as these mountains!" Or, possibly not. Whatever fever-dream of massive vehicles drove this madness, Hitler instructed Krupp to turn his beloved 800mm Dora artillery piece into a self-propelled weapon.

With Krupp's plans for the supertank Ratte a recent memory, the designers at Krupp set to work on the P. 1500, christened "Monster." A monster it would have been: mounted to its railway car, the 800mm gun tipped the scales at 1,344 tons. Each high-explosive shell weighed 4,800 kilograms and each of the armor piercing rounds weighed an astonishing 7,502 kilograms. For comparison, the famed British Tallboy bomb, so adept at bunker-busting, weighed a mere 5,443 kilograms.

No known drawings of the Monster survived the war, but it is known that Krupp completed its design in December 1942. It proposed a heavily armored and tracked gun carriage, weighing over 1,500 tons, and armed with secondary artillery and machine guns. Hitler was quite excited by the design, but the eternal killjoy Albert Speer forbade Krupp from committing its resources to the construction of a prototype. Speer was well aware that Der Fuehrer would greenlight a tracked baby pram if it were proposed on an impressively large scale. Hitler sulked, and Krupp returned to work on other projects.

Technical Mumbo Jumbo

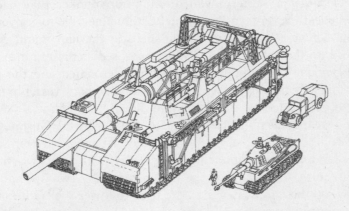

The P. 1500 traveling with stabilizers stowed and cranes folded. A nearby King Tiger heavy tank and a truck demonstrate its immense scale.

The P. 1500 was to be powered by "two to four U-boat engines." The most appropriate of these was the U-boat fleet's workhorse MAN M9V40/46 six-cylinder diesel. Each of these 6 meter-long and 2-meter-wide engines produced 2,200 horsepower. Two were used in U-boats, usually with one powering the boat and the other charging up the batteries. The Monster would have required four to keep its immense bulk heaving over land. Even then these four mighty naval engines would have given the Monster only power enough to reach 10 to 15 kph.

The Monster's treads would have been even wider than those seen on the Ratte, possibly with four or five of the 1.2-meter-wide treads on each side of the vehicle. Any less surface area and the weight of the Monster would have sunk it into the ground like an immense shovel head, compressing dirt until the vehicle was sitting in a pit several meters deep. Like the Ratte, even this generous weight distribution would have functioned as a whole press gang of men with pickaxes if the vehicle traversed over pavement. Monster commanders could forget about bridges unless they wanted to do a lot of collateral damage and slide into a river or gorge.

At the heart of the Monster was Krupp's artillery masterpiece, the 800mm Dora K (E), capable of lobbing 7-ton shells 38 kilometers. Two of these 800mm railway guns were built, the Dora and Schwere Gustav, and both saw very limited service. Notably, Schwere Gustav participated in the siege of the Soviet city of Sevastopol. On June 6, 1942, after days of successful shelling, the Schwere Gustav was ordered to target a subterranean ammunition bunker that had been buried beneath Severnaya Bay to make it invulnerable to conventional shelling. Schwere Gustav fired nine shells at the aim point. All nine plunged into the bay, through 30 meters of sediment, and into the armored bunker. The ammunition stockpile detonated and the bunker was completely destroyed. An unfortunate merchant vessel in the bay was also obliterated by a shell passing directly through it.

For a weapon as immense as the Dora and Schwere Gustav, a nine-round volley could occupy an entire day. At its peak, the Schwere Gustav fired fourteen rounds in a single day, with an exhausting rate of fire of only one round every fifteen minutes. Two special cranes mounted on these railway guns were used to lower shells into position onto a powered cart, that in turn assisted loaders manhandling the shells into the breach. These guns were served by a crew of more than 500 men. Some of these positions could be done away with for the Monster, but the ranks would have still had over 100 men. It can be assumed that a convoy of antiaircraft vehicles, tanks, infantry, maintenance crews, ammunition trucks (carrying one round each), and huge fuel bowsers would have followed behind the Monster.

When the Monster moved into a firing position, an entire encampment would have been erected, complete with field kitchens and latrines for the hundreds of men involved in the vehicle's operation, maintenance, and protection. The Monster was technically mobile, but firing on the move would have likely been catastrophic. The railway versions required two parallel rail tracks that had to be specially reinforced, as firing on them while straddling four normal rail lines would have splintered the metal rails like dry timbers. Firing the gun mounted on the Monster without preparing and bracing the vehicle would have likely had a similarly disastrous effect on the tank.

Nearly all large railway guns employed huge hydraulic dampeners to compensate for recoil. Because the Monster could not rely on recoil movement on a rail to supplement these dampeners, a tank-mounted version of its 800mm gun would have required much more in the way of recoil compensation. This might have included stabilizer jacks or booms that could be extended from the side of the vehicle as well as a sliding gun carriage and a hydroneumatic counterrecoil mechanism. Imagine the huge cannon sitting atop a slide mechanism like you see on an automatic pistol. When it fired one of its bouncing baby boys, the whole gun platform would slide back several feet and then get returned to its firing position by hydraulic rams. This shoving might take a fair bit of time depending on the distance of the recoil and any movement of the tank itself. If things went well, the gun would be ready to deliver another round inside ten minutes.

Once the Germans had all that taken care of, all they had to do was develop an intercom system that would display text for the stone-deaf gun team.

Variants

The 150mm howitzers mounted on the Monster seem to be overkill. They do not give it the ability to effectively engage tanks, nor do they provide any sort of antiaircraft capability. With the whole vehicle built around a giant artillery piece, putting two normal-sized artillery pieces on it seems sort of like taking out the backseat of a car to put a motorcycle there. Antitank guns, antiaircraft guns, or both, make much more sense than just piling on the artillery. The best option would have probably been dropping the additional guns for more ammunition and spare parts storage. Without an entourage of defensive vehicles, the Monster would have been all too vulnerable to the enemy, so there would have been little point in poorly duplicating the roles of these vehicles.

Analysis

Leopold and Robert were the names the Germans gave to a pair of 280mm railway guns located near the beaches of Anzio. When the Americans landed troops at Anzio, the guns became collectively known as Anzio Annie and they plagued the beachhead until a break-out was achieved. Despite nearly total Allied air superiority, large amounts of artillery, and naval bombardment, Anzio Annie could not be silenced. When the Americans broke out of the beachhead in early June and found the guns, they realized why the German artillery had survived. The guns, mounted on their rail cars, would trundle out of a cave to fire on the beach. When counterbattery fire started to pound in or bombers were heard overhead, the guns would travel back inside the shelter of the cave.

The 800mm guns of Dora and Schwere Gustav were not nearly so flexible. Firing them required specially laid tracks and hours of preparation. In this area, and at staggering expense, the Monster would have been superior to the railway versions of the 800mm gun. Without the need for hours of preparation and rail lines, the Monster could have sheltered inside a specially made bunker or a really, really, really big cave, only to emerge and pummel any enemies in range of its massive gun.

Deployed in the field, the Monster would have been an even easier target for Allied airpower than the Ratte. Ponderously slow to the point that infantry might have outpaced it at a jog, and unable to fire on the move, the Monster would have fallen well behind any advancing army. Not that the Germans would have conceivably been advancing, no matter how fast the Monster was rushed into production.

The biggest weakness of the Monster would have been its 800mm cannon. This enormous target was virtually unarmored. Components could have been destroyed by enemy fire, and the crew serving the weapon would have been vulnerable to shrapnel. With the gun knocked out of action, the Monster would have been a crawling bunker. The wounded beast would have been intimidating even then, but not much of a threat to a commander with a few dozen brave men who could run fast and throw demolition charges.

Hypothetical Deployment History

Krupp's design for the Monster was approved in August 1942, and construction immediately began on the two artillery pieces. Development of the chassis became a joint project between Krupp and MAN engineers, who had developed the engines that were to be used in the Monster. A 1:24 scale model was produced at the Krupp special projects facility 23, and this met with the approval of both Hitler and, reluctantly, Speer. The first gun was completed in June 1943 and was christened "Friedrich" but nicknamed "Das Kleine Obergefreite" (The Little Corporal) as a joke. The nickname stuck, but the poor little corporal did not have a chassis.

Recoil compensation was inadequate on the full-sized chassis, and it was found that the pressure of firing the gun could deform or even shatter tread links. Throughout the summer of 1943, designers toiled away and tested more than a dozen systems that could reduce the recoil force on the chassis. The stress on the treads was ultimately reduced by adding four hydraulic jacks in 8-meter-long booms. These booms sat flush with the hull during travel and then would be rotated, extended, and slotted into grooves on the top armor with electric winches. Combined with the slide mount of the gun carriage and its pneumatic return system, the gun could be fired after only forty to fifty minutes of preparation with minimal damage to the chassis.

The second gun was finished in October 1943 and was later dubbed the "Berlin Gun" by Joseph Goebbels in a propaganda broadcast. In a twist of fate, it would be the Little Corporal that ultimately served in Berlin's final days.

The Little Corporal was fitted to its chassis in February 1944, and the vehicle was dispatched to France, where it was intended to serve as a part of the mostly imaginary Atlantic Wall. During transit, the Little Coporal was unintentionally bombed by a damaged British Lancaster that was simply jettisoning its bomb load. Luckily for the Germans, the Lancaster crashed and the crew was killed, although days later the Allies learned about the gun from French Resistance fighters who had witnessed its movements. The damaged Little Corporal was laboriously shifted back to Krupp facilities for repairs and an overhaul.

In May 1944, the Berlin Gun became operational and was given the task originally assigned to the Little Corporal. On May 28, as it trundled into France, the gun was sabotaged by French Resistance fighters assisted by British commandos. The raid ultimately failed, but the damage to the gun rendered it immobile until it could be repaired. The next afternoon, a massive American bombing raid descended on the Berlin Gun and utterly destroyed it.

Repairs on the Little Corporal were finally completed in late September 1944. Hitler, still stinging over the destruction of the gun's twin, ordered a special firing bunker built in the center of Berlin. This was completed with slave labor in January 1945, and the gun was shifted there with great difficulty. The sight of the massive vehicle slowly churning over bombed-out rubble was both awe-inspiring and terrible for the beleaguered citizens of Berlin. Though the firing bunker was repeatedly attacked by the Americans, British, and eventually the Soviets, the gun survived to shell the Soviet armies that encircled Berlin. From April 15 through April 19, the gun was in action for several hours each day. With German artillery forces in and around Berlin largely scattered and low on ammunition, the huge gun was in high demand with commanders. On April 19, with the Soviets threatening a breakthrough at the Seelow Heights, the crew of the Little Corporal launched a total of eighteen rounds. At one point, the crew desperately loaded and fired with artillery landing less than a 100 meters away.

On April 20, the Soviets began to shell the bunker itself, and their air attacks became more focused and persistent. On the 20th and 21st combined, the Little Corporal managed to fire a total of three rounds. The gun did not fire again until April 27, when it emerged amid heavy shelling under the direct orders of Hitler to "fire the gun or be executed for cowardice." Although the armed crew outnumbered the SS men sent to enforce the order by twenty to one, they complied. The gun spoke once before damage was sustained. In the time it took to fire, nearly a hundred crewmen were killed. That night, many of the survivors attempted to desert the Monster. Some succeeded; most were caught and hung from lamp posts or shot to death.

On April 30, the remaining crewmen and a Volkssturm unit battled against Soviet shock troops around the Monster and, in some cases, even on top of and inside the vehicle. The fighting was brutal and lasted late into the night. At 4:17 A.M., the last of the crew surrendered and the shell-pocked Little Corporal belonged to the Soviets. Berlin did not last much longer.

What Fight Have Been

7:03 A.M., May 1, 1945
First Ukrainian Front, Special Sniper Detachment
Central Berlin

Avdotya Donetskov staggered through the streets of Berlin, mindful of the convoys of tanks and formations of men singing happily as they marched toward the shrinking front line. Berlin was nearly in the grasp of the Red Army. Advotya did not know who was left to shoot, so she just walked, aimless and alone amid the rush of war. Gunfire and artillery was still pounding only a few kilometers away, but it all seemed alien and distant.

A big American truck with a Red Army star painted on the hood swerved to avoid her.

"Don't get killed now, beautiful," the driver shouted after her.

The streets belonged to the Russians. There were a few frightened Germans here and there, peering out of windows or running from one doorway to the next. The Guards troops paid them little mind. The few German faces she saw seemed relieved. *They think the worst is over.* Avdotya knew from experience that the next troops to sweep through would not be so focused and disciplined.

Avdotya made eye contact with a pretty blonde German girl talking to two Guards officers in coquettishly halting Russian. *Why should I protect you?* The girl smiled and Avdotya looked away.

Avdotya realized she was walking toward the city center. Unter den Linden and the Pariser Platz lay ahead, and the carnage of close-in battle increased, almost unbelievably, until almost every structure was just a jagged ruin chewed up by gunfire. Bodies had been cleared from the streets in most places, but the closer she got to the Pariser Platz, the more dead she saw. She was surprised when she bumped into a German soldier in a ragged Wehrmacht field uniform. He stopped and stared at her with wide blue eyes. His face was streaked with grime and blood.

"Surrender," he said in Russian. "Surrender. Surrender!"

He fell to his knees and grabbed at Avdotya's trousers. She hurried past him and did not look back.

The scene on the Pariser Platz was one of destruction nearly to match the worst days of Stalingrad. Killed tanks were everywhere. Bodies—both Russians and Germans—were still littering the wide boulevard. The Brandenburg Gate was blackened by soot, and the Reichstag was nearly gutted. Its entire facade seemed to be an overlapping series of craters. The flag of the Soviet Union fluttered in the air above the Reichstag, though gunfire still echoed from the building.

Down Unter den Linden, a number of tanks and infantry milled around the open front of an oversized concrete bunker. Avdotya was curious and approached until she could see within the mouth of the structure. She had to suppress a gasp when she realized that the entire concrete bunker was a gigantic shelter for the Legendary Little Corporal Super gun. Avdotya had seen photographs of the gun and had heard it mentioned on German propaganda broadcasts, but it had always seemed to be another one of the fascists' untrue boasts.

The barrel of the cannon was fully depressed and was so long that it protruded from the bunker. Guards soldiers were clambering along the barrel like gleeful apes, hooting and, in some cases, even attempting to stand and run along its length. The enormous chassis for the Little Corporal had sustained heavy damage. Its armored hide was peeled back in two large wounds on its top. Twisted plates, reinforcing beams, pipes, and wires protruded like splintered bone from a compound fracture. The tanklike machine bore many lesser scars, as if a battle had raged across its back and along its flanks. Avdotya spotted heaps of dead Germans and a gaggle of disheveled prisoners and realized that the Little Corporal had been fought over, quite literally.

There was a loud pop that echoed through the cavernous bunker and sent a shiver of unease through the Germans and Russians. Guns bristled and searched for the source of the noise.

"The radio!" The shout was followed by another loud pop. "Hitler is dead!"

A burly officer with a mustache emerged from a maintenance bay behind the Little Corporal with arms full of French champagne.

"Whole coal cars of this stuff back there!" He laughed and began to hand the bottles to the men. "Let's have a drink to poor old Hitler."

Champagne corks popped and the men booed good-naturedly.

"Shit," the officer frowned. "To the Motherland! To victory!"

Avdotya was drawn in to the celebration. One of the soldiers handed her an oil tin filled to the brim with champagne. They laughed and cheered. Someone produced an accordion and someone else began to play the guitar. Another fool sat atop one of the automobile-sized shells of the Little Corporal and pounded it with a hand spade. He was promptly dragged down and kicked in the backside by a comrade.

With the battle still raging nearby and surrounded by corpses and forlorn prisoners, the soldiers danced and laughed. Avdotya sipped the champagne and let the soldiers kiss her on the cheek. An officer with a bit of foresight began marching the German prisoners away before the rest of the men got drunk enough to do something stupid. Avdotya watched them go and was reminded of the Germans who laughed and drank when they thought Stalingrad was all but won.

She threw the rest of her champagne out on the ground and left the party behind.

SECTION II

AIR

Chapter 7 ———————

Weser WP 1003/1

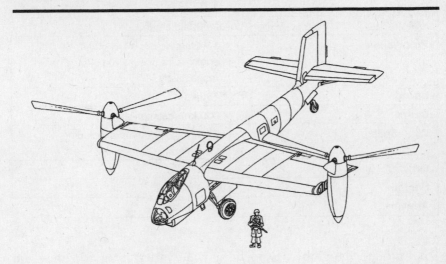

Overview

There were a number of vertical take off and landing (VTOL) vehicles attempted or built during World War II, and none proved deadlier to the enemies of Germany than the WP 1003. Not in the way the Germans had intended, because the WP 1003 never actually took off from a landing pad. The tiltrotor Weser WP 1003 served as an inspiration to an entire line of failed tiltrotor aircraft in the United States, culminating in Boeing's V-22 Osprey. Between 1992 and 2000, this aircraft's dismal service record resulted in the death of thirty crew and passengers and experienced many more nonfatal accidents. The aircraft was recommended for cancellation due to technical and safety issues in 1986. The aircraft is now entering production to serve as the main airborne transport of the U.S. Marine Corps.

Development History

There was great interest in VTOL vehicles near the end of World War I. In the interim years between the two world wars, various designers

Category:	Tiltrotor VTOL aircraft
Phase of Development:	Preprototype
Development Start:	1938
Development Team:	Weser Flugzeugbau GmbH
Crew:	2
Weight:	2,000 kg loaded
Propulsion:	1 × Daimler Benz DB 600 or 601 engine producing 910 or 1175 hp, respectively
Speed:	650 kph
Range:	800 km (estimated)
Wing Span:	7.00 m (11.00 meters including propellers)
Length:	8.30 m
Height:	3.10 m
Armament:	Unarmed

from around the globe developed a wide variety of gyroplanes and crude helicopters. The most successful of these was the Fa-61, which was developed in the late 1930s by Heinrich Focke. It was the first truly stable helicopter design and was capable of the extended flight and hovering, which had eluded early pioneers. The Fa-61 was even famously flown inside the Deutschlandhalle sports stadium by Nazi aviatrix Hanna Reitsch.

Focke's later designs included the highly successful Fa-223 Drache helicopter. Before the Drache, the Fa-61 and other early German helicopters were small and underpowered, leaving them to serve as reconnaissance aircraft and glorified messengers. The Drache was comparatively large and powerful and was capable of carrying as much as a ton of payload. Not a great deal by fixed-wing standards, but still an impressive achievement for early helicopters.

In 1938, the Weser WP 1003/1 was to have been the next evolution in VTOL technology. The WP 1003's fuselage closely resembled a fixed-wing aircraft with large-diameter rotors positioned similarly to the boom-mounted rotors of the Drache. These engines were mounted in nacelles at the wingtips, and the wings themselves were each divided at approximately the halfway point. Half of each wing and the engines could tilt up to 90 degrees to allow the WP 1003 to theoretically take off vertically and then fly like a fixed-wing aircraft.

The allure of the lift capacity, range, and speed of a fixed-wing aircraft combined with the vertical take off capability of a helicopter is undeniable. But the engineers at Weser had unwittingly created one of the most problematic configurations for a VTOL aircraft in history. The WP 1003 never advanced far enough in development to make this clear, but it undoubtedly inspired very similar aircraft like the experimental XV-15 and its production cousin the V-22 Osprey. The Osprey, planned to replace many of the ageing helicopters of the U.S. Marine Corps, has been a program plagued by disastrous crashes and overly complicated flight mechanics. Osprey pilots have to be especially well trained and aware of the dangers of their unique aircraft. One can only imagine the sort of skill that would have been required to handle a WP 1003 with similar capabilities and more simplistic 1940s' technology.

Technical Mumbo Jumbo

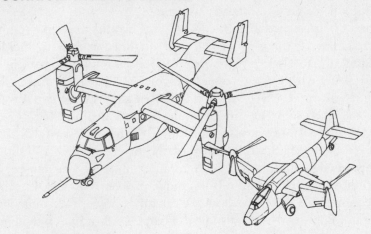

The preproduction WP 1003/1 (right) next to the modern V-22 Opsrey.

The Weser WP 1003/1 was designed with the aerodynamics of a fixed-wing aircraft and the capabilities of large-lifter helicopters (at the time) like the Fa-223 Drache. The two-man cockpit was located high in the forward fuselage of the aircraft and directly fore of the centrally located engine. A single Daimler-Benz DB 600 was selected to power both of the 4-meter diameter rotors mounted in nacelles on the aircraft's wingtips. At the time, the DB 600 was the logical choice for the engine, but it was later supplanted by the more powerful DB 601, and this would have likely served in a prototype or production model.

To maintain its VTOL capabilities, the Weser was a light airframe with a conservative fully loaded weight of only 2 metric tons. The projected top speed of the WP 1003 was 650 kph, but given the engine, the large rotors, and the performance of fairly similar aircraft like the Drache, this seems wildly optimistic. Fully loaded, the Drache was capable of scarcely 150 kph. The WP 1003 was more aerodynamic, lighter, and had a more powerful engine, but it is unlikely it would have topped 300 kph with a full payload. Even the modern Osprey, powered by two vastly more robust turboprop engines, is only capable of about 580 kph top speed.

No armament was planned for the WP 1003. Specific cargo capacity and troop-carrying capabilities are unknown. The Weser was well suited to serve as a light infantry transport, carrying perhaps as much as a full squad of Fallschirmjägers or other airborne infantry across the battlefield. This is purely conjecture, as at this early point in the history of helicopters, they had not been utilized or even widely considered for the role of massed infantry assault.

In terms of the technical difficulties Weser would have inevitably encountered, the Germans were the best qualified nation to tackle them at that time. The Fl 282 Kolibri, for example, approached torque problems with large intermeshed rotors. This small and agile observation helicopter served well with the Kriegsmarine, where it was used to spot Allied shipping, and it could be launched and recovered from the top of a turret on a warship. Although the success of this aircraft does not directly address many of the problems the WP 1003 would have encountered, it does serve as an example of German engineers' technical understanding of the unique problems of VTOL technology. Despite this experience and Germany's sometimes amazing leaps in technology, the Germans faced a black void of understanding when it came to tiltrotor technology. It took the United States almost twenty years of on-and-off testing to fashion a safely working prototype and another two decades to approach production readiness.

In the end, this technological deficiency would have likely kept the WP 1003 confined, at best, to unsuccessful prototypes.

Variants

No variants were planned for the Weser WP 1003. Had the design proven airworthy and had the Nazis fully grasped the incredible potential of VTOL-mounted shock troops, a lightly armed variant with an increased payload may have been developed. The exact troop capacity of the WP 1003/1 is not known, but even generous estimates make the aircraft large enough to accommodate only a handful of light troops in cramped conditions. An enlarged fuselage and more powerful engine would have enhanced this capability.

By contrast, the Nazis turned the Drache into a bombing helicopter, so who knows what they might have really done with the WP 1003. Maybe they would have strapped rockets to it and sent it after bomber formations.

Analysis

The Weser WP 1003 was an innovative design that was almost certainly out of the technical reach of the Germans. Many good aircraft suffered from this same problem, and fortunately for Germany and pretty much no one else, the WP 1003 was recognized as unfeasible. Had the Germans poured time and resources into the development of the WP 1003, we would have a cool prototype in a museum and a few days or weeks shaved off the length of World War II. For this reason alone, it is important to remember the macabre positive side of German wonder weapons. Without projects of questionable military utility like the V-2 or the Maus, there would have been many more fighters, bombers, and tanks that were proven to be good at killing Russians, Americans, and Brits.

Hypothetical Deployment History

The preproduction prototype of the WP 1003 was completed in May 1939. This aircraft was plagued with technical problems, and during its third unsuccessful attempt at sustained flight the aircraft lost all stability during rotor transition and crashed badly, destroying the prototype and killing the test pilots. The Luftwaffe did not show interest in a production order.

Despite these major setbacks, Weser Flugzeugbau continued to refine the design, and in late 1939 began construction of a second prototype. This design rotated only the wingtip nacelles rather than half of each wing and made the aircraft less prone to instability during transition. The prototype was completed and test-flown successfully in July 1940. A second test flight resulted in a hard landing and damage to the fuselage and landing gear. This was repaired, and in August

1940 a demonstration was given to Reichsluftfahitministerium (Reich Aviation Ministry; RLM) officials. They were impressed with the aircraft and ordered a production run of fifty to serve as light troop transports for a possible airborne invasion of Great Britain.

The first order of six aircraft, designated the We 266 Libelle, (Dragonfly), was delivered to training units in February 1941. The aircraft proved difficult to master, but very capable when mastery was achieved. Two of these training aircraft were lost in fatal crashes before the second order of eight combat aircraft was delivered in late April 1941. By then, Operation Sealion, the German invasion of Britain, had been canceled. Further production deliveries were to be allocated for the upcoming invasion of the Soviet Union. The aircraft entered service as a transport for shock troops and also saw use as an observation vehicle on the eastern front in June of that year.

The purpose of the We 266 took a dramatic turn in August 1941 when SS commando Otto Skorzeny approached Hitler with a daring plan to assassinate Winston Churchill. Operation Kälte-Dämmerung (Cold Dawn) was approved and six recently completed We 266s were earmarked as transports for the operation. With their undersides painted black, the We 266s of Skorzeny's commando teams took off at two in the morning on October 9. Using crude radio guidance, the aircraft managed to cross the Channel and sweep in at low altitude toward London in the predawn hours. An enormous fighter and bomber raid served as a radar diversion.

Poor navigation delayed their approach until dawn just broke across the city of London. As the We 266s made their final approach for landing, they were jumped by British fighters. Three managed to put down in the streets near 10 Downing Street, but one experienced a malfunction during rotor transition and crashed into the Treasury Green, and two were downed over the city by Spitfires. The shocked inhabitants of London watched in stunned terror as the German paratroopers piled out of the planes and engaged in a furious gun battle with the defenders of 10 Downing Street.

The beleaguered British troops put up a stiff resistance, killing several of the Germans and lightly wounding Skorzeny. In minutes, however, the Germans stormed the residence of Winston Churchill and began a mad search of the building for the prime minister. Unbeknown to Skorzeny, Churchill had watched the approach of the aircraft from the window of the Number 10 annex, where his family had taken up residence for safety purposes following the outbreak of war.

"I suppose I'll take my breakfast in the bunker, then," Churchill remarked before being whisked to safety by guards.

Skorzeny's force, stymied by the absence of Churchill, attempted to escape along preplanned routes. Most were killed by the British troops rushing to the scene. A few, including Skorzeny, eluded capture for several days. Skorzeny was eventually rounded up by the British, spotted drinking bitters at a pub while waiting for a steamer to arrive that would take him to Portugal. He was imprisoned for the remainder of the war despite three partially successful escape attempts, including one that took him all the way to Morocco before being recaptured. Skorzeny eventually escaped for good in 1948 and fled to Argentina.

Despite Skorzeny's failed mission and the constant technical issues, the Wc 266 remained in service until production was canceled in September 1943. Though the We 266 served fairly well, it was hated by air crews and was termed the "jumping casket" by nervous Luftwaffe personnel. Airborne infantry often complained of the poor survivability of the We 266 compared to conventional transport aircraft and requested parachute drops whenever possible. The usage of the We 266 as an assault transport was halted in July 1944, when an entire force of six aircraft, laden with infantry, was lost to a pair of American fighters over France.

What Fight Have Been

11:26 A.M., September 6, 1941
Eastern Front, I./JG51
Schatalowka-East Airfield, 5 Kilometers South of Dankowo, Belarus

Konrad Fleischer was up and out of the cockpit of his fighter before the ground crew had the blocks under its wheels. He tore off his flight cap and tossed it back into the cockpit then yanked down the zipper of his leather uniform jacket to let his chest air out a bit. Leathers were well and good at 5,000 meters, but the late summer Russian heat was unbelievable once you got a bit closer to the ground. Konrad had been forced to fly the last twenty minutes back to the airfield at treetop level with not enough fuel left to climb.

"Gave it to them, oberleutnant?" Manfred Schilling handed Konrad a grease-smeared package of Junos.

Konrad nodded and smiled with a sense of elation. The adrenaline was still thick in his blood.

"Got three and one on the ground." Konrad lit the cigarette and took an appreciative drag before continuing. "After the Channel this is fantastic stuff, Manny. Every time I go up, I send Russians back down the hard way. Even when you think the odds are against you, they aren't."

"If you say so, Konrad." Manfred opened the engine compartment on the Bf 109F, careful to keep his hands clear of the hot engine.

"Everyone else make it back before me?" Konrad surveyed the landing strips and open hangars, looking for the familiar markings of aircraft in his flight group.

"Sorry, sir." Manfred kept his back turned. "They said Lurtz was killed and Mehlinger went down ten kilometers east of here. They've got people looking for him, but Oberstleutnant Beckh saw him go down and said it didn't look like he bailed."

"Tough luck," Konrad said with a flicker of sadness that vanished after a moment. "I'm surprised Friedrich could see anything but the ground."

"He scored two tank kills," Manfred offered a weak defense of the acting commander.

"Oh yes, he would have made a fantastic panzer commander." Konrad gave Manfred a salute and ducked off toward the canteen.

On his way toward a bit of relaxation, he caught sight of his favorite person on the base. Lilli was in her gray auxiliary's uniform looking like something from an American film reel. Konrad took a moment to admire the modest cut of her uniform. It was hardly Hitler Youth enough to hide all of her assets. She was walking away with a pile of forms stacked on top of a clipboard and had not caught sight of him yet. He snuck up behind her and covered her eyes with his hands.

"Guess who?"

"Konrad, for God's sake, you stink like a pig in a petrol station." She smiled all the same when he let her go. "Beckh is going to feed that Iron Cross of yours up the wrong end for the stunt you pulled today."

"What? No 'Hello Konrad, so good to see you made it back safely' or 'Oh, Konrad, you look so fit in those leathers! Let's stop off and have a roll behind the hangar'?"

Lilli slapped at his chest as best she could with her arms full of papers.

"Just because the Russians can't kill you doesn't mean I can't."

He grabbed her upper arms and kissed her, smashing the papers up against her chest and nearly knocking her cap off her blonde locks. She shoved him away.

"Not now!" Lilli hissed. "The SS are crawling all over those whirly-birds, and I'm going crazy taking care of paperwork. Something is up."

Konrad had already had a good look at the half-dozen strange air-craft with SS markings that had arrived the day before, but the news that they might be going into action had his curiosity piqued.

"Oh, really? Perhaps I should go have a chat with Oberstleutnant Adler."

He peered out at the dapple-painted aircraft with their twin upright propellers. There was a throng of soldiers around each of the planes. He had read about Skorzeny's mad exploits in the things, but these were the first he had seen in person.

"You had better go talk with *your* commanding officer. Beckh is mad enough to have a coronary and I think he means it." She softened immediately, "We'll have plenty of time for a roll behind the hangar later tonight. I checked, you're off the roster."

"The hell I am," Konrad muttered, already forgetting about Lilli.

He set off purposefully toward the nearest of the aircraft. A group of ten fully outfitted soldiers in Waffen-SS kit were idling by the open side door of one of the planes. These men were not the fresh-faced zealots the Waffen-SS tended to churn out as replacements; fools with more fascism than common sense in their heads. These men had the impassive faces and relaxed demeanor of battle-hardened soldiers. Their uniforms were concealed beneath their camouflage smocks and their NCO had the common sense to hide his collar insignia. Konrad picked out the man who looked like he had shaved most recently and offered him a cigarette.

"If I had known the Luftwaffe had such pretty cigarette girls I would have joined up," the man quipped, and the soldiers around him laughed, but he took the Juno.

Konrad lit the cigarette and then another for himself.

"If I had known the SS was letting any sack of jelly wear a uniform, I would have joined the Reds." That sort of comment would either get Konrad's eye blacked or win them over.

The soldiers stared at him icily for a moment and Konrad tensed, ready to throw up his guard. The man he had given the cigarette to let out a roar of laughter. The others mostly followed suit, though one or two continued to glare at the cocky Luftwaffe pilot.

"Odd bird you boys are flying in. What's the story?" Konrad

handed his pack of cigarettes to the nearest soldier and nodded for him to pass it around.

"Horrible things," said the man Konrad had taken for their NCO. "We trained on them a bit, but I don't trust them."

"And you're going out today then?"

"Guderian wants a bridge, so the SS will give him a bridge. I just wish we were headed to Makoshim on the back of a motorcycle." The man took another drag. "Or a horse."

"Or a pig," one of the other soldiers added and they all chuckled.

"I don't suppose you know who is flying escort for your little adventure."

"Fifty-second or something," the NCO shook his head. "JG fifty-second."

"Yeah, but do you know which group?"

"Second," the pilot of the aircraft said as he stepped around the nose.

With a jolt of recognition, Konrad realized that the aircraft's pilot was a friend of his from Gymnasium. Reinhardt Steinhauer, apparently an SS-Untersturmfuehrer, looked none the worse for wear.

"Why you goddamn traitor!" Konrad laughed.

"All this?" Reinhardt looked down at his uniform. "Nah, just a fresh coat of paint. I'm only a shade off gray. They asked if I wanted to fly something new, and after bailing out over the Channel, it sounded like a fun time."

"It's good to see you again!" The two men embraced briefly. "I heard your plane went down, but I never knew if you got fished out of the Channel."

"I meant to come say hello to you. I was hoping you boys would be flying cover, but it looks like we got second group."

"Oh," Konrad beamed, "I wouldn't worry about that. I'll see you in the air."

Reinhardt gave Konrad a quizzical look, but the Luftwaffe pilot offered no explanation. The truth was that he knew exactly who to talk to. Konrad knew the right man—or woman—to get him very temporarily reassigned to a new group within the squadron.

"It looked like you're up there almost all day and night." Reinhardt ran a hand across the cockpit canopy of his aircraft. "When do you rest?"

"Rest?!" Konrad acted indignant. "I'm lagging behind. I haven't even broken a hundred yet."

Both pilots erupted with laughter. The Waffen-SS soldiers stared at them like they had just fallen upward out of a tree.

Chapter 8

M1932 Christie "Flying Tank"

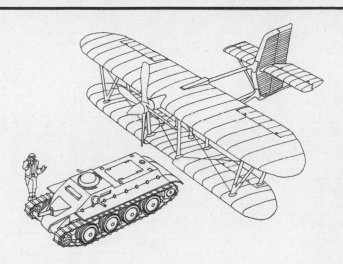

Overview

If you have heard of the U.S. inventor J. Walter Christie before, then you automatically fall into one of two categories. On one side, there are the people who think that J. Walter Christie is the forgotten genius of World War II. These folks believe that Christie's silent contributions to the development of armored warfare are virtually unmatched. Opposing these scoundrels are those who brush aside Christie's inventions and contributions as deservedly forgotten by most history books. The truth is probably somewhere between the two, but I lean more toward "Christie was a moody ass who allowed his egotism to interfere with his genius."

Christie is best known for the "Christie suspension." Invented in the 1920s to improve the cross-country performance of armored vehicles, Christie's revolutionary suspension employed a bell crank and individually mounted large rubberized road wheels. The addition of the bell crank allowed for a much greater range of motion in the suspension and the large road wheels eliminated the need for return rollers. Suspensions are pretty boring stuff, but at the time Christie's was something worth getting excited about. All he had to do to impress

Category:	Light airborne tank
Phase of Development:	Functional prototype
Development Start:	1932
Development Team:	J. Walter Christie
Crew:	3
Weight:	4.5 metric tons
Propulsion:	Hispano-Suiz 12-cylinder 750 hp
Speed:	Road (wheeled): 160 kph Cross-country (tracked): 95 kph
Range:	Road: 180–220 km Cross-country: 120–150 km
Length:	6.71 m
Width:	2.13 m
Height:	1.73 m
Armament:	1 × 75mm M3 (or similar) 2 × .30cal M1919A4 MG
Ammunition:	75mm-50 rounds (approximate)
Armor:	10mm ranging to 15mm

spectators was take one of his little tanks for an 80 kph test drive across a rough course.

Christie had a good, marketable invention to sell to the government, and you would have thought that he could arrange some sort of deal. Christie wanted to make tanks, not just the suspension, and he spent more than a decade trying and failing to sell the army on various designs. Christie's problem was that he refused to bend to the requirements of the army. He had a vision of hundreds of his small and very fast tanks swarming across a battlefield and exploiting every opportunity with their maneuverability. The army tended to disagree with his vision and was less than pleased whenever Christie back-sassed them over a modification request. Christie had a litany of failed prototypes that he began to shop abroad, selling a chassis here and there to the United Kingdom and the Soviet Union, among others.

Christie's obsession with mobility over armor and firepower culminated in the development of a series of flying tanks, but the U.S. military shunned these dubious innovations. The Soviets had successfully incorporated Christie's suspension into the BT-7 fast tank and pursued a line of airborne tank research similar to Christie's. World War II

A Panzerkampfwagen VIII Maus engages in street fighting in Poland.

The Landkreuzer P. 1500 Ratte nicknamed "Little Rosie" travels with a convoy.

A look down one of the gun tunnels of the V-3 Hochdruckpumpe in Mimoyecques.

Rotkäppchen launchers lash out from concealment at advancing Soviet armor.

An SS Soldat fights using a Vampir scope on the grounds of the Reichstag.

Bad news for someone down range as this P. 1500 Monster unleashes its 800mm gun on the enemy.

Skorzeny's commandos dismount from their Weser WP 1003/1 within sight of 10 Downing Street.

An M1932 Christie Flying Tank prepares to make an unscheduled landing over Normandy.

A member of Haubschrauber-Jäger-Regiment One executes a flawless landing with his Heliofly III/57.

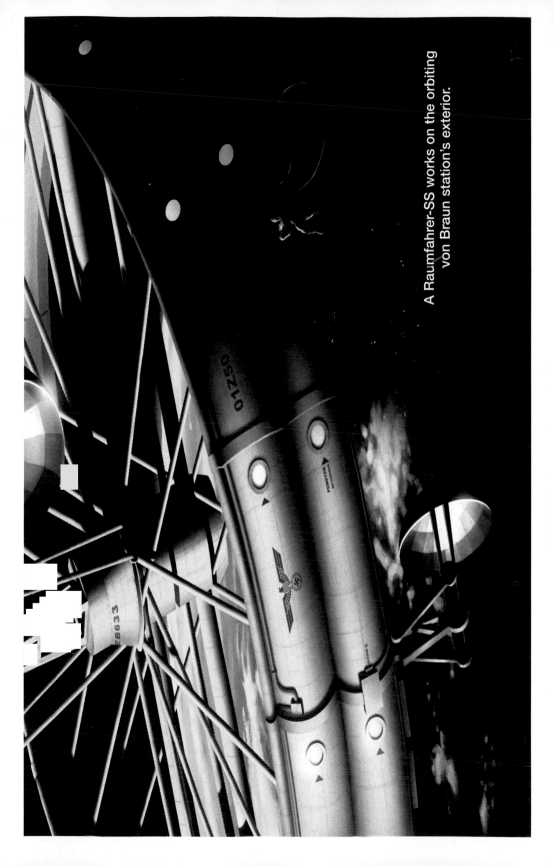

A Raumfahrer-SS works on the orbiting von Braun station's exterior.

Ho IXBs prepare to pounce on a formation of Allied bombers.

Project F suicide rockets make an attack run under heavy fire.

The Sänger Silbervogel S-1 activates its internal booster and soars away from its discarded first stage.

VS8 hydrofoils approach the burning piers of Narvik.

The Type XI-B U-cruiser U-113 begins its surface attack on an Allied convoy.

The HMS *Habbakuk*, turned USS *Avenger*, sails on through icy waters despite torpedo damage.

A Seeteufel amphibious submarine finds a ripe target moored in a liberated port.

The Diebner atomic bomb detonates over downtown New York City.

ended with two fundamentally identical flying tanks that were also nearly identical in their uselessness on the battlefield.

Development History

Christie's stormy relationship with the U.S. Army began in the aftermath of World War I. In 1919, the army determined that it was in need of a medium tank to fulfill all the requirements of its future armored forces. Christie was experienced with tractors and simpler armored vehicles, and at the army's behest, he cobbled together a prototype he called the M1919. Christie handed over the rushed prototype, but it had a variety of glaring flaws such as the usual suspension problems of vehicles at the time, poor maneuverability, and very low speeds. Oh yeah, it was almost impossible to gain access to the engine or transmission because of the hurried nature of its construction. Whoops! Hope it doesn't break! The army handed the tank back over to Christie, and he set to work generating a revised prototype.

Christie's next version was the M1921, which was basically the same as the M1919 without a turret. The suspension was slightly improved, and you could actually get a wrench into the engine, but the performance was still unsatisfactory. The M1921 made the review and testing circuits, but the army was unhappy with Christie's work, and its attention drifted to superior prototypes.

Christie returned to the drawing board. In 1928, he produced the first tank that incorporated what would become known as the "Christie suspension." The creatively named M1928 lacked a turret and was lightly armed and armored, but it had incredible cross-country performance. The tank was fast and had a smooth ride. It also introduced one of Christie's obsessions: the idea of being able to take the tracks off a tank and drive it on its road wheels. Almost every subsequent prototype created by Christie would incorporate this interesting but largely useless feature.

The army was very impressed with this prototype and sent Christie back to his mad scientist lair with design changes. Christie's relationship with the army grew increasingly contentious over the M1928, but he went on to produce what probably became his masterpiece. The M1931 was similar to the M1928—it had the same engine, transmission, and suspension—with a marked increase in operational range and the relocation of the 37mm main armament to a small turret. Just as Christie and his tanks were coming to the attention of governments around the world, Christie's relationship with the U.S. Army became untenable. In a series of transactions, some of them legally questionable, Christie produced and sold unarmed versions of the M1931 to Poland, the United Kingdom, and the Soviet Union. In Poland, the M1931 essentially became its 10TP light tank. England used the M1931 as the starting point for its Cruiser tank.

It was the Soviets who got the most mileage out of the Christie prototypes. The Christie M1931 became the basis for an entire series of BT "Fast Tanks," which eventually evolved into the legendary T-34. The T-34, the vehicle that famously gave the Germans a shock when they encountered it, was based on Christie's work. That's what the Christie-loving camp would have you believe, anyway. The truth is that the T-34 was a divergence from the sort of armored vehicle Christie himself advocated. It was fast and used a modernized version of his suspension, but the similarities ended there. After the T-34, the Soviets dropped his suspension entirely.

Following the export of his prototypes, Christie began to entertain increasingly idiosyncratic design ideas. In 1932, he began work on an all-new tank that took the best aspects of the M1931 and combined them with what Christie felt a tank would need to fly. The M1932 was born. It was a turretless design that incorporated a light field gun in the front section of a greatly elongated hull. The tank was sleek, extremely fast, and featured an impressively durable suspension designed to take the great stress of an airborne landing. Christie completed a prototype along with a supposedly functional flying frame that consisted of a reinforced biplane design and oversized propeller driven by the tank's engine. That wasn't as crazy as it sounds, since the M1932's engine was a large 750 horsepower aircraft engine.

Though there is no record of the M1932 ever successfully flying, Christie became infatuated with the idea of an airborne tank. Over the next decade, he developed no fewer than six unique prototypes based around this concept. Some were designed to use flying frames like the M1932, others were designed to be carried by transport aircraft and dropped from very low levels. The Soviets somehow caught this bug as well and developed a vehicle called the KT-40. They once again purchased a prototype from Christie and set to work testing and modifying it. The Soviets not only built a glider flying frame for an existing tank, the T-60 light tank, they actually managed to fly it in 1940.

Not surprisingly, the Soviets came to the same conclusions the U.S. Army had years earlier: Christie's flying tanks were completely idiotic.

Christie died in 1944. Perhaps, like Icarus, he had dared to fly his tank too close to the sun.

Technical Mumbo Jumbo

The M1932 was a light 4.5-ton tank with a hull nearly 7 meters in length. The unusual length of the tank was necessitated by a need for space to mount the large Hispano-Suiz aircraft engine and the 75mm gun. Crew conditions inside the M1932 were every bit as cramped and uncomfortable as they were on pretty much every Christie design. The powerful 750 horsepower engine was necessary to power the flight propeller and allow the tank to run-up its treads to maximum speed for drop landings. An interesting design feature of the M1932 was that unlike most airborne tanks, including most of Christie's later designs, the M1932 was capable of actually lifting off.

The disposable flying structure was a reinforced wooden biplane airframe with a large four-blade airscrew. It attached to the rear two-thirds of the M1932's hull at four points, and although provisions were not made for explosive bolts, these certainly would have been implemented had the M1932 ever gone into production. Power was provided to the propeller by attaching a chain drive to the rear drive sprockets of the M1932. Like most Christie tanks, the M1932 was capable of operating on its eight double-road wheels or using a full-track assembly. Crews could swap from one mode to the other in roughly ten minutes.

The M1932 was extremely fast on the ground. Christie famously test drove one of M1932's successors in 1937 and reached a rough cross-country speed of over 100 kph. Christie claimed that the M1932 was capable of speeds up to 160 kph when using its road wheels on paved surfaces.

Armor for the M1932 ranged from 10 to 15 millimeters, although this figure must be considered as an "unarmored" version of the vehicle. Christie planned for a more heavily armored production model of the M1932. Exact figures on this fully armored M1932 are not known, but it was calculated that the additional weight of even moderately useful armor could prove catastrophic to the flying and landing capabilities of the tank.

Weaponry on the M1932 consisted of a short-barreled 75mm gun mounted in a limited traverse ball turret at the tank's front. At the time, a 75mm gun had yet to be mounted in a U.S. tank. Production versions of the M1932 would have likely seen a low-velocity gun like the 75mm M3 used in the Lee and early-model Shermans. Browning .30 caliber machine guns were planned for ball turrets on either side of the hull, which was an interesting way of limiting the usefulness of a machine gun on a tank with no turret.

Variants

Though several prototypes of Christie flying tanks were produced, the only really remarkable distinction was that most of them were designed from the start to be dropped from a carrier aircraft. The logistics of executing a driving drop from a low-flying aircraft is even more horrifying to imagine than the crash landing of a truly flying M1932. At least in the M1932 the crew had some small degree of control over their fate. In tanks like the playfully named M1936 and M1938, the crew could do little other than hang on tight and watch as their carrier plane dropped them nose-first into a ravine at 150 kph.

Analysis

The M1932 flying tank was rightfully rejected by the U.S. military. Despite the conceptual coolness of a flying tank swooping onto a battlefield, the M1932 would not have made a very effective fighting vehicle. The first danger facing the crew of a M1932 would be simply surviving the towering peril of flying across potentially contested airspace. The tank would have been horribly unwieldy and nearly incapable of maneuvering at all. There were dozens of aircraft with heavier armor than the M1932 and hundreds with weapons easily capable of making the M1932 explode in midair. Once it had landed behind enemy lines, it could have been taken out by almost any weapon the enemy had. Fifteen millimeter-thick armor could be perforated by heavy machine guns and the lightest of cannons. Heavier armor would have increased the likelihood of a crash or a bad landing.

What the M1932 had going for it was its speed and maneuverability on the ground. Unfortunately, even these positives have to be tempered with the knowledge that the tank had a high possibility of sustaining some form of damage when landing. Christie-designed vehicles were also almost always mechanically unreliable. It would be great to be crewing one of these things, fly all the way across 50 kilometers of enemy territory to land, drive half a kilometer, and then lose the transmission.

The M1932 was so bad, and Christie had such an obsessive personality, that I would like to posthumously offer him five suggestions just as good as the flying tank:

1. Meat Tank—Save that metal for your bullets! The chassis of this tank would be made entirely out of meat. As an added bonus, it would smell so bad that the enemy would be uncontrollably sick when it rolled across the battlefield. Camouflage? Hey, look at that huge ball of vultures and rats!
2. Machine Gun Bottom—The M1932 had some pretty useless side-firing machine guns, but I think you could do better. Have all the machine guns fire directly downward. They'd only be useful when crossing a trench full of enemies suffering from catatonia or if the tank happened to fall off of a cliff and landed balanced upright.
3. Volcano Tank—Who would expect an armored attack to come from the magma-filled caldera of an active volcano?
4. Tree Tank—Find a good hollowed out tree, stick a cannon out of the knothole, and have the crew stand on one another's shoulders.
5. Falling Tank—Stick your tanks in a plane, fly up really high, and then just let the 15-ton chips fall where they may. It would take a miracle if even one of the tanks survived the drop, but you obviously believe in those if you think the U.S. Army is going to buy your goddamn idiotic flying tank.

The Christie flying tank would have technically worked, but the sacrifices necessary to make it "airworthy" crippled it as an effective fighting vehicle. I should say "hilariously crippled it" as an effective fighting vehicle.

Hypothetical Deployment History

The first production models of the M1932 (the AM2 Burnside) entered service after extensive testing and modifications in August 1938. The first batch of fourteen unarmed AM2s were delivered to the purpose-built Soft Sands Academy in the Nevada desert. Training accidents were initially frequent and serious until Soft Sands instituted the "5-feet policy." Crews being trained on the AM2 were ordered to never climb to an altitude of more than 5 feet off the ground.

Due to mechanical difficulties and crashes, a large portion of the production run of AM2s was diverted to replace training losses. The newly formed Ninety-sixth Special Airborne Armored Brigade (SAAB) was not fully equipped with combat-ready vehicles until 1941. The unit was on the verge of being disbanded just as it approached full organizational strength when the Japanese attack on Pearl Harbor drew the United States into the war. H Company of the Ninety-sixth SAAB was detached for a special mission assisting the British in North Africa in 1943. On their first mission, the fourteen vehicles sent with H Company were destroyed. Nine crashed and the remaining five were knocked out by the enemy. The unit did manage to preempt an enemy attack but was subsequently withdrawn for refitting to the United States.

The AM2 next saw combat during the ill-fated Dieppe raid when H Company again attempted an inland landing behind the beach location. This time, eleven vehicles were available for participation. Two crashed into the English Channel en route to landing sites, and seven AM2s were shot down by a single German Me-110 returning from a mission. The two surviving vehicles were both disabled during landing and their crews were forced to surrender. The remaining eighty-six AM2s of the Ninety-sixth SAAB were for a time slated to participate in the D day landings but General Dwight D. Eisenhower decided against it in the spring of 1944. The Ninety-sixth SAAB was formally disbanded in July 1944. The crews of the AM2s were given crash courses in the M4 Sherman and served with distinction as replacement crews.

What Fight Have Been

9:06 A.M., December 22, 1941
Ninety-sixth Special Airborne Armored Brigade
Soft Sands Academy, Nevada

The sergeant driving the jeep looked back over his shoulder and said, "Quite a name you got, Mister Lincoln."

"My parents were fanatics for irony," Robert E. Lincoln replied. "My bylines read R.E. Lincoln: You can call me Robert."

"You're going to want to get your camera as low to the ground as possible!" Captain Philip Gondry shouted over the constant rattle of gravel. "Make it look like the damn thing is high as an eagle."

R.E. bit down on his pipe hard enough to taste the cracks in the wood and glared at the dust-covered public affairs officer.

"I don't take pictures," he finally replied.

"Oh, well that's just fine, Mister Lincoln." Captain Gondry smiled like a man who'd just won himself a dance with Rita Hayworth. "We've got some *Stars and Stripes* folks here. I'm sure they won't mind sharing."

After the papers had finished screaming their headlines off about Pearl Harbor, they had gone looking for morale-raising public interest stories. The Ninety-sixth had been a comical oddity when it was formed in 1939. Then R.E. had the misfortune to recall the unit during a meeting of the editorial staff at the *New York Record*. The next morning, he was cursing his big mouth aboard a rickety army cargo plane bound for the ass end of the Nevada desert.

The jeep ride took them to an isolated expanse of flat hardpan earth. Trucks, jeeps, and staff cars formed a loose perimeter around what appeared to be a munchkin village. The structures of the village were done in a vague Hollywood version of Japanese style, with rice paper walls and wood roofs painted to look like clay tiles. The entire village was done at about 1:2 scale and R.E. had to control his laughter as he climbed out of the jeep and began jotting down notes. When he spotted the Japanese civilians, he abandoned all hope of controlling his laughter and just tried his best to conceal it from Captain Gondry.

There were two dozen or so pajama-clad Mexican children with big fake wooden teeth and mustaches. A little girl had her face painted to look like a Geisha, but it just made her resemble a miniature clown.

"Get the civilians into their places!" Captain Gondry shouted and the army men began to herd the Mexican children into the village.

The point of the whole charade was the flying tank concealed by canvas. Gondry had taken up a position next to the vehicle and with a flourish he and several other men unveiled it for the cameras.

"The AM2 is the ultimate firepower rapid deployment system of the United States Army." Captain Gondry began speaking directly to a newsreel crew. "No arsenal in the world can match our ability to forward-deploy armor assets not just to the front, but *behind* the front lines."

An army photographer snapped pictures, but R.E. had seen it all before, so he just scribbled down that the AM2 looked about the same.

The tank's engine roared to life as the demonstration began. It was a loud and higher rumble than most tanks and the chain connecting the huge biplane frame to the transmission began to spin. The propeller started to rotate and the tank began to pick up speed in the direction of the village. R.E. noted that along the tank's intended path was a second newsreel camera just three feet off the ground and angled slightly upward.

The AM2 trundled toward the village and tentatively began to bounce into the air. Each of these bounces became longer as it picked up speed. The kindest thing R.E. could think to say about it was that it looked like it absolutely did not want to fly but could be intimidated into doing it by the reinforced flying frame. When it finally lifted off the ground and stayed in the air, there was a murmur of genuine surprise in the audience. Dust swirled around it as it lifted up into the air one foot, then two feet, then three feet.

Then, with a terrible crash, it struck the newsreel camera meant to embellish its flight, shattering glass and knocking the terrified crew back. The AM2 flopped down hard, catching the back end of a slight dip in the ground, so that when it launched back into the air, it was at a 20-degree angle. The flying tank sailed ten feet high and then came crashing back down to earth. It spun wildly as it skidded across the ground. The Mexican children in the village fled and the tank crashed dramatically into the tiny wooden buildings.

R.E. flipped his notepad closed and began walking over to the sergeant and the jeep that had brought him to the demonstration. As he passed by Captain Gondry, he heard the insufferable officer asking if the newsreel crews could edit their footage to make it look impressive. R.E. thought it was pretty impressive, just not the sort of impression that the U.S. Army wanted to be giving.

Chapter 9 _____

The Heliofly III/57

Overview

I have always wondered what it would have been like to be one of the early astronauts, blasted into space with only a vague idea of what awaited you. Even the slightest mistake, miscalculation, or mechanical failure would result in you turning into a flash of exploding fuel. That's if you were lucky. If you weren't, space could probably find a way for you to die that involved searing blasts of radiation combined with your eyes exploding. I think it's pretty much impossible for people who haven't flown into space to understand this keen sense of mortality that surrounds every space mission. The one exception to this is for those unfortunate few who served as test pilots for the Heliofly.

An astronaut protected by modern space suits and insulated pressurized capsules can't hope to compare with a guy in a leather flight suit strapped to 6-meter-long rotors spinning into a blur less than 20 centimeters above his head. Every second of every flight would be like reliving the scene from *Raiders of the Lost Ark* when Indiana Jones is fist-fighting a Nazi next to an airplane propeller. You're not Indiana Jones; you're the big bald Nazi who actually gets a face full of rotor.

The Heliofly was the first in a series of failed attempts at creating a

Category:	Strap-on helicopter
Phase of Development:	Prototype
Development Start:	1942
Development Team:	Paul Baumgartl
Crew:	1
Weight:	30 kg without pilot 120 kg estimated max takeoff weight
Propulsion:	1 × Argus 8 hp engine
Speed:	100 kph (estimated)
Range:	10 km (estimated)
Rotor Diameter:	6 m
Armament:	Pilot's personal armament only

man-portable helicopter or "Hoppicopter" during and after World War II. The Austrian inventor Paul Baumgartl pioneered the idea of a backpack personal aerial transport and later abandoned the concept in favor of extremely lightweight conventional helicopters. The designer Horace Pentecoast essentially started the Heliofly project over from square one in 1945 and reached a similar conclusion to Baumgartl's. Pilots seem to have some sort of weird aversion to trying to land on their feet with rotors spinning directly over their heads.

Development History

Baumgartl was one of many European designers and amateurs fascinated with helicopters and various other rotary-wing aircraft in the years leading up to World War II. Unique among these designers, Baumgartl had a vision for a strap-on helicopter capable of being carried by a single man. The complex problems inherent in helicopter designs were further complicated by finding a way to lift and transport a man safely with a unit weighing less than 50 kilograms. Baumgartl began work on his first strap-on aircraft at a time when more conventional helicopters were still crude and dangerous. Taking these crude helicopters and translating them into a functional prototype of a strap-on helicopter would be akin to studying the human genome and then creating a living centaur.

Baumgartl operated out of a modest workshop near Vienna without the endorsement or sponsorship of the German government. In

1941, he completed his prototype of the Heliofly I, but this aircraft presented several major problems for a pilot with no reasonable solutions. Despite these problems, Baumgartl himself "successfully" flew this prototype in a demonstration for Luftwaffe officers and RLM officials. The Heliofly I was a single-rotor design and had basically no means beyond the pilot's brute strength to cancel torque. This made the Heliofly wildly unstable and capable of only making very short aerial "leaps" of no more than 25 meters.

Even limiting the Heliofly to a sort of super trampoline was not really a pleasant experience for the pilot, who had to wrestle the aircraft in the desired direction and then slow its descent during landing. The biggest danger for the pilot came at the moment of landing when a bad angle or slippery footing might make him fall. If he fell, the blade would strike the ground and splinter into hundreds of fragments, any one of which could prove fatal. Despite all these ruinous flaws, the RLM awarded Baumgartl a study contract and allocated him the funding and resources necessary to produce a new prototype. He was either a really smooth talker or some kind of master mesmerist.

Baumgartl began work on the Heliofly II, but this disappeared without ever seeing the light of day. He completed the Heliofly III/57 in 1942 and tackled the torque problems by mounting counterweights to two single-blade rotors. These two rotors rotated in opposition so that one rotor came very close to canceling the other's torque. Instability was still an issue, but the design was a major improvement over the first prototype, and its stability problems were manageable in the hands of a skilled pilot.

The Heliofly III/57 remained intolerably dangerous during landings, and Baumgartl gave in to pressure and scrapped the strap-on design. The final iteration of the Heliofly was the Heliofly III/59. It consisted of a framework of hollow tubes, a canvas seat, and a universal stick. The multiple blades of the rotor were angled forward on a boom and counterweighted by the new 16-horsepower Argus engine. This aircraft was really just an ultralight helicopter and was similar to other designs like the Nager-Rolz ultralights. It proved more stable than its predecessors, but it was still difficult to fly and it was unpleasant for test pilots. The lack of a fixed aircraft structure to align with the horizon and the constant powerful vibration of the airframe caused disorientation. Try skateboarding on the edge of a cliff the next time you get fall-down drunk and you'll have a good idea for how enjoyable this was.

The Heliofly project was canceled and Baumgartl went on to work on more traditional helicopter designs during and after the war. It should be noted that most designers who have since attempted to construct a strap-on helicopter have followed almost the exact same development arc as Baumgartl.

Technical Mumbo Jumbo

The Heliofly I (left) and the Heliofly III/59.

The Heliofly III/57 was the last of Baumgartl's strap-on helicopter designs. It was powered by an 8 horsepower Argus engine mounted almost immediately behind the pilot's head. The engine turned two separate single-blade rotors that rotated in opposing directions to counteract each other's torque. Each blade was balanced against a rotating counterweight. The aircraft was secured to the pilot's back by means of a canvas harness and was controlled with a universal stick that came down over the pilot's shoulder.

The aircraft carried minimal fuel and was capable of making "leaps" of roughly 100 meters at a time. It could not hover because of its instability and its operational ceiling (read: the apex of a particularly good jump) was less than 50 meters. The Heliofly III/57 was capable of carrying approximately 90 kilograms of weight or the weight of a single light infantryman and sparing equipment. The Heliofly III/57 could be broken down and stowed: the engine and controls inside a rucksack and the rotors and counterweights in a canvas sheath. These two parcels weighed no more than 30 kilograms. This was a manageable weight for a man carrying little else, but a true burden for an infantryman already hauling even a lightweight kit.

Variants

I selected the Heliofly III/57 to be the focus of this chapter rather than the Heliofly III/59. I felt that with the III/59, the Heliofly was transformed from something unique and strange into something conventional. Many designers seem to agree with me, as a good deal of effort over the years has gone into emulating the Heliofly III/57. To this day, research is continuing on strap-on aircraft designs like Michael Moshier's not-really-man-portable SoloTrek. Ultralight helicopters like the Heliofly III/59 have been built and flown successfully for several decades.

Analysis

Because it was incapable of reaching even modest altitudes and it could not hover the Heliofly III/57 was not particularly useful as an observation platform. It was also not a contraption that even an elite infantryman like a Fallschirmjäger could strap on and use without thorough training. Physical strength and above-average piloting skills were both absolutely required to handle the Heliofly. One of these two traits was not in great supply among most infantry formations in the German military.

With these considerations in mind, the Heliofly could have been used by specially trained commandos for special operations. There could have been a unit of helicopter-wearing shock troops drawn from the ranks of the Luftwaffe, but the Heliofly would not have been a lot of use in most assaults. You could jump really far, but you also made a lot of noise and as you flew through the air, you followed a very predictable trajectory. Perhaps they would have been useful for jumping over the moat and curtain wall of a castle. Look out, Jericho!

Enormous static fortifications like the Maginot Line could have fallen to massed assaults by the Heliofly, but casualties would have been heavier than they were with more conventional airborne troops. The poor soldiers with their disaster backpacks would have exposed themselves to heavy fire and had difficulty landing without injuring themselves or nearby troops.

Hypothetical Deployment History

Baumgartl's preprototype work on the Heliofly I attracted the attention of the Luftwaffe before it had even left the drawing board, and Baumgartl accelerated development of the aircraft to meet the demands of the RLM. Trials of the first prototype in mid-1940 were exciting but ultimately unsatisfactory. After a second failed prototype, Baumgartl returned to the proving grounds in February 1941 with the prototype for the Heliofly III/57. This new model was deemed acceptable. A production order was placed for 3,000 to be manufactured by Heinkel at its Oranienburg factory under the designation of the He-148 Floh (Flea). Baumgartl was subsequently hired as the chief engineer on the project.

While the Floh was under production by Heinkel, the Luftwaffe began to recruit volunteers from its pilot-candidate and airborne infantry programs. A total of six infantry companies, one artillery company, and one command company were raised to become Haubschrauber-Jäger-Regiment One. This independent regiment began mustering in Pomerania in July 1941 to operate as an independent force for assaulting Soviet strong points. Marching a long distance while carrying the Floh would completely exhaust troops. For strategic purposes, Haubschrauber-Jäger-Regiment One became one of the first fully motorized German infantry regiments. A number of training casualties were suffered, and by April 1942 the regiment was at only 70 percent of its paper strength due to injuries, deaths, and fail-outs. Despite this, the regiment exhibited considerable esprit de corps.

In May 1942, the regiment was transferred to the command of the Thirtieth Army Corps besieging Sevastopol. Dense fortifications in and around the port city and determined Soviet resistance had stymied German efforts to secure the area. The Thirtieth Army Corps requested the assistance of the regiment for a daring assault on a key complex of artillery bunkers before the launching of an all-out offensive in early June. Under General-Major Ernst Tannert, the Haubschrauber-Jäger-Regiment One launched its surprise attack on Soviet fortifications designated "The Wall." The Thirtieth Army Corps provided a diversion by unleashing a massive artillery barrage and attack on the Inkerman and Balaclava high ground near the city.

At 5:08 A.M. on June 12, with artillery crashing nearby, 288 men representing 2 companies launched themselves from their start positions into the fiery dawn sky. The astonished Soviets were caught almost completely by surprise, and the first wave managed to bypass the Soviet front lines with only a handful of casualties. A few jumps later and these two companies had settled on and around the artillery bunkers where they engaged in a fierce close-range battle with the defenders. The second wave of two companies began its attack on schedule, but this time the Soviets on the front lines were ready. Machine guns and a hail of rifle fire raked the leaping German forces, killing or wounding nearly half before they reached the objective.

Despite the casualties inflicted on the second wave, the German troops stormed the complex of bunkers with ruthless efficiency. Using grenades and satchel charges, they blasted their way inside, knocked out the artillery, and killed or captured the defenders of seven of the eight large bunkers. The final bunker took more than two hours to overrun, and by that time the Thirtieth Army Corps' feint had been aborted. Frontline troops rolled back in on the bunkers, now held by the Germans, and the already fierce battle became a maelstrom. The Germans were badly outnumbered and outgunned, but they held their own through the day, despite nearly all the soldiers being wounded in some way by that point. With most of his regiment cut off, General-Major Tannert convinced the Thirtieth Army Corps to launch a concerted attack in his sector. In the meantime, he committed his last reserves to the battle.

The final two assault companies leapt toward the shell-pocked bunkers under cover of smoke and darkness. Casualties from small-arms fire were light, but the pitch-black urban environment proved disastrous for dozens of men in this final wave. More than fifty were killed in accidents before reaching the bunkers or during their final approach. The Germans remained besieged for three full days with no food or water, save for what they could scavenge from the Soviets.

On June 16, elements of the Thirtieth Army Corps launched an assault on the sector as the surviving elements of the besieged German force prepared to link up. By pooling fuel from the surviving Floh aircraft, some sixty men were able to use the aircraft to attack from within the bunker complex at a critical moment. This surprise attack was nearly suicidal—only four men survived—but it threw the Soviet forces encircling the bunkers into hysterics just as the tanks of the Thirtieth Army Corps came crashing through. An additional seventy-six men, including General-Major Tannert, held the bunkers until being relieved by the Thirtieth Army Corps.

The Haubschrauber-Jäger-Regiment One achieved its goal but was nearly wiped out in the process. With less than 25 percent of his assault force intact, General-Major Tannert was commanding a ghost regiment. He did regroup his forces and participate in the assault that developed into the planned offensive, but only as conventional infantry. Sevastopol fell to the Germans on June 28, and the regiment was withdrawn to Poland for what amounted to a new forming. The new regiment served with distinction until its annihilation in December 1944.

What Fight Have Been

3:34 P.M., June 18, 1942
Eastern Front, Thirtieth Army Corps, Twenty-second Air Landing Infantry Division
Approaching Naval Fortifications in Sevastopol

The flying men with their buzzing machines had silenced the guns that overlooked the enemy entrenchments. That seemed to make very little difference to the Russians, who were pouring fire in on the panzers from every conceivable angle. Through the smoked-vision blocks of the Panzer IIIJ's turret, Viktor Fleischer could see that they had more than a kilometer of entrenchments to go before they broke through to the gun bunkers. Bullets ricocheted from the tank's armor almost constantly, and the nasty dug-in antitank guns had wiped out his entire platoon.

On his left flank, the assault guns attached to Twenty-second Infantry were faring a bit better with their heavier explosive rounds. To his right was nothing but Russians and the only surviving Panzer III in his platoon. Behind him the infantry were advancing, clearing trenches, and trying to solidify the breakthrough.

"Watch the ditches!" Vitktor shouted.

The panzer veered in the able hands of Jacques "Franky" Meijer and brought them around a nasty antitank ditch filled with infantry. There was a familiar clank on the hull.

"Grenade!" The blast rang the tank's bell, momentarily deafening them all, but seemed to leave them otherwise unscathed.

". . . un, ninety meters ahead!" The voice over the radio belonged to James Kraus in the Panzer III on their right flank. "Say again, gun ninety meters ahead!"

"Give him a high explosive," Viktor spotted the gun pit and barrel through the viewing blocks.

There was a loud report and Viktor's view was obstructed by a burst of smoke. It cleared in time for him to see the plume of dirt settling from behind the gun.

"Depress the gun a bit and—" Viktor was cut off by an explosion near the tank, followed by the sharp twang of debris hitting their side armor.

"HE loaded!" Gunther called from the loader's position.

"Give it to him again, Heinrich."

Heinrich fired again and the low-velocity shell thumped out of the 50mm barrel and landed dead center on the gun position.

"Got him!" Heinrich cheered.

"Give them something to think about from the coax and we'll run on past them."

The turret-mounted machine gun raked fire across the gun pit for several seconds. Franky threw the panzer into fifth gear, and the engine roared ahead at nearly top speed, trailing a tangle of barbed wire. Kraus's panzer was just pulling parallel to them on the right, and the assault guns were lagging a bit behind on the left. Viktor stole a look at the carnage in the gun pit as they passed it by. When he looked back out of the front block, he saw, to his horror, the flash of two more antitank guns firing on them. There was a loud bang and the tank jolted and turned 30 degrees. Viktor felt a vague pain in his thigh. Franky instinctively revved the engine, and the tank rattled as it spooled its right tread out.

"We've lost a tread!" Franky shouted.

"Get an explosive shot in those guns, hit them with the MGs!" Viktor popped the top hatch on the turret and fired a long burst from his machine pistol into the nearest trench.

Bullets smacked into the tank in response, and Viktor dropped back down into the turret, wincing as something dug into his leg, and secured the hatch behind him. Before he could repeat his orders, Heinrich loosed another high-explosive round.

"Got one!" Heinrich shouted and continued to fire the coaxial machine gun as he swept the turret toward the other enemy position.

"Reloading!" Gunther shouted.

"Radio's gone!" Willi Bayer shouted.

"Get on that hull machine gun," Viktor instructed and pressed his face to the vision blocks.

The remaining antitank gun fired again, putting a shot dead center into Kraus's panzer. The engine immediately vomited fire and smoke and hatches popped on the tank as the crew bailed out. Kraus and his gunner landed on the side facing Viktor's panzer and were somewhat sheltered from gunfire, the rest of the crew clambered out on the other side of the tank or the front. They were gunned down almost instantly. Kraus's driver slumped half in and half out of the driver's hatch, spilling blood across the tank's hull.

"HE loaded!" Gunther cried.

Heinrich fired again and the explosive round thumped out and burst near the remaining antitank gun. For a moment, the enemy gun was motionless, but then it began to turn slowly toward Viktor's Panzer III.

"Come on, Heinrich!" Viktor urged. "Gunther, get him loaded!"

Fire erupted in a great geyser from the enemy gun position. With a roar, the two assault guns surviving on the left flank charged past Viktor's immobilized panzer. Behind the enemy trenches, a wild front of turbulence began to coalesce on the ground. Dirt and debris swirled like dozens of tiny tornadoes, and like that, the battle was joined by the men of Haubschrauber-Jäger-Regiment One. They braked their rotors and dropped in on the rear of the enemy lines. For a few seconds, they massacred the Russians. Then the Soviets began to split their attention between the advancing assault guns and the sudden enemy presence in their midst.

"Crazy!" Viktor laughed. "They're mad!"

"Sir?" Heinrich looked up and wiped sweat from his brow.

"Damn it, give them all the fire support we can!"

Viktor hoped that the advancing German infantry would reach his immobilized tank before a Russian with a satchel charge or a firebomb did. He was too full of adrenaline to even notice the 10-centimeter-long sliver of metal that had shattered his femur.

Chapter 10 —————————

German Space Program

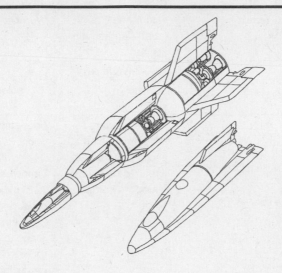

Overview

In the long shadows cast by *Sputnik*, the moon landings, and the space shuttle, it is sometimes easy to forget that it was in many ways the Germans who ushered in the space age. Germany's unique interest in rocketry can be traced to the Treaty of Versailles, which placed strict prohibitions on the types of weapons that Germans could develop. Rockets were not explicitly forbidden under the Treaty of Versailles, and they could therefore be developed openly by the German government. In the burgeoning science of rocketry, Adolf Hitler saw the potential for a whole new breed of weapon.

Many of the inventions included in this book were on the cusp of realization, or at least feasible designs were being seriously considered. The Nazi space station existed as a fleshed-out concept that caught the attention of a handful of luminaries of German rocket design. It was not given much consideration for production and was not even close to being within the wartime reach of German technology. The Germans did have a serious interest in various space projects including the Sänger antipodal bomber (see chapter 14), intercontinental ballistic missiles, and manned flights into space. The space station was seen

	Braun Station	A9/A10/A11/A12
Category:	Geosynchronous armed space station	Four-stage orbital launch vehicle
Phase of Development:	Conceptual	Partial prototype
Development Start:	1928	1940
Development Team:	Hermann Oberth and Wernher von Braun	Wernher von Braun
Crew:	2–12 (variable)	2–4
Weight: (estimated)	Unknown	4.1 million kg
Propulsion:	None, powered systems fueled by solar boilers and secondary fuel supplies carried as cargo	Four-stage orbital boost Launch stage: 50 × A-10 rocket motors producing 10 million kg of thrust Stage 2: 6 × A-10 rocket motors producing 1.4 million kg of thrust Stage 3: 1 × A-10 rocket motor producing 235,000 kg of thrust Final Stage: 1 × A-9 rocket motor producing 29,000 kg of thrust
Speed:	Geosynchronous orbit	29,000 kph estimated peak velocity
Range:	n/a	500 km orbit
Wing Span:	n/a	23.0 m
Length:	n/a	70.0 m (vertical on launch)
Diameter:	75 m	11.0 m
Armament:	Theoretical, see description	10,000 kg lift payload (including A9 craft weight)

as a distant dream by even the maddest of minds in the German High Command.

The German dream of a space program began in earnest in 1923, when Hermann Oberth published his historic book on space travel, *The Rocket into Interplanetary Space*. Oberth's book was expanded on by an Austrian military officer named Hermann Potocnik (pen name Hermann Noordung) in *The Problem of Space Flight*. Both of these volumes became inspirations for a young Wernher von Braun, whose name is probably familiar to most as the inventor of the V-2 missile and immigrant father of the U.S. space program. A connecting thread for these three pioneers of space travel was the idea of a space station for observation, science, exploration, and eventually war.

Development History

A somewhat fanciful depiction of a Raumfahrer-SS.

Science fiction and science reality have long had a symbiotic relationship in which ideas shared between the two can propel one or the other to great achievements. Visionary science fiction writers have often influenced the work of real scientists, and in turn many of these scientists have built the foundation on which the writers are free to do their speculating. In the early 1920s, dreams of space in science fiction had begun to see results in the science of rocketry. In this environment, great minds that straddled the fence between both worlds began to produce speculative works about the future of space travel.

One such scientist and writer was Hermann Oberth, and in 1923 he published his milestone work *The Rocket into Interplanetary Space*. Among the questions posed and possible answers offered by Oberth was a rough plan to construct a manned station in orbit around the earth. Oberth imagined a space station similar in purpose to the current International Space Station. It was to be a place for experiments, weather forecasting, and a jumping-off point for missions to explore the solar system. One of Oberth's most interesting ideas about this station was constructing the station as a rotating toroid (think delicious doughnut) that would generate its own gravity.

Oberth's work served as an inspiration to an Austrian military officer named Hermann Potocnik, who penned the book *The Problem of Space Flight* under the pen name Hermann Noordung. Within this book, Potocnik greatly expanded on Oberth's plan for an orbiting space station. The version outlined in Potocnik's book was a 30-meter wheel-shape similar to Oberth's, with a central docking pylon and airlock located beneath a huge parabolic mirror. The mirror would be used to fire a primary solar boiler and hundreds of smaller mirrors on the station's rim would similarly heat pipes for an auxiliary boiler. These boilers were part of a self-contained steam-engine system providing power for the station's systems. Theories for supplying crew with air on a station such as this ranged from the unusual (pumpkin plants) to the feasible but technically difficult (air filtration units similar to submarines). Provisioning flights from earth would have been regular, keeping the station stocked with potable water, food, and compressed oxygen.

Potocnik died shortly after his book was published, but Oberth continued to influence his young protégé Wernher von Braun. Where Oberth excelled at theoretical science, Braun was an engineering genius capable of overcoming almost any mechanical problem he encountered. As rocketry came into favor in Germany, so too did the Nazi Party, and it turned an encouraging eye to Braun's work. With an amoral ends-justify-the-means mentality, Braun set to work on top-secret rocketry projects for the German military. He served in the Luftwaffe and was later commissioned with a rank in the SS as a part of the Special Projects Group operating at Peenemünde.

Braun's most famous line of research at Peenemünde resulted in the A4 rocket, a potent liquid oxygen–fueled rocket that would later become infamous as the V-2 missile. Impressive as the V-2 was, it lacked the lift and thrust capacity to serve as a vehicle capable of carrying men into space. In 1940, while work on the A4 rocket was still ongoing, Braun began to focus some of his attention on using his knowledge to develop a two-stage rocket capable of functioning as a crude intercontinental ballistic missile (ICBM). Originally known (and later known) as the A9 rocket, development on this ballistic missile was halted by the German government in 1943. By renaming it the A4b, Braun was able to continue work on the rocket.

The A9 was an interesting vehicle capable of achieving an altitude of 390 kilometers and then gliding back through the earth's atmosphere. The first stage, known as the A10, consisted of six A4 rocket engines feeding into a single exhaust nozzle. This would have lifted the futuristic-looking strake-winged A9 to its maximum altitude and then separated. The piloted A9, filled with explosives, would have then glided back through the earth's atmosphere guided to a target by radio signals. The pilot would have either died or ejected from the A9 before impact.

The A9/A10 soup-and-salad combo actually reached the late pre-prototyping phase, with full-sized engine tests and wind tunnel tests of the glider portion. Braun had more grandiose plans. He had designed a third-stage booster (the A11) that was capable of boosting the A9 to even greater heights for the purpose of placing satellites into orbit. A massive A12 booster was also planned, and this was where Braun's designs began to overlap with Oberth and Potocnik's. The A12 could carry the A9 all the way up to an altitude where a manned space station could be constructed, and this was no doubt Braun's intent for the A12.

Following the war, Braun and many of his researchers (including Oberth) went to work for the United States after eluding capture by the Soviets. He brought with him his invaluable research. Among the studies and schematics were plans for Braun's space station, a concept that he later expanded on for the United States and made famous in the media.

Braun's station was to have been nearly two-and-a-half times the size of Potocnik's, but was otherwise of very similar design and construction. A parabolic mirror and smaller mirrors would have heated boiler pipes for power, and regular provisioning missions would have brought food and other supplies. The large mirror is often mistaken for a weapon, as it has since been written about as such, but the real armament would have probably been simple explosive charges launched from rockets or dropped in shielded capsules through the atmosphere. In the hands of the United States, the obvious implications were for a means of attacking anywhere in the world with nuclear weapons that could not be shot from the sky.

What Braun had designed ended up as an early roadmap for the entire U.S. space program, and Braun was at its helm most of the way.

Technical Mumbo Jumbo

Braun's A9-12 and space station both evolved into various projects with the National Aeronautics and Space Administration (NASA), but how might Braun have achieved his goals within the context of World War II?

As planned by Braun, the A9-12 was capable of reaching a maximum escape velocity of 29,000 kph. This would have been sufficient to get the crew of the A9 up into orbit, but problems developed when the A9 had to come back down. Braun believed that it could be constructed of steel like the A4 and could withstand surface temperatures of around 1,000 degrees Kelvin.

In reality, the A9 would have been subjected to surface temperatures of more than 2,000 degrees Kelvin during reentry, as was the case with the Dynasoar, a glide reentry spacecraft developed from the legacy of the A9. In the case of the Dynasoar, the outer surface was constructed of molybdenum, a transition metal often used as a replacement for tungsten. Molybdenum was somewhat rare, but could have been made available for Braun. He would have to discover this requirement before the first A9 reentered the atmosphere as a molten ball of metal.

Considering the technology of the time, the A4 was a reliable rocket, but the A12 first-stage booster consisted of the staggering equivalent of 300 of the A4 engines vectored down 50 thrust nozzles. Making 300 rocket motors fire reliably would be no easy task for Braun and would require complex failsafes and mechanical switches, in the event that some failed to ignite. The equipment Braun would have needed to wrangle the entire 70-meter-tall and 4.1-million-kilogram A9-12 assembly into place on a launch platform is beyond the realm of hypothesis. The only real possibility at that time would be to construct the rocket, piece by piece, on the launch platform.

The process of launching the material needed to construct the Braun station would require dozens of fully manned missions, because of the lack of guidance mechanisms. This would be expensive and difficult during peacetime and basically impossible during wartime. It would require billions of reichsmarks, long periods of good weather, and a magical lack of Allied bombing. Maneuver outside the earth's atmosphere would have been nearly impossible, even if crude maneuver thrusters had been fitted to the A9. Each mission to construct a portion of the station would have been difficult and fraught with danger because of the rushed equipment. Many missions, particularly early on, would probably be considered suicide missions.

This brings up the question of what sort of equipment German Raumfahrers might require. Their suits would likely be made from rubberized body gloves beneath a treated canvas outer shell with oxygen lines linked to their tethers and feeding back to an air compressor stored in the A9's cargo bay. Sun protection would be limited to glare goggles they could slip over the lenses of their hoods and protection from the cold could have been as simple as insulated jackets and trousers. Radiation exposure would have been a deadly risk to the Raumfahrers, and mobility would have been terribly limited by their suits as well as by their lack of specialized extravehicular activity equipment. Later missions would have access to the limited amenities of a partial station, so that Raumfahrers could at least take breaks from the dangerous task of zero-gravity construction. Even then, casualties among invaluable trained crews would have been high.

Braun's design for the station itself, based as it was on the work of Oberth and Potocnik, was fundamentally flawed. Braun imagined a single wheel in space rotating to generate artificial gravity through centripetal acceleration. The real problem was that a single-wheel design was prone to something known as progression—the same effect caused early single-rotor helicopters to be highly unstable—and could potentially wobble or move out of orbit. No doubt, this would be a great event for the people trapped inside the station as it broke apart and burned on reentry. In helicopters, this problem is solved by adding a tail rotor to counter the progression force generated by the main rotor. In a station like Braun's, the solution would be to double the number of wheels and have them spin in different directions.

Double the station means double the missions to lift its components into space and double the number of people killed during construction. Luckily, Braun had designed the station large enough that the station did not have to spin so fast that it would make occupants physically ill: a real risk later demonstrated by NASA testing.

Armament for the station would have consisted almost exclusively of rockets capable of bombarding targets back on earth. Without nuclear weapons or modern precision guidance, these missiles would have inflicted damage scarcely worse than a normal V-2 bombardment. The only conceivable advantage would have been their ability to strike at more distant targets than normal V-2 missiles. That was something that could have been achieved by Braun through much less ambitious projects.

Variants

The key variant to the A9-12 would be NASA's Dynasoar series of glide-capable space planes, though their intended mission was closer to the Sänger antipodal bomber (see chapter 14). The Dynasoar was a space-capable bomber designed to be launched by a Phoenix A-388 booster. The Dynasoar project began in 1958 and was canceled following prototype testing in 1966.

The most well-known variant of the Braun station appeared not in reality, but in the book *2001: A Space Odyssey* by Arthur C. Clarke and its film adaptation directed by Stanley Kubrick. The currently orbiting International Space Station is actually much more simplistic than a Braun station when you exclude the modern technology that it is packed with.

Analysis

Despite the miracles of sinister Nazi superscience, the Braun station was a pipe dream far out of reach for Germany during World War II. Few, including Braun, thought otherwise by the time the V-2 was fully operational. By that point, the construction of an armed space station would have been a folly that eclipsed any other superweapons even considered by the Nazis. Whole segments of industry would have ground to a halt to provide the necessary material and expertise for the project. The benefit of observation and bombardment with impunity would have been of little use to a nation coming apart at the seams.

Perhaps the final act of Hitler's drama would have been played out not in a bunker beneath Berlin, but above our planet. Imagine the syphilitic madman launching himself to his final redoubt—his Space Eagle's Nest—and then shooting himself in the temple with a pistol as his empire unravels beneath him. Now that would be an awesome movie!

Hypothetical Deployment History

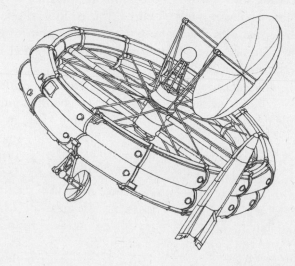

The Braun station design with an A9 launch vehicle in the foreground.

The A9 launch vehicle and its booster components completed testing in July 1942 and were approved for a production run of forty units, which was believed to be sufficient to complete construction of the armed space station. Construction began on four launch and booster assembly platforms throughout Germany in September 1942, and work began on the first of the rockets in late October. The entire operation became known as Project Valkyrie and was under the auspices of the SS Special Projects Group, although the quantities of resources being dedicated to it meant Armaments Minister Albert Speer became heavily involved.

While construction was under way on the first group of four rockets, screening, testing, and finally training began for 360 volunteers for the Raumfahrer program drawn from the Waffen-SS. Training facilities and barracks had been constructed by slave labor (now toiling on the rockets) in the vicinity of each launching platform. As the eager space pioneers completed their two-month courses, they watched as their vessels began to take shape on the platforms nearby. When training was completed, each group of Raumfahrer cadets was reorganized into a Sterngeschwader.

The first A9-12 became operational and ready for launch on August 7, 1943. Newsreels filmed the two chosen crewmen as they stood outside the elevator at the base of the embarkation tower in their brilliant white canvas suits. Both waved to the cameras and then to the audience in the distant reviewing stands. Hitler himself looked on. Minutes later, *Valkyrie 1* lifted into the air atop a roaring column of flame. At 27,000 feet, it exploded in a flash, raining debris and fuel for miles around and setting 200 acres of grassland ablaze.

Nine days later, *Valkyrie 2* lifted off under the guidance of Raumfahrer-SS Willi Heitz and Raumfahrer-SS Joachim Steiner. It successfully completed all stages of its orbital burn and Heitz and Steiner began their five-day mission in space. Communications with operations control at Kummersdorf were intermittent and often unpleasant, as Steiner and Heitz related a series of failed attempts to assemble the first crew module of the Braun station. They returned to earth successfully—almost miraculously as both lost consciousness for a large portion of reentry—but with little progress made on the station.

From 1943 through January 1945, the Sterngeschwaders of Project Valkyrie completed six successful missions to the construction site, although the crew of only two of these missions survived to return to earth. Five failed launches resulted in the death of both crew members and the destruction of the launch vehicle. By the end of January 1945, the Braun station was roughly 10 percent completed.

In January 1945, Hitler ordered the project discontinued and instructed that the two Valkyrie rockets under construction should be completed for use as ballistic missiles.

One was destroyed by a British bombing raid before completion. The remaining rocket was launched on February 23 with an A9 shuttle loaded to its maximum capacity of 4,420 kilograms of explosives. Steiner volunteered for the mission and successfully piloted the reentry vehicle to within one mile of Washington, DC. Onlookers watched in amazement as the German spacecraft dove from the sky and into the ground of Virginia, where it exploded with a thunderous clap and spray of fire and dirt. A few minutes later, Steiner sailed into downtown Washington beneath a parachute and was applauded by bystanders. Shortly thereafter, he was taken into custody by a police officer who paused to pose for a photograph with the stone-faced German pilot.

What Fight Have Been

8:14 A.M., August 7, 1943
***Valkyrie 1* Launch Center**
Near Sachsen, Germany

The SS guard handed back the stack of identification books and waved the gray Citroen through the gate. Konrad Fleischer parked the car in a meadow that was overflowing with officers' staff cars. Next to the gleaming Mercedes and Daimler limousines, his secondhand French sedan looked shabby. Konrad was unconcerned. He cut a fine figure in his dress uniform, and his brother had enough medals to make any of the staff officers jealous. Viktor's wife, Anna, was sitting in the back with their children. Little Josephine was appallingly cute in her little church dress, and Felix looked smart enough in his Hitler Youth uniform.

"It looks as though the entire high command is here," Viktor gestured to the sea of automobiles.

Konrad reached over and flicked at the medals lying across the breast of Viktor's jacket.

"They will be asking for your signature, big brother."

"Do you think the Fuehrer will be here?" Viktor's son asked.

"Without a doubt!" Konrad exclaimed as they climbed out of the car. "Did you see that soldier at the gate? That was a member of the honor guard."

"I'm sure all the greats will be here," Viktor frowned. "Göring, Goebbels, Himmler, they'll all want to show off."

"Always the cynic," Konrad lifted Josephine up onto his shoulders and Felix clung adoringly close to him as they made their long way to the reviewing stands.

Vitkor hobbled a few steps behind, putting his weight on his cane, with Anna at his side. It was quite a walk for someone still convalescing from an aggravation of a wound that had nearly needed an amputation, but Viktor did not complain and Konrad seemed not to notice. Long before they reached the reviewing stands, they could see the rocket. Josephine squealed with delight and amazement first, and Felix asked to be lifted up as well so that he could see. The magnificent spacecraft was taller than the Reichstag and even though it sat on its pad more than 5 kilometers in the distance, it was still an impressive sight.

"My God," Viktor said, "it's monstrous."

"It's fantastic!" Konrad countered. "I wanted to strangle Reinhardt when he told me about this. If I had known joining the SS would get me into—"

Konrad cut himself short as they passed a trio of thick-necked SS officers chatting near the entrance to the reviewing stands. Vitkor recognized Sepp Dietrich, but not the other two. Though he was not fond of Dietrich, he respected the man's ferocity on the battlefield. He seemed the sort who would rather be strangling an enemy in a trench with his bare hands than poring over maps.

It took some time to find their assigned seats. The stands were already nearly full to capacity, and every few steps required the formality of a salute. Normally, such a thing would not be required, but this was considered an official event, and most of the officers took sadistic pleasure in being saluted by the pair of decorated veterans. Reinhardt Steinhauer's position as one of the crew of the rocket had managed to get them tickets to the event, but he had not managed to get them good tickets. They were nearly as far in the back as possible, and the special box where Hitler would sit when he arrived was hardly even visible.

Music played over enormous loudspeakers on electric poles, and most of the crowd amused themselves by watching the whirling aerobatics of the fighter planes overhead.

"I barely got out of doing that myself," Konrad gestured up to the swooping Messerschmitts. "They must have two hundred fighters up today."

Felix hung on every word Konrad said and asked him a ceaseless stream of questions about his exploits over Russia and Britain. Josephine enjoyed a sweet and then fell asleep with her head against her uncle and Anna nestled in against Viktor, just happy to have him back.

After more than an hour, a voice boomed out of the speakers and announced that the Fuehrer would be arriving shortly. An SS band marched out and began playing various patriotic tunes. Hitler came next, sitting in his limousine with Heinrich Himmler, Reinhardt, and Eugen Burg. The Raumfahrers wore white space suits without the face pieces, and Hitler seemed ill at ease sitting with them. Hitler's limousine made a circuit past the reviewing stand while everyone saluted him and then he was driven out to the rocket. Viktor watched through field glasses he had brought along as Hitler shook hands with the Raumfahrers for the newsreel. Reinhardt and Eugen began to ascend a large staircase to a platform that led into the capsule atop the rocket. Hitler climbed back into his limousine and returned to the reviewing stands.

The two Raumfahrers boarded the craft, and the platform they had ascended began to fold in on itself. Some in the crowd gasped at this, but when the rocket began to smoke from various fueling lines and hatches, they were positively awestruck. Himmler and Hitler both gave brief speeches. Viktor judged Himmler's speech a bit too self-congratulatory, but Hitler's was stirring.

"Only the bold deserve what they dream, and only the will of the German people will see those dreams made real!" Hitler shouted. "Today, we are the first to conquer the heavens and look down on the lesser nations of earth! Today, we shout to the world that Germany's destiny is greater than mere soil and sand! We walk with Gods!"

The audience erupted in a chorus of enthusiastic salutes and Viktor could not resist joining them.

"Heil!" Viktor shouted again and again with a smile on his face. When he looked over at Felix doing the same, Viktor felt strangely ashamed at how caught up he had become.

The crowd quieted and Hitler took his seat. After more music and murmured conversation, the voice announced that the launch would begin in fifteen minutes, then ten, then five. Then the voice began to count down from one minute. The audience fell silent and stared at the rocket.

". . . seven . . . six . . . five . . . four . . . three . . . two . . . one . . . ignition!"

Smoke burst from the base of the rocket and spread out in all directions.

"Lift off!"

There was a bright flash that resolved into a burning tail at the base of the rocket. The stands rumbled, and the towering vessel seemed to slowly lift up off its launch pad. It plunged into the clear skies at the top of a pillar of fire and thick white smoke. The crowd cheered wildly and waved little flags above their heads. For a few moments, the rocket was obscured by its own trail of smoke, but as it curved toward the heavens it became visible again. Even Konrad was without words to describe the majesty of the rocket.

Felix reached across Konrad and prodded his father for the field glasses. The boy watched the distant speck of the rocket for a few moments.

"Something has come off!" he exclaimed.

The rocket flared high in the sky above.

"That's just the next stage of the rocket," Konrad explained. "You see, they have them stacked like . . ."

He trailed off as people began to gasp and point up into the sky. Konrad snatched the binoculars from Felix and looked again. The rocket was gone, its last place in the sky was marked by a puff of smoke. But there was more. Burning fuel-drenched pieces of the rocket were falling back to the earth. Each meteoric chunk of the rocket trailed flames and smoke as it descended.

"Oh God, Reinhardt," Konrad lamented and handed the binoculars back to Felix.

Viktor looked away as the wreckage plummeted toward a grassy field and turned his attention to Hilter. The Fuehrer was obviously furious, but he kept silent, turning his back on Himmler and stalking away from the reviewing stand with his entourage of aides and guards.

"Everything is normal." The voice from the loudspeakers sounded unconvinced by its own words. "Please remain in your seats."

Many members of the audience began to flee in fear of the falling debris, though it was obvious that they were at a safe enough distance. Viktor calmed little Josephine who began to cry at the commotion. SS guards stripped the film from the newsreel cameras. Music began to play from the loudspeakers.

Chapter 11

Horten Ho IXB Nachtjäger

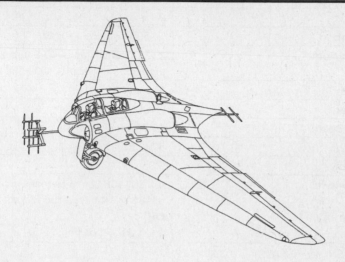

Overview

Had Batman been around during World War II to kick the Germans right in their fascist rear ends, he might have been surprised to find kindred spirits in Reimar and Walter Horten. The pair managed to be truly indie aircraft developers in a country where the economy was run like a birth control wheel. Operating outside the state-sponsored development industry, Reimar provided the brains behind the operation and Walter, a veteran pilot, provided the face and sales pitch. Without state funding, the Horten brothers designed and built nearly a dozen prototype aircraft. They were operating so far outside the norm that they were not even allowed time in the government-run wind tunnel facilities.

Like Batman overcoming the Joker's henchmen, the Horten brothers overcame these and other difficulties, and over a period of roughly a decade they constructed eight predecessors to the Horten IX. Reimar Horten loved the graceful and sinister flying wing design and employed it in several gliders before using it in the Horten IX. This batlike shape would have appealed to Bruce Wayne's chiropteran sensibilities and its performance would have (and did) impress Luftwaffe planners.

	Ho IXB
Category:	Turbojet night fighter
Phase of Development:	Functional prototype
Development Start:	1943
Development Team:	Reimar and Walter Horten
Crew:	2
Weight:	10,500 kg plus fuel load
Propulsion:	2 × Junkers Jumo 004B-2 turbojets producing a total of 1,820 kg of thrust
Speed:	950 kph
Range:	2,080 km
Wing Span:	16.76 m
Length:	8.50 m
Height:	3.05 m
Armament:	4 × MK 108 30mm cannons 24–36 × R4M unguided rockets OR 2 × 1,000 kg bombs

The Dark Knight might have similarly approved when Gothaer Waggonfabrik74, or Gotha for short, was selected to produce and build the Horten IX. Gotha was similarly enamored with flying wing aircraft, but the designers there had their own ideas about what makes a good bat plane. Gotha put erasers and pencils to work on the Horten IX schematics and planned to transform the Ho IX into the Go 229B production model. At the same time, Gotha also cribbed heavily from the Horten IX design in the creation of their proposed P. 60A heavy fighter. This probably caused some throwing of lamps and harsh words at meetings between the Horten and Gotha design teams during the preparations for Go 229 production. When the war came to a dramatic end, three prototypes of the aircraft had been built, and a pre-production series of four aircraft were in various stages of completion.

Development History

Reimar and Walter Horten had an unusual development process that involved leaping almost straight from drafting schematics to constructing a prototype. In the case of the Ho IX, the drawings were completed in 1943 and drew primarily on their previous success with all-wing glider aircraft. At the time that work was underway on the design, metal in Germany was at a premium and wood was more readily available. Based on successful conceptual tests of rocket- and jet-powered wooden aircraft, the Hortens proceeded with plans to construct the aircraft from treated plywood and a special wood composite called Formholz, which would be wrapped around a hollow steel frame.

Following the war, the Horten brothers claimed that this decision was also influenced by their knowledge of the radar-absorbent properties of wood versus metal. Whether or not this is true, the Ho IX would have had an increased ability to evade Allied radar because of its wooden construction.

In mid-1943, work began on the VI prototype at Göttingen without any Reich financing. This first prototype would forego the planned BMW 003 turbojets because of cost, stability concerns, and perhaps because they were completely unavailable. Following in the footsteps of previous Horten creations, the first Ho IX prototype would be a glider towed into the air. This version was completed in less than six months and took to the skies in early January 1944.

The RLM became aware of the Horten design and participated with interest in further trials of the glider airframe. Following extensive testing throughout the spring of 1944, approval was given to proceed with a powered prototype. Hermann Göring, who had been courted by fellow pilot Walter Horten, gave the project his enthusiastic personal endorsement. Gotha was awarded the contract for full-series production of the Horten design and construction of a powered prototype proceeded.

Unfortunately, the BMW 003 engines were still unavailable, and the Junkers Jumo 004 engines to be used as replacements were substantially larger, forcing a redesign of the aircraft and a delay in construction of the second prototype. The V2 was completed in January 1945, and test trials began at Orianenburg in early February 1945 with test pilot Erwin Ziller behind the yoke. The first test flight went well. The aircraft frame held up to stress maneuvers, was fast, responsive, and maneuverable. A second test flight resulted in damage to the landing gear, and the third test flight had a small incident in which the engines flamed out, the aircraft crashed, and Ziller was killed.

Despite Ziller's demise, Gotha moved ahead with the production series. The prototype shop was relocated to Gotha's facilities and work began on the first A-series production prototype designated V3. Within days, work was also underway on the V4 and V5 B-series prototypes.

These were of a slightly modified all-weather fighter design requested by the RLM. The V6 prototype was a second A-series model, and the V7 prototype was intended as a trainer. Of these prototypes, only the V3 was completed before the Gotha Friedrichsroda plant was captured by American forces. These troops found the V4 and V5 in final assembly and the other prototypes in various stages of partial completion.

The V3 prototype was taken to the United States for study and survives to this day at a preservation facility in Maryland. It has not been maintained or restored and is in a state of disrepair. Perhaps Bruce Wayne could finance the restoration project.

Technical Mumbo Jumbo

The Ho IX was designed as a flying wing to reduce every possible bit of drag on the aircraft. The aircraft had no real fuselage, just a lump in the center for the cockpit and the inboard engines mounted on either side. Control surfaces included spoiler flaps that extended across the center of the wing, elevons commonly seen in delta wing aircraft, and plain flaps. Whether or not these would have been adequate to make the Ho IX combat capable is a point of some contention with historians. However, the aircraft's maneuverability must have been at least adequate, or it would not have been approved for series production. Reports from Ziller following his nonexploding test flights seem to corroborate this.

The two Jumo 004 engines mounted in the Ho IX were proven power plants functionally identical to the engines used in the Me 262. Unlike the 262, which had its engines mounted in external nacelles, the inboard engines of the Ho IX would have provided improved flight performance and lots of headaches if major maintenance was required. The derivative Gotha P. 60 took this into account and mounted its engines inline with the cockpit in nacelles above and below the aircraft.

One of the most impressive flight characteristics of the Ho IX was its theoretical operational ceiling of 16,000 meters. No aircraft during the war even came close to this operational ceiling and this distinction would have allowed the long-ranged fighter to cruise safely above enemy airspace and swoop in to attack when an opportunity presented itself. Even the B-29 Superfortress reached its operational limits somewhere around 10,000 meters.

The Ho IX was constructed of a tubular steel framework skinned in treated and lacquered plywood. The aircraft's leading edges were composed of Formholz, a sort of molded wood pulp mixed with resin with characteristics not unlike plastic or fiberglass. Metal was only used on the exterior of the aircraft to shield the wooden skin from the engine exhausts.

The Go 229B was conceived of as a night fighter and categorized as an "all-weather day and night fighter" to please the RLM. The B version included a second crew member seated behind the pilot and was intended to mount the FuG 244 Bremen 0 radar set. With large reserves of fuel in its wings, the Go 229B was well suited for the endurance missions required of night fighters.

Armament for the Go 229B consisted of four 30mm cannons mounted just outside both engines and recessed in the leading edge of the wing. Either bombs or air-to-air rockets could be mounted on hard points beneath the aircraft with corresponding decreases in overall performance.

Variants

With a long loiter time and a large bomb capacity for a fighter, the Go 229B might have eventually seen a naval bomber version fitted with a guided antishipping missile to be operated by the second crewman. If the claims about the aircraft's operational ceiling were confirmed, there also would have likely been an aerial reconnaissance version built.

Analysis

Many historians argue that the Me 262, though a successful aircraft, was a colossal waste of resources at a time when Germany would have been better served by focusing on proven piston-driven aircraft. The Ho IX was an even more colossal waste of resources, because it never actually fought in combat. That means that it was a complete and total waste of resources.

In any event, Hitler was sure he was going to win the war with superweapons right up until the very minute before he ate a bullet.

Removing the Ho IX from the context of the war, the aircraft seems dramatically ahead of its time. Sleek in ways that most modern aircraft still are not, the Ho IX in flight must have been quite an amazing thing to behold, as long as you weren't Erwin Ziller watching the ground approach through your cockpit window.

Some of the claims about the Ho IX's capabilities must be viewed with a healthy dose of skepticism. The operational ceiling is a good start, since it so dramatically eclipsed all other active aircraft. The B-2 Spirit—the obvious ancestor of the Ho IX and aircraft like it—has a service ceiling of just over 15,000 meters. While the Germans were ahead of their time in many areas of technology, it's best to assume that the 16,000-meter claim of the Hortens is fanciful. Other estimates, including the aircraft's range and speed, also seem overly optimistic, if at least more feasible.

Even if the Go 229B failed to fully meet the promises made by the Horten brothers, it still might have proven a peerless aircraft with little to fear from Allied fighters and bombers.

Hypothetical Deployment History

Delivery of the first batch of four Go 229B training aircraft was made to JG 284 on August 6, 1944. Based in Aache, JG 284 served as a short-range interceptor squadron tasked with protecting the Reich and was unprepared to deal with long-range night fighters. Training progressed slowly and was compounded by frequent air raids and attrition. When the first delivery of six combat aircraft (designed Go 229B Krähe) was made in September, there were only three pilots fully trained on the aircraft.

On September 17, the Go 229B flew its first combat mission. Four Go 229Bs from JG 284 escorted a reconnaissance aircraft over the portions of France liberated by the Allies. The mission was a disaster. The reconnaissance and escort aircraft were jumped by American P-51 Mustang fighters before they even crossed into territory held by the Allies, and two were shot down before the fighters of JG 284 could dive on the enemy. The Go 229Bs inflicted casualties on the Mustangs, which were forced to break off because of low fuel, but found themselves in the midst of an inbound bomber raid. More P-51s jumped the reconnaissance formation before the Go 229Bs had a chance to climb to attack altitude.

A lucky hit from a P-51 machine gun caused a catastrophic fuel explosion in the lead Go 229B. The lead's inexperienced wingman stalled out in an effort to climb and was forced to abandon his aircraft. The surviving two fighters engaged in a whirling high-speed dogfight with the American Mustangs in an effort to give the remnants of the reconnaissance flight a chance to escape. The Go 229Bs managed to get the better of the P-51s, downing eleven and forcing two away, but superior numbers prevailed and both Go 229Bs were shot down.

On learning of the loss of all four fighters, JG 284 dispatched teams to find and destroy the evidence of the crashed aircraft. Though all four were believed to have crashed behind German lines, the swift advance of an Allied armor column cut off the team at one of the crash sites. The team managed to destroy the Go 229B before it fell into enemy hands, but their subsequent capture and interrogation led to vital information about it being divulged.

A total of 157 Go 229B Krähe were produced. The aircraft was unmatched in the air during the war, but was plagued by mechanical difficulties and proved difficult for pilots to manage. Despite these difficulties, the aircraft earned a fearsome reputation among Allied pilots (particularly bomber crews) who came to call them "Hitler's Vampire Bats."

What Fight Have Been

9:51 P.M., October 11, 1944
Western Front, I./JG 284
Somewhere over Eastern France

"If we throttle down anymore we're going to stall out." Thomas Reincke's voice was strained with tension and hoarse from shouting over the aircraft's engines.

"You worry too much, Tommy." Konrad Fleischer waved back at his radioman and navigator. "You just tell me when the radar finds us something and I'll worry about stalling or outrunning our little friends."

"Yes," Thomas seemed to regain his confidence, "they're still down there. Chattering away like damn fools."

Thomas tapped his earphones, though Konrad missed the gesture. The airwaves were buzzing with the inane conversation of the pilots flying the formation of Stukas thousands of meters beneath them. The poor saps were half-trained and flying obsolete models rigged with fake bombs. They were flying with strict instructions to talk as much as possible on their radio. Konrad was surprised they had not been jumped by the Amis yet. The Americans usually threw swarms of fighters up after a lone Storch.

Konrad glanced out the curved canopy of the Krähe and past his black wingtip at the faintly glowing engines of his fellow night fighters. He was in the lead position of the schwarm, guiding all four aircraft into the attack, at which point they would separate into pairs.

"Contact!" Thomas's excited announcement cut through the haze and Konrad was focused in an instant. "Bearing down from the northwest. Altitude . . ."

Thomas fidgeted with the temperamental radar.

"Shit!" he exclaimed. "They're ah . . ."

"They're plucked geese," Konrad finished as enemy cannons began flickering thousands of meters below and ahead of the night fighters. "Hang on to your lager, Tommy."

Konrad keyed the radio as he throttled the jets up to speed.

"We're hitting from the two o'clock." The engine noise grew from a deep pulse to a high-pitched whine in the span of a second. "Let's give them something to write home to their wives about. Then break and engage at your pleasure."

The American fighter formation was veering apart to engage the Stukas individually when the Go 229Bs struck. The night sky above the P-51s seemed to burst with fire as tracers flashed from the wings of the black fighters. Konrad swept up the formation, raking his gun sight across three of the American planes and grinning with unabashed glee as the third Mustangs exploded in spectacular fashion. The Mustangs could out-turn him, so he began his wider curve before they had a chance to react. Otto Schwarz, his wingman, deftly followed the maneuver while the other pair swung away in the opposite direction.

Konrad craned his neck to keep an eye on the Mustangs. Several were already breaking off in disarray, either too damaged or too frightened to continue. The numbers still favored the Americans, however, and Konrad knew the P-51s would be at their most dangerous in this close. An enemy fighter zoomed past too near for Konrad to track with his guns, but Otto managed to put a burst into the aircraft's tail and sent it spiraling toward the ground. A white silk canopy flapped open in the sky.

Thomas grunted under the G-forces as Konrad executed another sharp turn and came in on the tail of a pair of P-51s still madly gunning for the retreating Stukas. Konrad's first squeeze of the trigger put burning projectiles over the top of the Mustang and nearly hit a hapless German dive bomber. The American pilot dove hard for the deck and Otto zipped past in hot pursuit. The American's wingman stayed on one of the Stukas and shredded its wing with guns. The Stuka flopped over shedding fiery debris. The pilot leapt from the cockpit and was struck by the spinning aircraft before he could open his chute. Konrad lost sight of the bomber, but he doubted the pilot survived the impact.

Revenge was served quickly for the American. Konrad squeezed the trigger three times and sliced apart the P-51 before it could pull away. It went down nose first, the entire fuselage disintegrating in clumps of burning wreckage.

"Seven o'clock!" Thomas called.

Tracers zipped under the Krähe's right wing, and Konrad resisted the urge to jerk the stick in the opposite direction. Instead, he gave the Mustang a surprise and threw the jet on its tail in a brutal climb. Konrad's vision faded out and the engines shrieked and spit white hot exhaust. The pursuing Mustang's pilot had a split second of perfect gun coverage on Konrad's aircraft, but he was green and broke away, fearful of the unknown capabilities of the strange German aircraft.

Konrad smoothed out the climb and left the swirling melee below. None of the Americans gave chase. Otto formed up on Konrad's wing, his fighter holed in a few places but otherwise unharmed. Konrad leveled out well above the Mustang's operational ceiling and then brought the Go 229B around looking for new targets. He intended to break through the 200 mark before the night was over, and he still had four to go.

Chapter 12

German Atomic Bomb

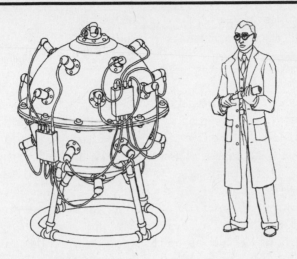

Overview

No book on wonder weapons of World War II would be complete without a chapter on Germany's mysterious atomic bomb project. For academic and amateur historians, the true story of the German atomic bomb has remained elusive and controversial. Every few years, new discoveries are made and new research is put forth that almost completely rewrites the narrative. How close were the Germans to developing an atomic bomb? Why did they fail when they had a head start and some of the greatest pioneers of atomic energy? Many authors have tried to answer these questions, and there has yet to be a real consensus beyond the fact that Germany never dropped an atomic bomb on an enemy.

Obsessively deconstructing a scientific research project that took place more than half a century ago may not seem too exciting to you, but you haven't heard about the orgies. The Kaiser Wilhelm Institute was *the* party school of the Third Reich and its director between 1941 and 1945, Werner Heisenberg, organized toga parties that devolved into legendary bacchanals. Heisenberg's parties were extremely open-

Category:	Fission/fusion implosion device
Stage of Development:	Live testing (controversial)
Development Start:	1941
Development Team:	Kurt Diebner and Research Center E
Yield:	1 kt
Estimated Blast Radius:	650 m
Estimated Fatal Radiation Radius:	1 km
Fissile Payload:	U-285 and deuterium/tritium

minded, given the environment, and Heisenberg himself would offer to "wrestle" any man or woman who challenged him.

Perhaps luckily for Germany, new evidence has surfaced that the besotted and stankified Heisenberg was not really the leader of Germany's atomic bomb efforts. It was the staid and scholarly Kurt Diebner—who shunned "the devil gin" and fornication in favor of Pervetin and carefully scheduled atomic experiments—who may have advanced Germany to the cusp of the atomic age.

The story of German atomic weapons research is convoluted, but also exciting, like a game of naked twister. So strip down, grease up, and get ready for *history*.

The Catcher in the Rhineland

Yankees manager Casey Stengle once described Morris "Moe" Berg as "the strangest man to ever play baseball." Berg was a Princeton-educated catcher for the Boston Red Sox and became almost legendary for his appearances on a radio quiz show during which he demonstrated genius-level intelligence. Berg was Jewish and spoke a variety of languages fluently, including German. When war came to the United States in 1941, Berg offered his services to the U.S. government, first as an advisor and then eventually as an Office of Strategic Services (OSS; a precursor to the Central Intelligence Agency) agent. He participated in spying operations in South America and Yugoslavia, but his most infamous mission was an assassination that never took place.

The OSS assigned Berg to the secret mission Project Azusa in May 1944. The operation sent Berg to Europe to attempt to gain intelligence about the scientists working on the German atomic energy project, determine the likelihood of a German atomic weapon, and convince European nuclear experts to defect to the United States. In

December 1944, Berg learned that Werner Heisenberg, the head of the German atomic energy project, would be giving a lecture on nuclear energy in Zürich.

Berg was ordered to attend the lecture and ascertain whether or not Heisenberg believed that an atomic bomb could be constructed in the immediate future. If Heisenberg mentioned that such a development was likely, Berg had orders to assassinate him. Berg attended the lecture with a pistol in the pocket of his coat.

Heisenberg's unknowing evasion of the assassination attempt owes more to the failure of his domain within Germany's atomic bomb program than any sort of innate physicist survival instinct. Heisenberg failed to convince Berg that the Germans were capable of building an atomic bomb, and the Red Sox catcher left the conference quietly. Things might have gone differently had Diebner been giving the lecture.

Development History

The development of a German atomic weapon is a subject of heated debate among historians. Some believe that Germany's research was stymied by ignorance, sabotaged to ineffectiveness by the Allies, and/or misled by well-meaning German scientists who sought to keep atomic weapons away from the Nazis. Others believe that Germany's atomic research advanced to the level of testing and production of small-scale tactical atomic warheads and so-called dirty radiation bombs. Some authors even believe the possibility that at least one of the atomic bombs deployed against Japan by the United States was partially or fully German in origin. It probably doesn't help clear things up when one of the world's leading historians in the field, David Irving, went on to become an adamant Holocaust denier.

The most comprehensive study of Germany's atomic weapons research will remain classified for several decades after the publication of this book. As a part of Project Alsos (Greek for "Grove" and no doubt a reference to Manhattan Project kingpin Leslie Groves), advancing U.S. forces were to confiscate any and all material relating to Germany's atomic research. German scientists who were working on the project were captured, interrogated, and kept under surveillance even after they had been released from captivity. The official standing of the United States was that Germany had failed to develop a functional atomic weapon, but the full findings of Project Alsos will not be available to the general public until 2045. Declassified documents related to Project Alsos suggest that either the Germans tested a small atomic bomb or were much closer to constructing one than has been the conventional wisdom.

Germany's atomic energy program was similar to Germany's rocketry program in that resources, manpower, and brainpower that could have been pooled were spread out among various facilities, research communities, and projects. For rocketry, it was Wernher von Braun's Peenemünde facility and Eugen Sänger's Trauen facility competing to develop strategic rockets. When it came to atomic research, it was Werner Heisenberg and the Kaiser Wilhelm Institute versus Kurt Diebner and the army-run (later SS-run) Research Center E in a race to atomic weapons development.

Heisenberg was one of the world's leading experts in atomic energy development—he was every bit as important as Maximilian Oppenheimer or Enrico Fermi—but Heisenberg was neither interested nor adept at maneuvering German politics. He frequently underestimated Germany's ability to produce a working reactor and greatly overestimated the amount of reactor-bred plutonium required to construct a bomb. Heisenberg was more focused on creating a postwar energy infrastructure for Germany than an actual weapon. When Heisenberg's researchers gave speeches to German officials, they were routinely unimpressive and deemphasized their ability to produce an atomic bomb.

Following the war, Heisenberg claimed that it was all part of a scheme to keep Adolf Hitler from having an atomic bomb. Heisenberg's own letters to badass Danish physicist Niels Bohr and others seem to contradict this claim, as he voices a firm commitment to "a Europe under German leadership." Whatever the reason for Heisenberg's failures, he routinely received less funding and support than Diebner's Research Center E.

Diebner and Heisenberg were nominally united under the umbrella of Germany's Uranium Project. Diebner worked on and off with Heisenberg from 1941 through 1943, but by late 1943 his ideas and political patrons like Hermann Göring had given him the financing and manpower to work completely independently from Heisenberg. The flow of information between Heisenberg and Diebner gradually constricted. Following the 1944 attempt on Hitler's life by army conspirators, Diebner's Research Center E was placed under the authority of the SS. Heisenberg was shut out almost completely.

Diebner's plan for a bomb used a gaseous centrifuge developed by

Erich Bagge and Paul Harteck in 1942 to refine uranium into U-235. In contemporary terms, 50 tons of pure uranium will yield roughly 350 kilograms of U-235 in a centrifuge. The Germans had an adequate supply of uranium, thanks to their annexation of Czechoslovakia. The isotope yielded by the centrifuge was then used to construct a reactor designed to breed plutonium for an atomic bomb.

In November 1944, Diebner wrote a letter to Heisenberg that implied that his plutonium breeder reactor in Gottow, near Berlin, had been brought online and suffered a possible critical failure. Soil surveys conducted in 2003 discovered traces of radiation in the Gottow area, though these two pieces of evidence should not be viewed as proof that Diebner's reactor achieved a chain reaction.

Besides the Gottow reactor and a 1955 Diebner design for a plutonium reactor probably derived from his research at Gottow, Rainer Karlsch's controversial book *Hitler's Bomb* contains an even more shocking incident. Karlsch collected declassified U.S. documents of eyewitness accounts of a supposed live test at Thüringia of a strange bomb by (reportedly) Diebner in October 1944. This information was derived from interviews with a German rocket scientist who was flying in the area at the time of the test and was regarded by U.S. military interrogators as above average in reliability. The scientist's account describes a white flash and telltale mushroom cloud, but on a smaller scale than yielded by the first American bombs.

Diebner's supposed 1944 test weapon was using an explosive-sphere design similar to that used by the Americans for the Fat Man bomb. Specifics of its design indicate that it was not intended to achieve, and probably not capable of, a large-scale supercritical reaction. Instead, the design called for large quantities of conventional explosives to trigger a series of smaller fission and fusion reactions. Based on the description of the pressure wave, Diebner's bomb had an estimated yield of only 1 kiloton. By comparison, the Little Boy bomb dropped on Hiroshima had a 13-kiloton yield and the Fat Man bomb dropped on Nagasaki had a 25-kiloton yield.

Further eyewitness accounts have also been published recently of casualties resulting from a supposed Diebner atomic bomb test in March 1945 at the Ohrdruf training ground. These accounts are fairly credible, but the exact nature of the device tested (on two occasions) is murky. Eyewitnesses claim to have seen the charred bodies of prisoners used to test the effectiveness of the bomb as well as several injured SS officers caught too close to the explosion. Radiation sickness was also reported to have claimed a number of lives among those injured from the blast. In March 1945, an atomic detonation would have been seen by Allied ground troops, so it is probable, assuming accounts are true, that this was a conventional device seeded with radioactive material.

Karlsch's revelation about the Diebner bomb and other bombs should be taken with a grain of salt. New evidence of a German atomic bomb surfaces roughly every decade, and it takes at least that much longer before the evidence should be deemed as truth, half-truth, or pure fabrication. As of 2006, there was no reason to doubt Karlsch or his methods, but this sort of dramatic discovery should always be viewed as a work in progress.

Technical Mumbo Jumbo

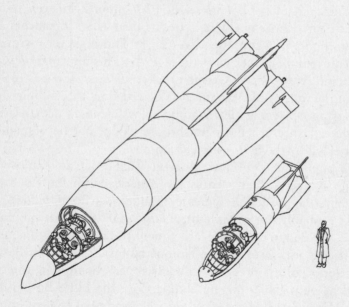

A modified V-2 rocket (left) and a gravity bomb represented two possible delivery vehicles for the Diebner device. Diebner has been included for scale.

Atomic weapons derive their destructive force from either nuclear fission or nuclear fusion. This is produced by forcing a radioactive isotope to achieve a supercritical reaction, during which it expels large quantities of destructive energy. The yields of nuclear weapons are measured in kilotons (1,000 metric tons of TNT) and megatons (1 million metric tons of TNT). This measurement refers only to the explosive force and heat energy of the bomb and does not indicate the amount of radiation released by the blast. It is possible to create salted atomic weapons that release much greater amounts of deadly gamma radiation than their yield would suggest. All atomic weapons developed during World War II were in the kiloton scale.

The two primary isotopes used in atomic weapons are uranium-235 and plutonium-239. Uranium occurs naturally and can be mined and refined to yield large quantities of U-238 and small quantities of U-235. Plutonium occurs naturally in only very tiny quantities, so the Pu-239 used in nuclear weapons is manufactured. This is done by bombarding U-238 with fast neutrons to create the unstable isotope U-239, which undergoes a rapid decay to Pu-239. It is difficult to extract Pu-239 from the mixed fuel elements of a nuclear energy reactor, although it is believed this happens illicitly at times. Reactors used to produce Pu-239 are generally designed specifically for this purpose and are known as "breeder reactors."

During World War II, the vast majority of atomic weapons development was focused on creating a fission reaction. Both of the atomic bombs dropped by the United States on Japan were fission warheads. It was not until the early 1950s that the United States and the Soviet Union began developing weapons that utilized a more potent fusion reaction. These weapons are more commonly known as "hydrogen bombs" and modern strategic weapons employ a fusion warhead that uses a still-secret process to magnify the explosive potential into the double-digit megaton range.

The U.S. atomic bombs used two different methods of detonation. The Little Boy bomb dropped on Hiroshima employed the so-called gun method that utilized conventional explosives to fire a bullet of uranium at a larger uranium target. The force of the collision caused a fission chain reaction and the release of 13 kilotons of energy. The gun design was so unstable that if the *Enola Gay* had crashed en route to Hiroshima, there was a high probability that the force of the impact would have set off the bomb. Not surprisingly, the gun design did not lend itself to safe atomic weapons and only appeared in experimental designs briefly before being phased out.

The Fat Man bomb was a much larger fission bomb built around a plutonium core or "pit." The volatility of the impure plutonium available at the time meant that the gun method was more likely to cause a misfire or premature detonation. The scientists working on the project ruled it out and opted for an implosion design. This involved constructing a core of plutonium and surrounding it with a thick shell of high explosives arranged from interlocking directional charges called "lenses." This shell was then studded with numerous and carefully placed detonators. The detonators would fire in unison and the explosive shell would have its energy focused inward toward the pit. This would increase the density of the plutonium by a factor of approximately two and prompt an immediate fission reaction. The Fat Man bomb turned out to have a 25-kiloton yield.

Diebner's design was similar to the implosion design used for the Fat Man bomb, but with several key differences. A normal implosion design constituted a pit of plutonium inside of a larger roughly spherical mass of explosives formed into lenses. Diebner's design was actually several nested spheres and in cross-section resembled the many layers of a big jawbreaker. The outer shell was an explosive charge studded with detonators. The next layer was a neutron reflector, probably made from beryllium metal (although there are many alternatives), that cut roughly in half the amount of fissile material required to achieve critical mass. The next layer, representing a majority of the pit, was a fissile layer consisting of either plutonium or enriched uranium. Since Diebner seemed to have a bit of difficulty with his breeder reactor, it's fair to assume that it was uranium. The final layer was a pit within the pit made from a mixture of deuterium (heavy water) and tritium.

Diebner's bomb functioned by detonating the shell and increasing the density of the pits to prompt a series of fusion reactions within the deuterium and tritium inner core. The released neutrons would bounce around and off the neutron reflector (over a period of maybe 10 nanoseconds) and cause a series of fission reactions in the enriched uranium outer core. The advantage of this design was that it required only 2 or 3 kilograms of fissile material. The disadvantage was that it was basically a fizzle, yielding only a single kiloton. Another side effect of the design was that it would have probably functioned much like a salted weapon and released large quantities of gamma radiation in a messy and unpredictable fashion.

Variants

Diebner's bomb was just one of many possible configurations for an atomic weapon. Germany had access to uranium, the ability to enrich uranium, and, if Karlsch is correct, the reactor to breed plutonium. However, Allied bombing and sabotage had greatly reduced Germany's ability to produce the refined ingredients for an atomic weapon. Given the availability of the necessary atomic bomb ingredients, Diebner's low-yield design was actually a fairly good compromise between making a bomb that worked and writing about a much better bomb that could work in his dream journal.

Analysis

Heisenberg's team of researchers at the Kaiser Wilhelm Institute failed to develop a working atomic bomb for Germany. The level of Diebner's influence and success within the German atomic bomb project is less clear. Diebner's position as a power player has only come to light in the past several years. What is clear is that he was driven in ways that Heisenberg was not, and he had powerful patrons and financial backers in the Nazi government.

The capabilities of Diebner's atomic weapon claimed to have been tested in 1944 are largely unknown. It was weak by the standards set at Hiroshima and Nagasaki and scarcely a party popper compared to modern atomic weapons. The available information on the device simply prompts more questions.

If the Germans had the technical capability and fissile material to construct one such device, there is no reason to believe that they could not have constructed more. With Allied forces advancing on all fronts, why did the Germans not simply test their bomb on the Allies? If they could construct more bombs, why were these never used when the device's test seemed successful?

The obvious answer to these questions is that the account of the test in October 1944 is either intentionally misleading or simply incorrect. There is enough evidence to make the activation of the Gottow reactor plausible, but limited testimony from a leaked document is not sufficient evidence that the Germans live-tested an atomic weapon. Compared to the Manhattan Project in the United States, the Germans invested virtually nothing into atomic research. Even with a scientific head start and backdoor deals with officials, the Germans lacked the resources, in terms of matériel and, potentially, brainpower, to pull off a real functional atomic device.

Let's put all that aside for a moment and pretend that Diebner's bomb was real. Let's pretend that the Germans even had two or three of these "tactical" atomic devices by February 1945. With the German military being driven back into Germany from the east and west, the two probable uses of the weapons would be to slow the enemy advance or to enact a scorched earth policy on key cities or installations. In the former capacity, a handful of small atomic weapons would have given little more than pause to Allied planners. An atomic device with that low of a yield would only be able to destroy tanks out to a few hundred meters and would probably be more of a danger to troops advancing through the area irradiated earlier by the bombing. In the case of the Soviets, their numerical superiority over the Germans was so favorable that even losing 5,000 men to one of the bombs would do little to slow their momentum.

The bomb would have been slightly more effective as a threat—to the Allies and collaborators—that to surrender a city might mean the detonation of such a device in the city center. Historically, the Germans worked hard to instill fear in the mayors of cities on the brink of surrender by murdering public officials who were working with the Allies. German agents even assassinated mayors after they had surrendered to the Allies, and the possibility of using a device such as Diebner's bomb as an exclamation point would have been quite tempting. How much the threats would have actually done to stiffen the resolve of the German people is difficult to estimate, but bear in mind that German cities that resisted the Allied advance were being bombed to rubble anyway. The Diebner bomb lacked the destructive power to level an entire city, but it might have been used to destroy key installations like factories and oil production, to prevent them from falling into enemy hands.

A third possibility, unlikely historically, would have been to use one of the experimental projects discussed in this book as a vehicle for delivering atomic weapons around the globe. Hitler was obsessed with the idea of striking terrifying blows at his enemies and weakening morale, regardless of the strategic significance. His ultraexpensive V-2 rocket campaign against England terrified only a small percentage of the population and merely angered most, even in the areas around London most likely to be attacked. The attacks did little or nothing to disrupt production, training, or the course of the war and amounted to violent gestures of defiance. Such a gesture using a new super-weapon in the dire days of 1945 would have been almost irresistible.

One scenario for the use of a small late-war atomic weapon against the United States would be to employ a submarine-launched rocket. Plans existed for a submarine-launched version of the V-2 that could be towed into position. The idea of marrying a small atomic payload to such a rocket is covered more fully in chapter 19.

What Fight Have Been

4:17 P.M., January 22, 1945
Fuehrerbunker, Waiting Area
Berlin, Germany

Konrad Fleischer did not need a thermometer to tell that the atmosphere was chillier deep inside the Fuehrer's bunker than it was out on the snow-lashed streets of Berlin. An emergency meeting with Heinrich Himmler and Albert Speer had preempted Konrad's visit with the Fuehrer. That alone would not have bothered him much, but the delay had cast him into purgatory with a gaggle of fawning officers and a weary sprinkling of fellow unfortunate visitors.

"The Fuehrer would have liked very much to have awarded you your medal on the moment of your glorious three-hundredth victory over the enemy," effused a jowly SS officer who Konrad assumed he should recognize. "Heroes of your stature are barely known in the history of war."

Konrad nodded vaguely to whoever the lickspittle was and absently examined his pocket watch.

It was an obvious gesture of contempt, but none of them other than General Heinz & Guderian seemed to notice. He shot Konrad a baleful look but kept his mouth shut. Guderian probably sympathized in his own tight-assed way. Konrad was about to ask Guderian how he liked regaining the Fuehrer's favor after every other general worth a damn had been sacked, when Traudl Junge returned with coffees. Konrad winked at her as she handed a cup to a dour member of Speer's relatively tiny entourage. She blushed at that and leaned in to offer Konrad a splash of cream. He bit his tongue and nodded with a grin. Konrad reckoned her a bit mannish in the jaw, but otherwise quite a fine one.

He watched her go and then turned back to stare at himself on the cover of *Ein Volk, Ein Traum*. The same jowly officer was holding the magazine and a grease pencil up for Konrad to sign it.

"My daughter would love it if you signed this to her." Konrad took the magazine and began to write. "Her name is Helen."

Ein Volk, Ein Traum supposedly told the story of Germany's dream of the stars and how the first successful Raumfahrer had flown higher than Icarus and returned to the Fatherland to tell the tale. There was also an entire spread of photographs of Konrad, accompanied by an article detailing his heroism and trumpeting him as the man who would bring the war to the faraway shores of the United States.

Konrad's favorite photograph was a fantastic shot through the airlock porthole of Obersturmführer Ritter Matzig aboard the station under construction in orbit. He was removing his helmet in the airlock after welding a radio antenna, according to the caption. It was a good picture, but Konrad liked it because someone at the press office had done a horrible job of covering Matzig's beard with paint. The poor man looked like he had an immense goiter.

Konrad handed the magazine back to the SS officer just as an outburst from the Fuehrer's private chambers caught his attention. It was muffled by the thick steel door, but the Fuehrer's voice cut through the metal.

"If we have such a device, I demand we use it! We do not hesitate! The German people will triumph—I will triumph—when the fools think our defeat is at hand."

Himmler or Speer replied, but Konrad could not make out the words.

"Bah!" Hitler raged. "Heisenberg! You say Heisenberg? But where is our bomb?! He whines and complains that it is too hard and promises power that we can bury in a mountain and use to run our factories, and he cannot do even this!"

There was a barely audible reply.

"I should have him shot is what I should do! I tell you this, Albert: If you think—"

There was a slightly sharper interruption, but Konrad still could not make out what was said.

"If Stalin had it, he would have used it. If the Americans or the British had one, then they would have used theirs, as well. This is ours and ours alone." Hitler paused for a moment and when he spoke again Konrad had to strain his ears to hear what was being said. "Faithful Heinrich, Germany has led the world into a new age. Outside that very door is one of our new space pilots. No other nation can claim such an achievement. It is ours alone. Now this . . . this bomb. This belongs to us as surely as the stars. But we will share it with our enemies."

Konrad recognized Speer's voice. He could not quite make out what the man said, but he knew he heard the word *gas*. Whatever the architect said it threw Hitler into another of his fits.

"Not the same at all! And that will not do, Speer! That will not do. We have a bomb, you find a way to drop it. No matter the cost." Hitler muttered, and there was a rattling of papers being thrown. "Look at it again! Look at that great ball of fire and those burns! A kilometer away! Stalin will tremble and beg us for terms! The Americans will run back to their country and hide!"

A moment more, and the argument began to grow circular. Konrad excused himself from the waiting area and found Traudl and two of the other secretaries smoking cigarettes in the generator room.

"I fly out of Berlin in two days," Konrad smiled at her in the winning way he had practiced for the film reels. "I would experience the most profound joy a man can know, if you would accompany me to dinner this evening."

The girls giggled and Traudl blushed. He knew he had her. He did not have to wait for an answer.

Chapter 13

Daimler-Benz Carrier and Parasite Project Series

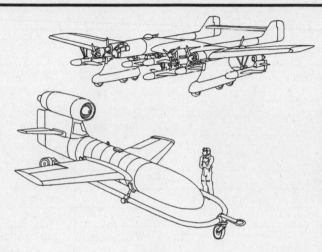

Overview

The concept of a parasite aircraft was not new to aviation during World War II. The British had been launching Sopwith Camels from blimps since 1918, and nearly every nation with the economy to support an aviation industry had tried to marry a small air-launched aircraft to a larger carrier aircraft at one time or another. Following World War II, this concept would gain even more traction, not to mention usefulness, when the United States would air launch the famous X-1 from a B-29 and break the sound barrier. During the war, designs for parasite and carrier aircraft were taken to their greatest extremes by Nazi Germany. Big surprise there.

Daimler-Benz's excitingly titled "Project" series of carrier and parasite aircraft are practically a study in the shifting needs of Germany's Luftwaffe. Begun in late 1942 as a means to ferry a jet bomber across the Atlantic to strike at the United States, the twin designs shifted dramatically over the years. By 1945, the idea of a huge jet carrier aircraft had been replaced with a huge propeller-driven aircraft, and the fast jet bomber had become six swept-wing flying suicide bombs.

It went from bold plans to bring the distant United States to its

	Project C	Project F
Category:	Carrier aircraft	Expendable flying bomb
Phase of Development:	Preprototype	Preprototype
Development Start:	1945	1945
Development Team:	Kurt Tank Focke-Wulf/Daimler-Benz	Kurt Tank Focke-Wulf/Daimler-Benz
Crew:	3	1
Weight:	122,000 kg fully loaded	10,000 kg (estimated)
Propulsion:	6 × Daimler-Benz DB DB 603 1,750 hp engines	1× BMW 018 jet engine producing 3,500 kg of thrust
Speed:	500 kph (estimated)	1,050 kph
Range:	17,000 km	50–100 km (estimated)
Wing Span:	54 m	9 m
Length:	35 m	12.96 m
Height:	11.2 m	Unknown
Armament:	Point defense only	3,000 kg shaped charge warhead

knees all the way to a desperate gambit to stem the enemy tides in the span of just three years. By the time the Project C and Project F were preparing to make the jump from the drawing board to the skies, Germany had fallen and it could not get up.

Development History

Long before Daimler-Benz AG jumped into the cozy bed of capitalism with Chrysler, it was in the business of manufacturing vehicles and components for the German military. In keeping with the expertise of Daimler-Benz, the majority of these contracts focused on the terrestrial, with a handful of forays into aircraft engine development. It was not until late 1942 that Daimler thrust itself wholly into the aircraft design arena, by pairing with Focke-Wulf superstar designer professor and schematic progressor Kurt Tank.

Daimler-Benz had been quietly working on a design for a long-range bomber parasite and carrier before 1942. These concepts were progressing well, but under the urgings of Reich officials the team under Fritz Nallinger and Erich Übelacker joined forces with Focke-Wulf to advance plans for a bomber that would allow Germany to strike at the United States. Kurt Tank from Focke-Wulf oversaw the technical aspect of the design process, and it was his responsibility that the Project be capable of attacking targets in the United States or deep within the Soviet Union without refueling.

By the spring of 1943, the Daimler team under Tank had completed design and preprototype testing on the Project A-I and Project A-II. The Project A-I was an ambitiously scaled carrier aircraft powered by jet engines with a staggering 17,000-kilometer range. The Project A-I carried the twin-engine jet bomber Project A-II slung beneath its fuselage. This smaller bomber aircraft sacrificed fuel in exchange for a larger bomb load and powerful BMW 018 jet engines.

A number of factors lowered the priority of the matching set of Project A vehicles: the worsening situation in the air and on the ground, an increasing emphasis on fighter production, and, most important, the sheer number of components the Project A required that were unavailable. Taking these factors into consideration, the Project A was projected to be ready for production by 1947.

Instead of being completely shelved, the research done on the Project A was put to good use in the Project B. For the Project B the first step in a move toward realism was scaling the aircraft down by nearly 50 percent from a wingspan of 94 meters to 54 meters. The jet engines powering the Project A were replaced with four puller and two pusher piston engines, and the huge wings were completely overhauled. The A-II bomber was similarly given a new coat of paint, including a new tail assembly and the removal of the two engines in favor of a single massively powerful Daimler jet engine.

In 1945, the Project drifted in a grim direction that mirrored the broader position of Germany in the war against its enemies. The Project B was transformed into the Project C that—records being what they are—was pretty much the same as the Project B with a different name. The more dramatic change was replacing the A-II/B jet bomber with five Project E flying bombs.

The Project E was a very small jet aircraft similar in appearance to Germany's Komet rocket fighter, with a large engine situated beneath the tail of the aircraft. Appearances aside, this was no fighter. The fuselage was packed full of 2,500 kilograms of explosives acting as a shaped charge that would magnify their effect. These aircraft were suspended from launch posts beneath the Project C, which would taxi them to the target area and release them for a suicide run.

The final iteration of the Project took shape in 1945. The Project C remained unchanged, but the suicidal Project E flying bombs were replaced with an equally suicidal Project F. This aircraft included a darkly amusing escape hatch that had about as much chance of saving the pilot as Germany had of winning the war. It was essentially a panel that fell out from underneath the unfortunate pilot, who was then sucked out into the open air, along with his chair and anything else in the cockpit. Perhaps the inclusion of the escape mechanism allowed Adolf Hitler to sleep a little easier at night.

The Project F boasted a much more powerful BMW 018 jet engine. This was the same engine that was originally included in the Project A-II bomber parasite. The really confusing thing about suddenly going back to that engine in 1945 is that in late 1944 BMW's facilities where the BMW 018 was being tested were obliterated by bombing. Very little additional progress was made on the engine before the war ended. Was this a lack of communication between the companies, wishful thinking, or an effort by designers at Daimler to sabotage their own suicidal aircraft? Reverend Kurt Tank saves the day!

Technical Mumbo Jumbo

The B-29 Superfortress was the largest production aircraft of World War II, with a 42-meter wingspan and a loaded weight of 54,000 kilograms. Had the Project C carrier aircraft ever been manufactured, it would have dwarfed the mighty Superfortress. With a wingspan of 54 meters and a fully loaded weight of 122,000 kilograms, the Project C would have easily claimed the largest aircraft title from its Allied competition. The Project C's dominant feature was its enormous wing area of 500 square meters. This was more than three times the wing area of a Superfortress and was key to the Project C's long range and stability.

The Project C was powered by six Daimler-Benz 1,750 horsepower DB 603 piston engines. The DB 603 was a large and, at the time, very modern twelve-cylinder liquid-cooled engine, incorporating a supercharger and fuel injection. These were configured to drive four puller and two pusher airscrews in the wings of the Project C and brought the Project C to a respectable estimated top speed of 500 kph.

One of the most unique and interesting features of the Project C and its predecessors was the elevated landing gear structures. These two widely set and heavily reinforced platforms were necessary in all versions of the Project carrier to support its immense weight and to allow the parasite aircraft to be loaded on the ground. They were sort of like a combination of knee braces and stilts for that crazy fat guy who wants to suspend a motorcycle from his groin. Each of these landing "pylons" contained three large-diameter wheels, and together raised the Project C's fuselage nearly 9 meters off the ground. They remained in place during flight.

No armament was planned in the designs for the Project C, although this almost certainly would have been altered to include at least some turret-mounted point defense. The three-man crew could have been supplemented as necessary to accommodate gunners.

The Project C was capable of carrying five of the Project E flying bombs or six of the Project F flying bombs suspended on drop racks beneath its wings. In the case of the Project F, one flying bomb hung beneath the fuselage with another Project F actually fixed below it.

The Project F had a missile-shaped fuselage with a reinforced forward portion containing the 3,000-kilogram shaped explosive charge. The cockpit was cramped and located just forward of the aircraft's tail assembly with the extremely large BMW jet engine located immediately above it. It would be an understatement to say that this configuration looked somewhat awkward. It probably would have been awkward to fly as well, but it was a bit of design genius that allowed for a larger explosive charge to be carried and simplified the manufacturing process.

The ejection seat, or in the case of the Project F, the "fall out of the aircraft seat," consisted of a fuselage panel that would fall away when a lever was pulled in the cockpit. Gravity and airflow would suck the pilot and his seat out of the cockpit and into the relative safety of the air outside of 3.5 metric tons of explosives. The Project F was nearly capable of breaking the sound barrier, so falling out of its belly either from low altitudes or in a steep dive could be a bit dicey, to say the least.

Variants

The Project C and F were the final installments of the Project series and never entered production. As such, their variants are only limited by the infinite power of your imagination!

Analysis

In its earliest incarnation, the Project series was merely eccentric. The concept of using a massive jet aircraft to ferry a smaller and faster jet bomber across the Atlantic was not terrible. Over the United States, a jet bomber would have at least briefly wreaked absolute havoc. It almost certainly would have had an opportunity to release its bomb load on its own terms, and because of the speed of the bomber and even its carrier jet, they would have likely made good their escape. As with most German superweapon projects, this one falls apart once you look at the resources-to-benefits equation. This equation became less and less favorable for the Germans, the further the Project progressed.

Being the biggest aircraft in the world would not have made things easy for the Project C when it was on the ground and subject to Allied air attacks. If a Project C miraculously survived marauding bombers and fighters long enough to take to the skies, its odds only improved slightly. Allied fighter power had a stranglehold on the Reich by 1945, and any aircraft as large and vulnerable as the Project C would have had to fly with a formidable escort formation or else be easy prey. Mustering an escort like that in 1945 would have been no simple task for Germany and would have cost it heavily when the inevitable air battle resulted.

Let's just say the escorts manage to fend off the Allied fighters long enough for the Project C to approach a target. This would have either been a ground target, like a bunker, headquarters, or armored formation or a naval target. The 3,000-kilogram charge in a released Project F would have done a good deal of damage to ground targets, but unless the intelligence information guiding the attack was exceptionally good, the effort would be wasted. A trained pilot and a jet aircraft traded for a handful of tanks or infantry? Not worth it.

Naval targets would have been the most worthwhile use of the Project C and Project F. The high speed of the Project F would have made it exceedingly difficult to shoot down on approach, and the large size of its warhead could have devastated a carrier. The Project C had an unmatched ability to remain airborne without refueling for roughly 36 hours. If a Project C could make it to open waters undetected, it could have operated much like a submarine hunting for Allied naval convoys. The Project C would have never made it near a carrier group, but if it had, the Project Fs it carried might have dealt a crippling blow to the U.S. or British navy.

Hypothetical Deployment History

Two operational prototypes of the Project C completed testing in January 1945 and were shifted to the formative Fifth Squadron of KG 200 for use in secret missions. These joined nine operational Project F flying bombs. In late February 1945, V/KG 200 undertook a long-range naval interdiction operation from two separate bases in western Germany. This was planned as Operation Ball Lightning and involved elements of two Jagdeschwaders, including some twenty-seven fighter aircraft.

Lightning A, mounting four Project F flying bombs and escorted by twelve fighters, departed for the Atlantic coast of France at 7:00 P.M. At 7:20, *Lightning B* departed for the North Atlantic, accompanied by fifteen fighters and also mounting four Project F flying bombs.

Lightning A successfully crossed to the Atlantic undetected, although its fighter escort was jumped and badly mauled during its return trip. Over the next 18 hours, *Lightning A* managed to cripple the heavy cruiser USS *Bethesda* and sink the British destroyers HMS *Impenetrable* and HMS *War Dog*. The fourth flying bomb launched from *Lightning A* malfunctioned before impact and detonated prematurely. *Lightning A* was intercepted during its return flight and was shot down over occupied Germany. The crew did not survive.

Lightning B suffered a similar fate. Its escort fighters became embroiled in a major dogfight over German airspace and most were shot down. The remainder escaped with *Lightning B*, which had sustained significant damage to its engines. Realizing that the North Atlantic hunt was impossible, the crew of *Lightning B* requested available targets and was vectored to an ongoing Allied bombing raid over Pforzheim. Allied fighters intercepted *Lightning B* just as it made visual contact with the bomber formations. It launched all four of its Project F flying bombs in the direction of the bomber formation and was shot down shortly thereafter.

The Project F flying bombs slammed into British Lancasters and managed to destroy five. Miraculously, one of the Project F pilots survived and returned to KG 200 a few days later. The Project C never entered production. A crash program attempted to modify the Project F for launch from more conventional platforms, but this did not produce results before the end of the war.

What Fight Have Been

7:49 P.M., February 23, 1945
Area Bombing of "Yellowfin," Bomber Group Five, Lancaster *My Salty Lady*
Approaching Pforzheim, Germany

"Hang on to your tackle," the pilot advised. "We're about to get shot to ribbons."

The nose machine guns clattered. Something crashed against the Lancaster and the whole aircraft rocked violently.

"Aw, quit windin' 'im up, Sully." The copilot leaned back and gave R.E. Lincoln a crooked grin, "We only been 'it a bit. Nothing we can't soldier through."

"Tell that to the number three." The pilot feathered the prop and with a jerk it coughed and sputtered back to life.

R.E. fought down the vomit rising in his throat and grabbed one of the upright supports next to the bombardier's post. When he leaned back and looked to the front of the aircraft, he could see a constant flash of explosions and the deceptively slow arcs of tracers curving up through the sky. The view did little to calm his stomach.

" 'Ere we are then," the copilot gestured expansively, "lovely Yellowfin. Looks like we're a wee bit late fer the party."

"Try not to give me any bumps," the bombardier shot R.E. a serious look and dropped his earphones onto his head.

"Holy God." The copilot seemed at a loss for more descriptive words.

"Mister Lincoln," the pilot began, "you might want to pop up here and have a look."

R.E. reluctantly abandoned the relative reliability of his spot next to the bombardier and began to walk up the shaking fuselage toward the cockpit. He found handholds where he could and bit his tongue when something rattled the side of the plane and nearly bowled him over. When he was able to steady himself on the pilot and copilot seats, he looked through the windscreen. The view of the city below was nothing short of apocalyptic.

"That ought to pay Jerry back for London all by itself." The pilot sounded genuinely impressed.

"Caw, pay them back fer Ol' Trafford, more like," the copilot scoffed. "Burn 'em to a cinder, I say."

The city was one contiguous fire, raging high into the sky and dwindling to isolated fires around its edges. Every moment, another storm of incendiary bombs crashed down into the inferno and raised a plume of flames and a gust of black smoke.

"What's that?" R.E. pointed out the window.

"That's Yellowfin, the objective," the pilot explained.

"It's where we—"

"No," R.E. interrupted, "what is that?" He jabbed his finger against the windscreen.

There was another flare in the sky ahead of them. The burst was too small to be a flak explosion and it kept burning and growing larger. A third flare finally caught the pilot's attention.

"I don't—"

The aircraft passed them with a distinct engine roar. It was moving faster than anything R.E. had ever seen. It resembled one of the buzz bombs the Germans were still occasionally using, but larger and with what distinctly looked like a cockpit. R.E. pressed against the pilot and both men leaned to the side glass to watch the strange aircraft pass. It dipped its wings a bit and plunged straight into the cockpit of a nearby Lancaster. The big bomber dropped its nose, pulled up again, and then exploded. Not a single recognizable piece could be seen in the cloud of burning debris.

"Oh Christ," the pilot commented with remarkable dryness.

A second flying bomb zoomed past them as scarcely more than a blur of light. A third seemed to be headed directly at their aircraft.

"Ross," the pilot addressed the nose gunner. "If you would be so kind, please shoot Jerry's new bomb."

The Lancaster's nose gun began hammering. The tracers disappeared into the dark shape hidden by night at the end of the engine exhaust. They did nothing. As R.E. watched the flying bomb grow larger and larger, he felt as if he were in a dream. It was the sort of dream in which he would see a tornado drawing near, yet could do nothing to move or seek shelter. Fate could not be stopped.

Ross stopped fate with his twin .30 caliber machine guns. The flying bomb exploded in a brilliant flash and a moment later the Lancaster slammed through its debris trail. Something popped in the number three engine and it began to burn. There was a moment of stunned silence and then the pilot regained his senses.

"Not the end of the world," the pilot said, flipping switches on the control panel.

"Aw, be honest now, Sully." The copilot looked to R.E. and gave him another crooked grin, "We're proper fucked now, mate."

R.E. staggered back to his safe spot next to the bombardier and resolved to stare directly at the floor of the aircraft until it had landed.

Chapter 14

Sänger Silbervogel Antipodal Bomber

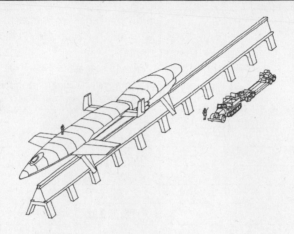

Overview

No German designer of secret projects deserves to have his story told in the form of a pulp-action movie quite like Eugen Sänger. The developer of the Sänger Silbervogel (Silverbird) Antipodal Bomber was a pioneer of rocketry and space exploration who collaborated with a sassy physicist whom he later married. Sänger and Irene Bredt designed a space bomber to attack New York City, wriggled away from American interrogators following the war to work for the French, and then dodged kidnappers sent by Joseph Stalin, only to flee to the United States to work for the Americans. Sänger, more than even Wernher von Braun, is the father of the modern U.S. space shuttle program. His revolutionary plans for a rocket-powered reusable space bomber heavily influenced the design of the Dynasoar and later both the Soviet and American space shuttles. The basic engine design cooked up by Sänger and Bredt remains in use to this very day.

Sänger created an immensely powerful self-cooling engine to provide the thrust to lift his flat-bodied bomber just above the upper atmosphere. The craft would arc up through the atmosphere, and, with the rocket motor's fuel supply exhausted, it would glide back down gracefully

Category:	Suborbital Amerika bomber
Phase of Development:	Preprototype
Development Start:	1933
Development Team:	Eugen Sänger and Irene Bredt
Crew:	1
Weight:	9,973 kg fully loaded
Propulsion:	Two-stage suborbital boost
	Launch stage: 1 × Sänger Monorail Launch Sled producing 700,000 kg of thrust Second stage: 1 × Sänger-Bredt Regenerative Engine producing 146,000 kg of thrust
Speed:	21,800 kph
Range:	23,400 km
Wing Span:	15.00 m
Length:	34.00 m
Diameter:	2.32 m
Armament:	1 × 3,600 kg bomb

toward the earth's upper atmosphere. Rather than diving through it, the bomber's trajectory would flatten out, and it would skip across the upper atmosphere like a stone over the surface of a really hot pond. The stresses placed on the airframe and shielded underside would have been immense, but the risks for the lone pilot were offset—to the strategic planners at least—by the global strike capabilities of the antipodal design.

Sänger's design was robust, and his engines would later prove ingenious, but much like Braun's orbital designs, the Silbervogel demonstrated a lack of understanding of some of the technical difficulties and dangers posed by reentry. The problems the Silbervogel design would have faced, like repeatedly skipping the craft across a high-friction barrier at an incredible velocity, were in many ways even worse than those faced by Braun's more straightforward rocket designs. The lower chances of success for the Silbervogel, compared to Braun's orbital rockets, were mitigated by the fact that available technology and resources allowed for an actual serious attempt at the craft. It was much smaller, required much less fuel, and although its launching method was basically a rollercoaster, it could at least be concealed from Allied bombers.

Development History

Eugen Sänger was to Steve Buscemi what Wernher von Braun was to Tom Cruise. Braun was out getting all the hot groupies, signing autographs, and trying to convert people to Scientology. Sänger was toiling away on his craft, innovating boldly, and slipping love notes to his physicist collaborator Irene Bredt. Like Braun, Sänger were inspired by the works of Hermann Oberth, and in the late 1920s Sänger decided to transfer to the Vienna Polytechnic Institute and change his major from party animal studies to aeronautical engineering. His bong firmly stowed away in a steamer trunk, Sänger went on to graduate with a degree in 1931 after having to redo his thesis paper, because his choice of rocket propulsion was considered too radical. They might have reconsidered that evaluation, if only they had known precisely how radical to the max Sänger's thesis had been.

Sänger continued to research and theorize on rocket development, and in 1933 he published a revised version of his rejected thesis entitled "Rocket Flight Engineering." Sänger's paper was revolutionary and approached many of the obstacles of rocketry and space flight with the hard math to match his big dreams. Sänger even hypothesized about ion engines and the advantages they might offer for long-duration space flights. The first ion-drive deep-space probe was launched in 1998, thirty-four years after Sänger's death in 1964. While Sänger's paper was of great interest to rocket enthusiasts of the time it wasn't until he published two articles in the Austrian aeronautics magazine *Flug* that he gained the attention of people with the money to help Sänger realize his dreams.

Sänger's articles focused primarily on his advances with Bredt in the development of a regenerative self-cooling rocket engine and the promising results of a series of static tests conducted with this engine from 1930 to 1935. In February 1936, the Luftwaffe cordially invited Sänger to come to Trauen, Germany, and attend the ground-laying ceremony at his new top-secret rocket research facility. Sänger headed the elaborate Trauen facility while Braun was the project director at the Peenemünde rocket site. Rather than pooling their immense talents on a single project, the Luftwaffe kept each largely in the dark of the other's work. Sänger and Braun had to fight with senior Luftwaffe officials to even visit one another's facilities.

While Braun focused on vertical rocketry, Sänger envisioned a space plane launched horizontally from a gradually inclining monorail rig. The facilities were constructed with a rail line for testing rocket motors and with large wind tunnels for testing the aerodynamics of the space plane design. The Silbervogel gradually took shape in the period leading up to the invasion of the Soviet Union. In 1941, projects deemed too ambitious to contribute to the war effort were canceled, and Sänger's attentions were supposedly diverted to more pressing problems. In reality, Sänger continued to work nearly full time on the Silbervogel and by 1944, he and Bredt had produced a fully fleshed-out and tested design and method for launching the space plane and attacking targets around the globe.

Sänger believed that the Silbervogel's velocity of nearly mach 20 would allow it to skip across the atmosphere. Sänger and Bredt also held the view that the large single-warhead conventional bomb the craft carried would be delivered to the target at a sufficient velocity to magnify its destructive power considerably. No significant work was completed on the project after 1944; when the war had ended, Sänger was in the employ of the French government.

Sänger's stint with the French did not last long. Their security forces uncovered a plot by Joseph Stalin, who had become obsessed with Sänger's Silbervogel, to have Sänger kidnapped and brought back to the Soviet Union. Sänger subsequently eluded his would-be kidnappers and fled to the United States, where he worked with the air force and NASA on various advanced space flight projects. Some of these borrowed heavily from Sänger's previous work. The Dynasoar was practically the Silbervogel launched vertically by one of Braun's titanic multistage rocket boosters.

Technical Mumbo Jumbo

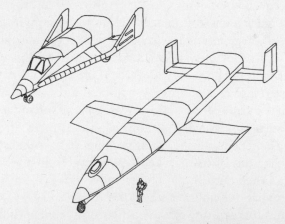

The Dynasoar (left) and the Silbervogel.

The Sänger Silbervogel was a two-stage boost-glide bomber capable of reaching a boosted velocity of more than mach 17. The craft was designed with a flattened fuselage to decrease drag and enhance lift capabilities and featured swept wings with a very low aspect ratio compared to the overall length of the Silbervogel. The spacecraft also had a small horizontal tail assembly. The pilot of the Silbervogel sat inside a small reinforced cockpit with almost no visibility and would instead rely primarily on radio signals and gyroscopic guidance to find his target. The fuel supply and rocket motor were mounted behind the cockpit, with fuel tanks extending above the bomb bay.

The Silbervogel's engine utilized the regenerative cooling technique pioneered by Sänger and Bredt, in which the pressurized fuel supply was cycled around the engine to prevent overheating. This innovative engine design was the most proven of all the Silbervogel's components. During the mid-1930s, Sänger ran a variety of tests on scaled-down versions of the engine and this continued up to full-scale testing at the Trauen facility.

The Silbervogel was launched by means of a 3-kilometer-long monorail that curved slowly up to a 30-degree incline. The Silbervogel was mounted on a launch sled immediately in front of a first-stage booster producing 600 tons of thrust for an 11-second burn period. At the end of this burn, the Silbervogel would fly from the rail, dropping the booster and sled beneath it. Once the craft had achieved a sufficient altitude, the pilot would activate the second internal rocket engine, producing 100 tons of thrust for a 3-minute orbital burn. At the end of this burn, the Silbervogel would hopefully be well above escape velocity and capable of beginning its up-and-down circumnavigation of the globe.

The distance and altitude of its atmospheric "bounces" would decrease as the Silbervogel shed speed. If the Sänger craft had achieved the adequate preorbital velocity to glide to its target in this fashion, it would then release its bomb through the lower atmosphere. The speed of the Silbervogel would be transferred to the bomb as it fell away, allowing its payload to slam into the ground at a speed much faster than gravity would normally permit. The force of this impact would then amplify the explosive force of the 3,600-kilogram bomb. In case you are not a bombologist, a 3,600-kilogram bomb is a really large bomb. Not nuclear bomb–level destruction, but large enough to inflict serious damage on an urban area.

As was the case with Braun's early spacecraft designs, the heat fluctuations facing a craft reentering the atmosphere were not fully appreciated by Sänger and Bredt. Though the Silbervogel was designed to withstand intense heat, it was not capable of actually surviving reentry (not to mention the atmosphere skipping) in even its 1944 configuration. Advanced materials like molybdenum could have solved these problems in much the same way they eventually did for the Dynasoar. Unfortunately for Sänger and the poor pilot of the first Silbervogel, only transatmospheric tests could have fully demonstrated the necessity for using them.

Variants

Early in its design phase, the Silbervogel was a much smaller and unarmed space plane, compared to the bomb-toting creature it would later become. It was enlarged to increase its global reach and to allow it to carry something that would make the Nazis want to send it into space in the first place. Had the Nazis ever developed an atomic weapon, the Silbervogel would have been a prime choice for a delivery platform. This would have likely required a specially made version of the craft capable of lifting a heavier payload, a matter of scaling up the design by 10 to 15 percent.

Analysis

The Silbervogel was an interesting vehicle, but of little practical value for the Germans and their shrinking empire. For an empire on the rise or an empire with resources the Germans lacked, it could have served as a crucial strategic asset. Had they possessed an atomic bomb, it might have been a nearly unstoppable delivery vehicle. Had they been mounting aggressive offensive abroad in the latter years of the war, the Silbervogel might have been a very effective surveillance vehicle. Had there been no better solutions, the Silbervogel might even have succeeded in its intended role as a strategic bomber. A lot of "mights" and a lot of money would get the Silbervogel off the ground, but it would have been a waste of resources eclipsed only by the Braun station for a nation already strained to breaking.

Hypothetical Deployment History

Tests of the Silbervogel airframe and its rocket motors were completed in August 1943 to the satisfaction of Sänger and Luftwaffe officials. In

September, the Luftwaffe approved an order for three of the space planes to be built at the Trauen site and for simultaneous construction to begin on a full-scale launch rail. The internal and booster rocket motors were completed in February 1944, and the Silbervogel airframe was completed in March. Construction of the monorail proceeded at an excellent pace up until late January 1944, when it was spotted and badly damaged by Allied bombers. The monorail site was shifted to the south, where a natural ravine was used to camouflage construction.

The launch rail and the first Silbervogel were finally ready to enter service on September 19, 1944. Albert Speer, Hermann Göring, and several other high-ranking party officials, as well as a newsreel crew, observed the launch from inside a bunker. With a brilliant jet of fire and roiling white smoke, the Silbervogel 1 streaked up its launch rail and into a clear mid morning sky. The booster and launch sled sailed through the air and splashed into a man-made pond as intended. The test pilot Klaus Reiter became the first human being to break the sound barrier. At 6,000 feet, the Silbervogel's internal rocket motor kicked in and successfully propelled the space plane to escape velocity.

Reiter lost consciousness due to G-forces twice during the assent and was just regaining his wits when the craft made the transition through the atmosphere to the silent darkness of space. Unfortunately for expectant ground crews, the radio inside the craft had been damaged and did not relay Reiter's statement that "the Reich eagle now watches over the whole of the planet." A more robust radio transponder did send back word that the craft broke apart during its second atmospheric bounce. It would take many weeks of investigation and research to determine that inadequate heat shielding had caused the craft's fuselage to fail catastrophically. Despite the death of the pilot, the flight was declared a success in the newspapers and on radio broadcasts.

Production on the partially completed Silbervogel 2 was immediately halted to allow Sänger and his development team time to come up with a way to avert a repeat of the disaster. Nearly six months later, the entire underside of the Silbervogel 2 had been covered in a heavy black skin of molybdenum. The added weight was compensated for in the plans for the Silbervogel 3, but the retrofitted Silbervogel 2 could only carry aloft a single purpose–made 1,250-kilogram bomb.

On February 19, 1945, under scattered snow showers and the constant risk of Allied bombing, the launch of the Silbervogel 2 went ahead despite protestations from Sänger. The space plane performed admirably through the first boost phase, but bad wing icing at higher altitudes caused the craft's trajectory to become unstable during the second phase. The pilot ejected at 21,000 meters and miraculously survived, though he fell into Allied hands. Worse than the loss of the craft was that the Silbervogel streaked wildly into Allied airspace and was fairly easily tracked to its source by the immense column of smoke it left in its wake.

Less than a week later, a massive bombing raid decimated the Trauen site, including some of the underground areas thought to be invulnerable to aerial bombardment. Bredt was killed and Sänger was badly injured. Sänger was so distraught over Bredt's death that he killed himself with cyanide while still convalescing from his injuries. The remaining staff of the Trauen facility was shifted to Braun's team at Peenemünde, in the hopes that they could accelerate development of projects there.

What Fight Have Been

7:04 a.m., February 19, 1945
Silbervogel 2 Launch Rail
Trauen, Germany

"Release!" Konrad Fleischer's yell was lost to the roar of the first-stage rocket motor.

He threw his palm against the release button and blew the explosive bolts that kept the launch dolly locked into place on the rail. G-forces immediately slammed their invisible hand against him as the Silbervogel was propelled down the rail at an incredible speed. The vibrations inside the cockpit were so intense that the curvature of the launch rail was felt, rather than seen, as a moving twist in Konrad's guts.

"All lights green," he gasped, his lungs straining against the force of acceleration. "Rail release in five . . . four . . . three . . . two . . . one . . ."

There was a thump and a receding clatter as the booster dolly flew away on its terminal trajectory toward the catch lake. The Silbervogel was fully airborne and it was up to Konrad to make the call of when to activate stage two. A simple gyroscope switch inside the controls would kick it in if he waited too long, but Sänger had confided no better than a 25 percent chance of survival if it was left to the automatic system. Konrad squinted at the angle and altimeter gauges. The vibrations had decreased to nearly nothing, but he was still on the verge of blacking out.

Is that a seven or a one?

It clicked over to an eight and Konrad smacked his hand across the internal booster activation.

"Primary booster go!"

There was a reciprocating thump that seemed to roll through the Silbervogel's fuselage and then back out its tail. With a roar, the internal booster fired and Konrad was once again pressed down hard into his seat. His helmet was fogging badly and the small canopy was so thick and ice-swept that he could barely see outside the aircraft.

"... atus. Repeat ... S-2 ... is your status?" The earpiece in his helmet crackled with static and was hardly audible.

"All green, Trauen!" With effort Konrad turned his head to see the altimeter through the fogged helmet. "Twelve thousand meters!"

One of the green lights on the console began to flicker out. Konrad shifted his head again to see which one it was.

"Climb angle indicator is going!" It blinked off and the yellow bulb next to it illuminated. "I'm losing my angle, Trauen. Say again, I'm losing my angle!"

"... peat. Please repeat, S-2!"

"I'm losing my climb angle and," Konrad struggled to see the airspeed indicator, "damn it. Shit. Trauen, my velocity is too low. Altitude too low!"

"... copy, S-2. Please stand by."

"Booster burn expiring in nine seconds!" Konrad reached out and grabbed the stick with both hands. "Attempting course correction."

"... egative ... ot to adjust course! Repeat, do—" the radio lapsed into silence.

Konrad knew he had to pull the aircraft up by 5 to 7 degrees and knew that he was strictly never to attempt to do it manually. He concentrated on the stick, focused his strength in his wrists, and with all his effort he pulled back on the stick as little as possible. The engine howled. Immediately, lights went red across his board. The primary emergency indicator began to flash red. There was a hideous thump and something snapped off the right wing. The vibrations doubled.

That's it, then?

Konrad yanked back on the cockpit canopy release, and with a whoop it was sucked away. He followed an instant later, pulled out and past the rocket engine. The intense heat rippled across him for only a fraction of a second, but it was enough to melt most of the outer layer of his padded flight suit. His pressure helmet popped and Konrad blacked out.

He awoke. He was falling. He was falling impossibly fast. His body was numb with cold and he was literally covered with a layer of ice. Konrad had no idea how high he was or where he was; his helmet was completely frosted both inside and out. Drawing a breath stung his lungs. He yanked on the main chute release and the powerful jerk of the canopy deploying knocked him unconscious again. Konrad regained consciousness and could sense the earth opening its arms to catch him. He braced his legs for landing and, within seconds, put down on hard-frozen dirt. The wind dragged him across the ground for several seconds as he fumbled with the chute release.

Konrad rolled over and got himself up on his hands and knees. Miraculously, he seemed to be uninjured. He tore off the helmet and gasped in a lungful of rich ground-level air.

"You a Yank?" the question was asked in English.

Konrad looked over at a young British soldier with a dirt-streaked face. Several other Brits were running to join the man.

"Too bad not," Konrad replied in his schoolboy English.

He pointed to the Reich Eagle on his upper arm and then, with a surprising flash of embarrassment, realized that the heat of the rocket had burned it away.

"German," Konrad smiled wearily. "Luftwaffe."

"What happened to you, Jerry?" The British soldier yanked Konrad to his feet. "You look like a cooked goose."

"Bad day," Konrad replied.

"Imagine that, mate." The Brit gave him a rough slap on the back, "Buck up then, you're out of the fight. You can kick up your heels in a prison somewhere far away."

Konrad squinted up into the sky. There was still a white track of smoke marking his aircraft's ascent and eventual wild descent. He looked back at the British soldier and grinned, the Brit half-smiled and prodded him with his rifle.

"On your way, then. Back of the lines."

Konrad staggered past the British soldiers with the infantryman who found him at his back. As he passed an idling tank, he began to wonder what the London girls would make of him.

SECTION III

SEA

Chapter 15

VS8 Tragflügelboot

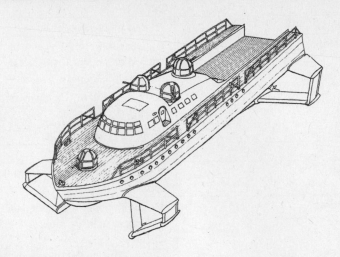

Overview

The VS8 Tragflügelboot was a large high-speed transport hydrofoil designed with an eye to carrying invasion forces across the English Channel, but later adapted for the transport of tanks from Sicily to North Africa along the treacherous Mediterranean shipping routes. Hydrofoil technology was in its infancy at the outbreak of World War II, and the Germans had in Baron Hanns von Schertel the leading pioneer in the technology and an almost pathological advocate of hydrofoil concepts. Hydrofoils are watercraft with winglike foils mounted on struts that extend beneath the hull of the vessel. As the craft picks up speed, the foils develop lift just as an aircraft wing does. This lift will bring the hull of the ship up above the waterline, greatly reducing drag and increasing the speed of the craft.

The idea that Schertel could, in essence, make a ship that would fly was not very well received by naval engineers and military planners. Sure, to jaded citizens of the twenty-first century like you or me, the idea of a hydrofoil is no more unusual than an automobile or a meson cascade chamber. To the primitive minds of the early twentieth century, Schertel might as well have been talking about leprechauns or trans-

Category:	High-speed hydrofoil transport
Phase of Development:	Limited production run
Development Start:	1940
Development Team:	Hanns von Schertel and Gotthard Sachsenberg
Crew:	22
Weight:	70 tons empty/90 tons loaded
Propulsion:	2 × Daimler-Benz 20-cylinder supercharged MB 501 diesels producing 5,000 hp
Speed:	45 kt projected (37 kt achieved)
Range:	325 km
Length:	32 m
Width:	10.25 m
Draught:	4.25 m hull/less than 2 m hydrofoil (at speed)
Armament:	4 × 15mm heavy machineguns 1 × light or medium tank OR 15+naval mines (for minelayer variant)

muting iron into steel through the occult processes of metallurgy. They were simply unimaginative, and for more than a decade, Schertel toiled away on his preposterous flying ships with only his own resources. Though a baron surely had vast coffers of gold ducats stashed away in his science castle's treasure room, these were quickly squandered, so he enlisted the aid of the dashing shipyard owner Gotthard Sachsenberg.

The Sachsenberg family controlled shipyards in Dessau-Rosslau, and Gotthard Sachsenberg was a true political rogue in a time when very few rogues survived. Sachsenberg was a decorated naval hero of the Great War, a member of the Reichstag, and he was once taken out into the woods to be shot by the Nazis, but convinced his captors to release him. Despite the fact that he was both vocally opposed to the Nazis and, almost unbelievably, of Jewish heritage, this incident was the only attempt made on his life by the Nazis. They valued Sachsenberg's contribution to the war effort (and feared the repercussions of killing multiple Sachsenberg family war heroes) more than their own grotesque ideological purity.

This unlikely pairing of Sachsenberg's resources and Schertel's genius produced some of the most revolutionary ship designs of World War II, of which the VS8 was the closest to realization.

Development History

Hanns von Schertel began his experimental work into the design and capabilities of hydrofoils in 1927, while attending college in Berlin. He drew on the work of earlier pioneers, including Alexander Graham Bell and his early HD-4 hydrofoil. Schertel's initial designs utilized exclusively surface-piercing foils. These foils partially emerge from the water when the craft is foilborne and can cause severe stability problems in heavy seas. After multiple partially successful prototypes, Schertel tried his hand at a submerged foil design that might remedy the stability problems. Due to a lack of adequate depth-sensing equipment, Schertel's submerged foil design was not ready for prime time.

Schertel returned to surface-piercing foils for his seventh prototype, combining a V-foil in the craft's front with outer trapezoidal foils in the aft. This craft was satisfactorily stable in test runs and reached speeds exceeding 30 knots. Schertel began to receive publicity over his latest creation, and further test runs attracted the attention of various officials, as well as a certain entrepreneur by the name of Gotthard Sachsenberg. Sachsenberg arranged for a distance trial on the Rhine in 1935 for prospective buyers from the Köln-Dusseldorfer Shipline. The hydrofoil's journey from Mainz all the way north to Köln was so successful that representatives from the ship line placed an order for a vessel for commercial use.

With a military mobilization taking place in Germany and signs of war in every paper, Sachsenberg began to draw naval engineering talent to a project under Schertel that would create, he hoped, the world's first military hydrofoil. The result of this hydrofoil dream team was a high-speed minelayer designated the VS6 that began prototype testing in 1940. It competed against a rival hydrofoil design by Oscar Tietjens in a review conducted by the Kriegsmarine. Tietjens's design was faster, but it was Schertel's more-maneuverable design that won the people's ovation and juicy naval contracts for Sachsenberg Shipyards. Although the Sachsenberg crew was the rising star of German hydrofoils, the Tietjens design received the designation VS7 and development and funding continued.

The high-speed hydrofoil transport was designated VS8, but it was still in the preprototype phases of development when Germany abandoned its plans for Operation Sealion, the invasion of Britain. A new purpose was found for the craft. British control of the Straits of Gibraltar and Malta and a large Royal Navy presence in the Mediterranean had made supplying the Afrika Korps from Italy a bit dicey. Ponderous freighters were often sunk by British aircraft or surface ships, and getting replacement tanks and parts to Erwin Rommel was increasingly difficult. The VS8 was ideally suited for high-speed runs between supply bases in Sicily and North African ports along the Mediterranean coast. Even aerial mining would hardly slow the flow of matériel into the region if delivered by a fleet of hydrofoil transports.

The prototype VS8 was completed in 1943, and tests were conducted that allowed S-boat (high-speed attack craft) crews to get a feel for and evaluate the performance of the hydrofoil vessel. The reviews were mixed. The S-boat crews were practically a breed unto themselves, as fiercely independent as U-boat crews and very bonded with their vessels. They were modern-day pirates and privateers, rogues of the sea, but they were not so favorably inclined to the radical differences in performance the VS8 offered. In light seas, it was a dynamo. It was almost 10 knots faster (on paper) than their S-boats and handled fairly well. However, in moderate seas it had difficulty becoming foilborne and was correspondingly slowed. Piloting the VS8 required a gentle hand as tight turns dropped it off its foils and back into its hullborne configuration. Perhaps worst of all, it had a very deep draft when maneuvering at lower speeds and even normally minor obstructions like dense kelp beds could cause damage to the lightweight foils.

Inadequate engines also plagued the VS8, as they did so many other German advanced projects. Instead of the dual MB 501 supercharged engines (sometimes known as the MB 511) supercharged engines with each pushing 2,500 horsepower, Sachsenberg was forced to settle for two 1938 model MB 501s producing a total of only 4,000 horsepower. Shaving off a fifth of the engine power certainly exacerbated the VS8's reported difficulties in high seas and tight turns. Following a final series of navy testing in 1944 during which the VS8 was reviewed as a possible minelayer, the project was canceled. The craft experienced engine failure in September 1944 and broke up during attempts to salvage the vessel. Another design, a 45-ton torpedo boat designated the VS10, had been destroyed during an air raid. Some further effort was made to return to the VS6 configuration, but the naval verdict was decidedly unfavorable, and all hydrofoil projects were terminated.

Work on hydrofoil designs continued at the Sachsenberg Shipyards until the end of the war, despite German instructions forbidding a waste of resources. Schertel escaped the advancing Soviets, and with the help of Sachsenberg, he received financing from Swiss backers and formed the hydrofoil development firm of Supramar. This firm successfully developed a number of designs and helped launch the world's first hydrofoil passenger line.

Though Sachsenberg's shipyards were stripped from him by the Soviet government of East Germany, he was allowed to keep his family castle. He offered shelter and space there to former Nazi scientists shunned by the new order of East Germany and helped finance their development of pharmaceuticals and medical treatments. It was their genius and that of Schertel at Supramar that fueled a new Sachsenberg fortune, though Gotthard did not live to see much of it.

Technical Mumbo Jumbo

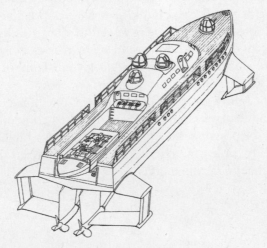

The VS8 with a Panzer II preparing to depart into shallow waters.

At 32 meters in length and displacing 70 tons empty, the VS8 hydrofoil was the largest hydrofoil constructed until the 1960s. Cabin space for a twenty-two-man crew as well as a handful of honored guests made the VS8 roughly analogous to an S-boat (or E-boat) in terms of crew compliment. It had a dangerous 4-meter draft when hullborne, but this became an acceptable 2 meters or slightly less when foilborne. This deep draft was mitigated by the fact that so little of the vessel made contact with the sea when foilborne, and it was so fast that it was extremely unlikely to set off naval mines.

Two supercharged MB 501 engines were to provide 5,000 horses' worth of thrust and two U-foils were to provide the lift. With their powers combined, the VS8 could reach a top speed of between 45 and 50 knots. Unfortunately, the supercharged Daimler-Benz engines were in short supply—especially for hydrofoil projects—and the VS8 had to contend with less powerful versions available in greater abundance. With a total of 4,000 horsepower, the VS8 could make it to a respectable 37 knots, but its surface-piercing foils struggled in moderate seas, and the underpowered engines made it difficult to become foilborne. Making turns greater than 5 degrees dropped the VS8 down onto its hull like a bunk bed collapsing under a moose.

Perhaps the VS8's most notable feature was its lowered rear decking, which was just large enough to accommodate a light or medium tank. Amphibious and diving versions of several tanks existed, but the VS8 was best equipped to contend with the 38(t) and Panzer II outfitted with pontoon flotation. Tanks were loaded by flooding the rear deck and allowing the floating tank to drive up into the back of the ship. The pontoons could then be removed in transit or, in the case of an amphibious landing, the VS8 would maneuver as close as possible to a landing site and then flood its rear deck to disembark the tank directly into the water.

The VS8 was lightly armed with four 15mm machine guns mounted in four glass- or Perspex-domed turrets designed to protect the guns from sea spray or rough seas. Overall, the VS8 was lightly armored and vulnerable to pretty much any armament heavier than its own compliment of heavy machine guns.

Analysis

The VS8 was ideally suited for getting a small and select cargo somewhere quickly. It was vulnerable to small arms, and with a deep draft that would have precluded getting very close to the shoreline, the VS8 would not have made a good landing craft. As a blockade runner for delivering tanks to North Africa, it would have functioned well enough, but to what end? The VS8 could carry a single tank or 10 to 20 tons of supplies. Hundreds of them would have to be built to make any meaningful impact on the supply situation in North Africa, and part of their advantage was that British ships and aircrafts would likely overlook a single small and fast boat. A steady stream of hydrofoils coming from Sicily would have been countered as surely as the larger merchants being sunk all too regularly.

My thought, and this is pure speculation, is that Sachsenberg didn't really want to make a useful vessel for the German navy. They took him out into the woods to give him a noodle through the neck. I think that sort of thing deserves a little revenge, and my romanticized vision of Sachsenberg is as a lovable scoundrel. If he could get paid and help his buddy Schertel live out his hydrofoil fantasy without ever actually providing the Nazis with a useful ship in a timely manner, then he was doing his own part to screw over the Nazis. Schertel got to advance the cause of hydrofoils and bring his dreams of flying boats closer to fruition. Despite the thumbs down from a few Roger Eboats, Schertel proved that hydrofoils did offer advantages in military vessels. They just didn't make good landing craft.

Hypothetical Deployment History

Following the successful Rhine test run of the VS6 in 1935, the Kriegsmarine placed an order for a high-speed landing hydrofoil in preparation for amphibious operations against Norway and Great Britain. The result of several test prototypes was 1938's VS8 transport hydrofoil, which was capable of carrying a single tank or 20 tons of men and equipment at speeds up to 40 knots. The projected 2,500-horsepower diesels had not been made available, so the ship continued to suffer from poor maneuver speeds and difficulties in rough seas. While the Schertel-Sachsenberg team continued to refine the design, an initial production run of seventy-five was placed for the VS8, with delivery to begin in August 1939. Construction of the first order of so-called Tragflügelboot (T-boats) began jointly at Sachsenberg Shipyards and Friedrich Lürssen Werft, though the latter gave second priority to its own S-boat construction.

Initial delivery of the T-boats began surprisingly on schedule in September 1939, just days after the invasion of Poland. Prospective training crews straight from S-boats did not appreciate the performance of the T-boats very much and were annoyed with being saddled with duty on what amounted to a small freighter. A few crews excelled at maneuvering the T-boat despite this bias, and as more crews began to show up, the negative reputation of the T-boat began to fade. The T-boats got their first taste of combat on April 8, 1940, when sixteen of the T-boats participated in the initial German landings in Norway. The T-boats were a special "Sturm Group" meant to confuse British naval forces and possibly seize the port of Oslo ahead of the main German invasion fleet. The goal of this small force was to bypass the coastal fortifications as rapidly as possible and capture the Norwegian royal family.

In high seas, the T-boats were unable to utilize their advantage of speed, and when spotted by British surveillance aircraft, they were run down by British destroyers of the Home Fleet. Five T-boats were sunk in a running battle before a window of calm seas allowed the T-boats to become foilborne (much to the surprise of the British) and escape the destroyers. The British abandoned the chase on the afternoon of April 8 as the German fleet moved into the fjords. The narrow fjords presented some difficulties for the T-boats, but the waters were deep enough and calm enough for them to remain foilborne.

At the fortifications of Oslo, heavy guns proved inadequate for engaging the fast and nimble boats. Smaller guns and small arms fire still exacted a heavy toll from the landing force. Two T-boats were sunk while offloading, and all but one of the six remaining Panzer II tanks were lost either to accident or fire. Additional rubber rafts brought in to land infantry proved so slow that nearly half of the infantry was killed before reaching ground. The attack was a failure by all accounts, but the troops succeeded in deploying a heavy smoke screen for the landing of a large force early on the morning of April 9.

Some naval strategists argued that the T-boats represented an excellent distraction. Most, including Admiral Erich Raeder, believed that the distraction was more than offset by the losses and the forewarning they gave enemy forces at Oslo. This forewarning allowed the Norwegian royal family to escape Oslo and flee to England. An additional eight T-boats were employed at the Narvik landings, just ahead of the main invasion fleet, and these proved much more successful. Only two T-boats were lost, and five of the eight tanks they carried reached the port safely and proved crucial in seizing the city. Despite protestations from individual T-boat captains, the T-boats were considered too fragile and too expensive to squander in large amphibious landings.

The initial production run of seventy-five T-boats was completed in October 1940. By October 1941, these had been largely converted to fill the same role as the S-boats. A handful of T-boats participated in operations on the eastern front in their intended role and were frequently pointed to by German commandos and Brandenburgers (naval commandos) as one of their preferred transports. The last T-boats still equipped as transports were deployed (and sunk) during a series of supply runs from Italy to North Africa in late 1942.

What Fight Have Been

4:01 P.M., April 9, 1940
Operation Weserübung, Twenty-first Army Corps, Third Mountain Division
Narvik, Norway

Heinrich Schöpke leaned against the treads of *Marlene* smoking a cigarette and flipping through an album of photographs that had fallen from the top of a nearby chest of drawers. Jacques "Franky" Meijer was fiddling with a phonograph machine next to the collapsed four-poster bed. *Die Moritat von Mackie Messer* began to play, a deceptively upbeat tune for all its lyrics about flashing knives and murdered women. An elderly husband and wife and their grown daughter stood against the far wall, backs stiff as boards and eyes wide with disbelief at the panzer that had crashed through into their bedroom.

"Do you have anything to drink?" Viktor Fleischer asked the man for the third time, adding a gesture that he hoped conveyed the idea of him drinking from a mug.

"Oh, for Christ's sake Viktor, just go and get something from their pantry." Franky had fallen back into his casual off-duty behavior once he realized the battle for Narvik was prematurely over.

"I would have thought they would speak a little German," Viktor ignored Franky's advice to go plundering.

"They will learn the language soon enough," Heinrich interjected. "A load of Wehrmacht mountaineers with fat paychecks and nothing to spend it on other than pretty Norwegian girls."

On cue, a line of smiling men from the Third Mountain Division marched past. It was an orderly march, but the men were chatting and relaxed.

"Get hit by a house?" one Gebirgsjäger shouted and the others piled on a chorus of good-natured jeers.

Franky glared and tossed a phonograph disc at them. It shattered on the pavement of the street and they hooted with laughter.

"I-I speak German," the daughter finally stammered, prompting a series of catcalls from the departing mountain troops.

"We just want some milk or water," Viktor explained.

"Or some beer!" Heinrich shouted after her as she shuffled through the door with her parents close at her heels.

She returned with bottles of milk and Viktor paid her a five reichsmark note without even considering what he was doing. The milk was from the icebox and it chilled his throat and eased his thirst. Heinrich began sneezing halfway through his bottle.

"I said beer!" He cursed and threw the bottle against the wall of a neighboring house.

Viktor strolled around the outside of the house, admiring the proud mountains that seemed to rise from the deep blue waters of the nearby fjord. As he completed his circuit around the property, he spotted someone he knew from the T-boat that had brought them to Narvik.

"Why aren't you with your ship?" Viktor asked the young engineer.

"Petrol," he explained. "Captain Ostman told me to get petrol, so I am going to find petrol. The bowsers have already worked over the harbor, and we need more if we're to put out to sea again today."

"You're too nervous," Viktor smiled and handed the younger man the rest of his bottle of milk. "Poland. Now that was fighting, but look at how fast that was over. This is just a show. The Norwegians are nearly finished in a day."

"Captain Ostman doesn't think so. We lost two of those T-boats today, and that was against those rust buckets the Norwegians had out there. The British are going to come, and he wants us out. We can't fight the Royal Navy in landing boats. Not even the ones we have."

"What about the supply fleet?" Viktor asked, suddenly serious and keenly aware of his ignorance of the strategic situation.

"Supply fleet?" The engineer laughed. "If there's one coming, chances are it's going to get caught up by the Brits. My advice to you: The British are coming, so learn to do what I'm doing."

"What's that?"

"Live off the land," the engineer tipped a nonexistent cap in Viktor's direction and set off again on his search for petrol.

Chapter 16

Type XI-B U-Cruiser

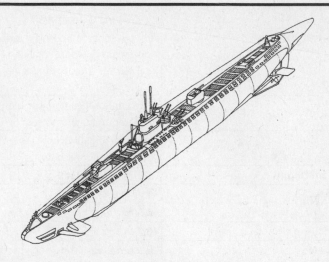

Overview

The Type XI-B U-boat or "U-cruiser" was concocted before the outbreak of World War II and was a modernization and enlargement of similar designs utilized with success during World War I. The Type XI mounted a pair of armored turrets containing twin purpose-built 127mm artillery pieces in each turret. The Type XI-B entered limited production shortly before the invasion of Poland by Nazi Germany, but with the beginning of the war, the production run was canceled and the four very incomplete hulls were abandoned. The enormous Type XI-Bs were deemed too costly an undertaking and were viewed as less useful on the modern seas than their predecessors had been. This assessment was accurate, and nothing further ever came of the interesting design, but the story of the Type XI-B does not end there.

A legend grew up around the Type XI-B that one of the hulls in the initial production run was completed and that the Type XI-B was sent to the United States on a highly secretive diplomatic mission. The most popular conspiracy theory involved Dutch royalty-in-exile, known to be somewhat ironically sympathetic to Germany, and a plan for a separate peace with the Western allies. This theory holds that the Type

Category:	U-cruiser
Phase of Development:	Partial production
Development Start:	1937
Development Team:	Kriegsmarine "K" Design Office
Crew:	110 and up to 60 passengers or troops
Weight:	3,630 tons displacement
Propulsion:	8 × twin shaft 12-cylinder diesel motors producing a total of 17,600 hp 2 × electric motors producing a total of 2,200 hp
Speed:	23 kt under diesel power (26 rumored) 7 kt under electric power
Range:	30,000+ km surfaced 100+ km submerged
Maximum Depth:	250 m (estimated)
Length:	115 m
Width:	9.5 m
Height:	6.2 m
Armament:	2 × armored turrets each mounting twin 127mm guns 2 × 20mm AA guns mounted on twin gun platforms 2 × 37mm guns mounted on twin gun platforms 4 × 53.3cm bow torpedo tubes 2 × 53.3cm stern torpedo tubes

XI-B was sent to Cape Cod to assist the Dutch royal family in their negotiations. It also supposedly broadcasted a diplomatic message to Germany and was then sunk by a U.S. naval airship. Then it was invited to tea with the queen and circumnavigated the globe in a zeppelin with a friendly powder-blue dragon named Twinkles. It was a very busy submarine!

Some sliver of authenticity was added to this theory, sans tea and Twinkles, when in 1993 a wreck of what seemed to be a U-boat was discovered off the coast of Cape Cod. Edward Michaud of Trident Research and Recovery was the man behind the discovery, and before long, he announced that a sonar survey of the wreck had revealed the U-boat to be much larger than a standard U-boat type. Michaud, who happened to subscribe to and also author many of the conspiracy theories regarding the Type XI, teamed up with another salvage company in 1997 to conduct a video survey of the wreck and begin recovery operations. That was the last anyone really heard from Michaud on the subject, and it seems unlikely that a recovery effort even began. No other divers or salvage operations have in any way corroborated Michaud's fanciful discovery.

Development History

The Type XI-B U-boat was not the first attempt by the German navy to combine the capabilities of a light surface warship with the advantages of a submersible vessel. The first U-cruiser was a converted transport submarine that had been drafted into the German navy. In 1917, the U-151 and a half-dozen of its sister ships were modified to include two 105mm artillery guns on their decks. At the time, this firepower was capable of inflicting severe damage on coastal defense vessels. The retrofitted U-cruisers were so successful that Germany went on to up-gun two other types of U-boats for a total of eleven U-cruisers throughout the war. These later modifications included 150mm guns that devastated enemy vessels.

At the end of World War I, the Treaty of Versailles heavily restricted Germany's ability to produce and develop new U-boats. However, by the mid-1930s, the Treaty of Versailles was often being ignored or subverted by Germany, and the Kriegsmarine's fancy once again turned to the concept of U-cruisers. The 1937 design for the Type XI-B was more than 20 meters longer than the Great War U-cruisers and displaced nearly twice the tonnage. This new U-cruiser design boasted armored turrets and bristled with antiaircraft armament. It was sleek, modern, and purpose-built to the task of engaging surface ships with its unique 127mm guns.

It also incorporated a vertical storage cylinder for the miniscule Arado Ar 231 float plane, theoretically improving the Type XI's search capability over its predecessors. I say theoretically because the Ar 231 was not a very good aircraft. Hauling the plane out of the storage cylinder and then launching it before the seas shifted from the nearly glasslike calm required by the Ar 231 would have been difficult. But that's another story for my next book, *Listen to Me Bitch and Moan about Float Planes*.

The design for the Type XI-B was approved for production by AG

Weser in Bremen, and the plans were completely finalized by January 1939. The initial production run consisted of four boats designated U-112 through U-115. By the outbreak of war in September 1939, the keels had been laid for all four boats.

With bombs flying and people dying, German war planners gave the Type XI-B project a long look and decided "nein." The boats were costing way too much money, and they were diverting resources. That often was not enough to give pause to the Germans, but in the case of the Type XI-B, early war U-boat experience had taught them that the days of submarines engaging military vessels with deck guns had basically come to an end. Improved antisubmarine warfare capabilities, longer range, more accurate guns, and better armor had rendered a boat like the Type XI-B prematurely obsolescent.

The true story of the Type XI-B ends with the dismantling of the incomplete hulls and the shift to more conventional U-boat designs. According to Michaud, one example of the Type XI-B was completed. His reason for believing this is a vague (very vague) reference to the Type XI-B reaching a surface speed of 26 knots. This supposedly occurred in the Weser River near the AG Weser facility, where the Type XI-B was being constructed. This one oddly unclear reference is the sole real evidence for the existence of the Type XI-B. Every other detail of the conspiracy theory surrounding the Type XI-B is conjecture.

Choice among these details are:

1. The Type XI-B was Adolf Hitler's escape submarine for leaving Germany for South America and establishing the Fourth Reich. Forget that the Type XXI U-boat would have been much better for this and that it actually existed.

2. The Type XI-B was a part of some inner conspiracy in Nazi Germany that was using the Dutch royal family to negotiate a separate peace with the United States. The evidence supporting this: on August 26, a U.S. naval search for a submarine turned up nothing and on the same day in 1944 that Princess Juliana left Cape Cod! Dun-dun-dunnnnnn! What are the odds that Princess Juliana would leave Cape Cod on the exact same day that the U.S. Navy searched for and failed to find a submarine? Unthinkable!

3. There is some other theory about a Type IXC/40 U-boat that was sunk a month or so earlier, which is completely confusing, because Michaud is inconsistent with the designations he uses for the U-boats. Imagine a bowl of spaghetti and then imagine labeling it "U-boat flow chart" on an overhead slide, that's #3 in a nutshell.

According to Michaud, some top-level White House cover up kept the *real* fate of the Type XI and the *real* truth of its mission from the public for more than fifty years. Now that he's found the wreck, the truth can be known. Too bad no one else can find the wreck.

Technical Mumbo Jumbo

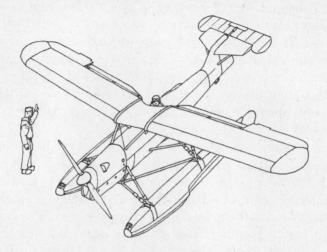

The unloved Arado Ar 231 float plane.

The Type XI-B was an enormous beast of a submarine, roughly the size of early generation postwar nuclear submarines. It would have been the second largest diesel submarine ever constructed, beaten out only by the Japanese I-400 carrier submarines. The Type XI-B's length of 115 meters was nearly twice that of the Germans' workhorse Type VIIC submarines, and it displaced almost five times the tonnage. The Type XI-B was powered by eight twelve-cylinder marine diesel engines separated into two separate engine rooms. A third engine room contained the twin electric engines that would power the submarine while it was submerged.

Because of its immense size and displacement, the Type XI-B was a particularly slow submarine while submerged and could manage only 7 knots on its overtaxed electric engines. The supposed river trials of the Type XI-B reported by Michaud indicate that the submarine was capable of a top speed of 26 knots while surfaced. Development documents indicate a rated speed of 23 knots on the surface, still respectable for a submarine.

The primary armament of the Type XI-B consisted of two heavily armored turrets mounted on the upper deck of the U-cruiser. One was mounted on the fore and one was mounted on the aft decking behind the conning tower. Each turret contained a pair of specially designed 127mm guns. By the standards of surface vessels of the time, these four guns did not amount to particularly heavy armament. The U-cruiser might have been able to engage a lone destroyer of older design on the surface, relying on its smaller profile to give it the advantage over the faster and more heavily armed ship.

The Type XI-B was also equipped with two 37mm guns and two 20mm guns mounted on two flak decks or Wintergartens to accommodate so much antiaircraft weaponry. Four bow and two stern torpedo tubes rounded out the armament of the U-cruiser, giving it the punch of more conventional submarines. A full set of torpedo reloads was stored beneath armored deck plates.

There was another trick up the Type XI-B's sleeve in the form of a pressure-sealed vertical storage cylinder containing a broken down Arado Ar 231 float plane. When hunting for targets, the submarine could surface, the crew could drag the Ar 231 out of the cylinder with the assistance of a folding winch, and then they could assemble and attempt to launch the aircraft. Odds were in favor of the sea being too choppy for the feeble plane to take off, and even if they managed to get it airborne, the Ar 231 had a bad habit of breaking into pieces when it landed. The Kriegsmarine briefly used the aircraft on surface vessels, but it was hated and was eventually replaced by the even smaller Fa 330 observation helicopter. The Fa 330 had its own set of issues, but was regarded as a major improvement over the Ar 231.

With 110 hands, the Type XI-B had a very large crew complement compared to other submarines of the time. It was once again beaten out by the 140-man crew of the Japanese I-400, but the Type XI-B could cram nearly 60 passengers inside. According to some sources, the reason for such spacious compartments on a submarine was to allow for an assault force of naval commandos (Brandenburgers). This also coincides nicely with the even wilder theory that the Type XI-B was intended as a VIP transport for gentle fellows like Hitler. A big wheel at the murder plant like Hitler would travel with quite an entourage of guards, personal assistants, and groupies.

Analysis

To put it delicately, the Type XI-B was an appalling mistake dredged from the septic brainpans of syphilitic mongoloids. The U-cruiser's amazing armored turrets would have done little more than perhaps give the boat's commander the mistaken impression that he could surface and engage enemy warships in a gun duel. The captain and crew would be sentenced to death unless they were exceptionally lucky or the captain of the enemy ship suffered a fortuitous pulmonary embolism timed to coincide with the first 127mm volley from the U-cruiser. As a commando delivery platform, the Type XI-B was outclassed by everything from aircraft to fishing trawlers. In its most dubious of roles—as a chariot for a fleeing fuehrer—the Type XI-B was a ridiculous stand-in for the vastly superior Type XXI boats under production in large numbers by the end of the war.

Hypothetical Deployment History

The keels for U-112 through U-115 were laid in February 1939 at the AG Weser yards in Bremen. The outbreak of war in September forced the Kriegsmarine to reevaluate the Type XI-B. Because of the submarine's extreme cost, it was decided in early October that the initial production run would be completed and all further production canceled. U-113 was the first of the four submarines to be completed in May 1940. A crew under Korvettenkapataen Uwe Kauffmann was assigned to U-113, and after basic training, the vessel became a part of the Fifth Flotilla out of Kiel. In June 1940, U-113 was given a training mission in the North Sea. Kauffmann's first cruise in the Type XI-B was highly successful as, at the time, merchant convoys were often unescorted and unarmed. From June 19 through June 24, Kauffmann managed to sink 68,000 tons of shipping using only his 127mm guns.

Kauffmann returned to Kiel victorious, just as U-112 and U-114 put out to sea. On July 1, U-112 suffered a disaster when it surfaced beneath the Norwegian merchant *New York* and damaged both of its turrets. Three crewmembers were badly injured in the accident, and the captain in command of U-112 was relieved of his duty by a political officer assigned to the vessel during training. The damage was repaired, but on its return voyage U-112 encountered the Polish destroyer *Burza*. The captain of the *Burza* attempted a torpedo run on the submarine, and when this failed, he launched depth charges. U-112 was struck almost directly by a depth charge and was forced to surface. Rather than allow it to be captured, U-112 was scuttled. U-114 had a largely uneventful tour, sinking a handful of Norwegian fishing trawlers with its guns and failing in a torpedo attack on the British merchant *Ivanhoe*.

U-115 entered service in August 1940, and for the remainder of the year, all three surviving U-crusiers served fairly well with the Fifth Flotilla. In January 1941, U-115 struck a mine near the northern Channel entrance, and it sunk with a loss of thirty-seven men. In March, U-114 attempted to engage the HMS *Insurmountable*, a tribal-class British destroyer. U-114 scored initial hits on the forward gun turrets and superstructure of the *Insurmountable*, but was forced to dive with damage after the British vessel out-turned the U-cruiser. U-114 limped back to Kiel, where its damage was deemed irreparable.

The last hurrah of the Type XI-B boats came in August 1942, when U-113 was guided by an observation aircraft to a major convoy heading for Murmansk. U-113 moved in among the ships of the convoy and opened fire with torpedoes, sinking an American escort destroyer almost immediately. U-113 sank two merchants and damaged a third before exhausting its torpedoes. Captain Kauffmann then ordered U-113 to the surface and began to engage the merchants, some of which were armed.

Two more merchants were sunk, and a British Hudson sent to assist was shot from the sky. Unfortunately for Kauffmann and the crew of U-113, a second destroyer had experienced engine trouble and lagged behind the convoy. With half of the convoy ablaze and Kauffmann mercilessly hammering the survivors, the American destroyer emerged from the smoke and flames and struck U-113 square in its conning tower with its opening salvo. An injured Kauffmann ordered a crash dive, only to surface minutes later with bad flooding. He attempted to maneuver the U-cruiser to a better firing position, but the destroyer and an armed merchant ranged him quickly and immobilized U-113.

Kauffmann attempted to scuttle his boat, but damage to the ballast tanks had somewhat ironically made it difficult to intentionally sink the vessel. U-113 was boarded by the American destroyer USS *Flint*, and its crew was taken prisoner.

The convoy was not in the clear. As U-113 was being towed behind the destroyer, German He-111 torpedo bombers arrived. They engaged and finished off all of the remaining vessels in the area, including

U-113. A freighter that had been wounded by U-113 earlier in the day arrived at the scene of the shipping massacre hours later. It was only able to fish three survivors from the ocean. All three were crewmen from U-113. Captain Kauffmann was posthumously awarded the Knight's Cross.

What Fight Have Been

2:31 P.M., August 8, 1942
North Front, 1./JG 5 Eismeer
Somewhere over the North Atlantic

Konrad Fleischer put his Fw 190 into a shallow dive. The engine noise deepened, and the burning freighter came into view. Machine guns winked on it like windblown candles. The fighter shuddered as the 20mm cannons in its wing roots came to life. The guns thumped the cockpit as they pounded out a stream of deadly tracers. Konrad banked the fighter to strafe along as much of the ship as possible before pulling up. Smoke swirled from the stricken ship's superstructure, and as he passed over the bow, an explosion lit the waves. Konrad pulled back on the stick, and the engine howled up to full speed.

The Fw 190 juddered.

"Still got a bit of fight left in them," Konrad said to himself as he glanced at the fresh perforation of his fighter's left wing.

"We're beginning our run," said the commander of the force of He-111s Konrad was supposed to be escorting. "Quit showing off and cover our tails."

"Copy that, bomber lead." Konrad climbed to a safe vantage above the convoy and began a wide circle.

The big twin-engine torpedo bombers were coming in from the south, low to the water and headed at the convoy's flank. They were majestic in their own pig-ugly and turtle-slow way. Konrad had difficulty appreciating them after spending most of his career tangled up in whirling air-to-air combat. He had played escort plenty of times over London, but in the empty wastes of the North Atlantic, his job was more akin to babysitting. The bombers got to paint little ships on the sides of their planes, and he watched his name slide down the kill board.

"I guess that's what you get when you're too good at what you do," Konrad murmured to himself.

Konrad began to let his mind wander off to another of his fantasies that inevitably climaxed with him shooting down Oberstleutnant Friedrich Beckh behind Russian lines. He was almost to the part where Beckh begged for him not to open fire when he noticed a strange shape on the ocean below.

"Bomber lead, this is escort lead."

"Go ahead."

"Do you notice anything strange behind that escort destroyer?"

There was a pause.

"Negative, escort lead. I see two destroyers."

Konrad spiraled in to get a better view.

"Torpedoes in the water," the bomber lead's voice was relieved.

The bombers began to climb just as they started taking fire from the destroyer and some of the freighters. Konrad banked over the destroyer, dangerously low, for a good look at the ship traveling in its wake. The vessel behind the destroyer was nearly the same size, but with a good deal of its hull visible beneath the waterline. It had two armored turrets; one was fore and one was aft of its superstructure. The forward gun was crumpled and smoldering. Konrad continued to bank, and in partial profile, the ship was unmistakably a submarine. It was flying an American flag, but the markings on its heavily damaged conning tower were definitely that of a U-boat.

Konrad considered whether or not to tell the bomber lead. The torpedoes were already in the water and there was nothing the idiots could do to stop them.

Tracers suddenly ripped past the windscreen on both sides and the fuselage shook with the force of impacts.

"You idiot, pull up!" the bomber lead shouted.

Konrad banked hard in the opposite direction and pulled his Fw 190 into a steep climb that forced it close to stalling. Flak bursts from the destroyer's guns were on him and when he looked back, the Wintergarten of the U-boat was ablaze with flashing gun barrels. More hits shook the fighter, and he watched as his oil pressure began dropping. Just as he felt sure he was nearly done, he outran the U-boat's antiaircraft guns. The destroyer's larger guns chased him for a few more seconds before he had fled outside their range as well.

"Hit! Hits!" the bomber lead cheered. "Look at those beauties."

Explosions tore through the convoy. One freighter sundered in two and disappeared beneath the waves almost immediately. The destroyer tried to turn itself away from the torpedoes, but it was too slow. One struck its hindquarters and lifted it up out of the water. The U-boat being towed behind it coasted right into the path of two of the torpedoes. When the bursts of smoke had cleared, the U-boat was only visible as a patch of burning oil and a dark, fragmented shape beneath the water.

"Escort lead, that is how it's done," the bomber lead said smugly. "I'll be expecting that bottle of cognac you've been keeping for your two-hundredth. That's if you don't want this reported."

Konrad bit his tongue.

Chapter 17

HMS *Habbakuk*

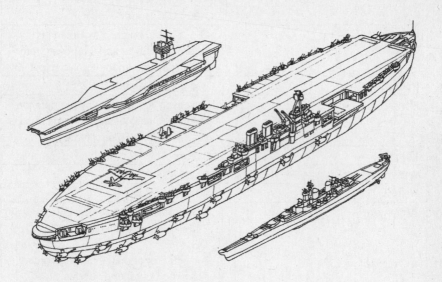

Overview

One of the most unusual military inventions of World War II was born from the verdant mind of one of the most unusual thinkers of the twentieth century. Geoffrey Pyke was literally crazy. You could be generous and say that Pyke was crazy like a fox, but some of the schemes he developed with Britain's Office of Combined Operations seem to have skipped the fox part. For example, Pyke's solution to overcoming the heavy defenses of the Ploesti Oilfields in Romania included sending commandos in fire trucks who would pretend to extinguish fires while shooting incendiary bombs out of their hoses. If that wasn't strange enough, Pyke offered an alternative ruse in which hundreds of dogs would be released with barrels of alcohol around their necks and these dogs would run into the oil field and the guards would become intoxicated.

Pyke's most infamous invention was also one of the few that actually progressed beyond the initial concept. With German U-boats

Category:	Ice aircraft carrier
Phase of Development:	Preprototype
Development Start:	1942
Development Team:	Geoffrey Pyke and the Office of Combined Operations
Crew:	1,000+
Weight:	2,000,000+ tons
Propulsion:	26 × electric engines mounted in external nacelles and fed power from an unspecified internal power plant
Speed:	6 kt under full power
Range:	Effectively limited only by the duration of the ice itself, lasting upwards of a year even in warmer climates
Length:	610 m
Width:	91 m
Height:	40 m
Armament:	Numerous light AA armaments 200+ × Supermarine Spitfires OR A mixture of aircraft including fighters, heavy bombers, and various antisubmarine warfare aircraft

plaguing Allied shipping, the need for a self-sufficient platform capable of protecting convoys and hunting submarines was obvious. Pyke's solution was to simply tow a massive iceberg to England, outfit it with engines, and use it as a mobile landing field. This proved unfeasible, but Pyke went on to suggest that a ship could be constructed from enormous blocks of ice. This concept met initially with doubt and then with wild enthusiasm from the sort of people who like big ideas and are generally unconcerned with the details. Those same people also tend to be in charge, and Lord Louis Mountbatten himself was an enthusiastic supporter of Pyke's scheme. Early tests at a secret location in Canada produced mediocre results. Pyke is often credited with coming up with the solution, but in reality, it was a team of American researchers who discovered the wood pulp mixture that created much stronger, more reliable, and slower melting ice. They named it "pykrete" in honor of Pyke and thus were ensured history would forever forget their contribution.

Pyke's creation was to be an immense ice aircraft carrier named the HMS *Habbakuk* after a somewhat obscure biblical prophet who foresaw a work "which ye will not believe." The scale prototype of the *Habbakuk* was fairly successful, but all was not well in the ice ship's future. The Americans had to take over the project because the immense drain on resources was too great for Britain to handle, and they were quickly realizing that destroyers, new sonar, and search aircraft were having an effect on U-boat operations that a single preposterously expensive ice ship could not hope to match. Pyke's dreamboat sank into Lake Patricia in Canada in a way that no other ship in history could hope to emulate.

Development History

"You need me on your staff because I am a man who thinks."

These words and an eccentric résumé of invention and innovation convinced Lord Mountbatten to hire Geoffrey Pyke for the Office of Combined Operations. Pyke's unusual suggestions as a scientific advisor and engineer with Combined Operations included a pipeline to transport men and equipment and a motorized sled that would roll a torpedo down a hill. Pyke's most famous creation was the immense ice aircraft carrier, the HMS *Habbakuk*, incorrectly named after the biblical prophet Habakkuk. Pyke originally envisioned using towed icebergs as airbases, but this quickly became the much more elaborate idea of constructing a ship from refrigerated blocks of ice. Both Mountbatten and Winston Churchill were quite taken with this idea.

In late 1942, Pyke and a team of experts traveled to Canada. There, they joined forces with the Canadians and Americans in a two-pronged effort to test the feasibility of the ice ship. One team headed to Lake Patricia in Alberta and began constructing a 60-by-30-foot mini-*Habbakuk* out of ice cut from the lake. Another team was assigned the task of determining the best way of reinforcing the ice sufficiently to allow it to withstand damage from bombs, cannons, and torpedoes. In the spring of 1943, two American professors working on this second team developed a new substance that consisted of 14 percent sawdust or wood pulp and 86 percent water. These were mixed into slurry and then frozen into solid blocks that could withstand much more pressure than normal ice and were virtually immune to the fracturing that makes ice so fragile. These wood-ice blocks were named "pykrete" by the scientists and deemed to be the perfect building blocks for the *Habbakuk*.

Lord Mountbatten famously demonstrated the resiliency of pykrete during a secret meeting of the Allied Chiefs of Staff in Quebec. Mountbatten had arranged a large block of ice on a pedestal next to a second pedestal supporting a large block of pykrete. The gathered top brass of the Allies watched with curiosity as Mountbatten took out his revolver and fired it at the block of ice. The ice shattered into pieces. Mountbatten then fired at the pykrete and the room flew into an uproar. Rather than shatter or even punch a hole in the pykrete, the bullet ricocheted off the block and put a hole in the trouser leg of Fleet Admiral Ernest King. He was relatively unscathed, and Mountbatten had made his point about the strength of pykrete in a dramatic fashion. The refrigerated ice ship on Lake Patricia was a similar success, surviving until the following summer, and capable of withstanding shotgun blasts with only superficial damage.

The cost of constructing a full-scale *Habbakuk* was far too great for the British to undertake alone. The Americans were suitably impressed with the project, so they took charge in a move that rankled with Pyke. Adding insult to Pyke's injury, the project was canceled not long after the Americans took charge and realized they had no good reason to spend tens of millions of dollars on an ice ship when regular ships were doing a pretty good job.

Technical Mumbo Jumbo

The HMS *Habbakuk* was to have been constructed on a staggering scale from more than 200,000 blocks of pykrete ice. This ice would have been used to construct a hollow hull with exterior walls some 12 meters thick onto which normal fixtures and surfaces could be attached. All pykrete portions of the ship would have been reinforced with a wooden framework and run through with a network of galvanized-iron pipes pumping refrigerant. Forty thousand tons of cork were required to provide the insulation for the exterior and interior of the ship. Cavernous hangars within the *Habbakuk* would provide ample space to store hundreds of fighters and even large aircraft such as Lancaster bombers. Aircraft could taxi onto side-mounted elevators and be carried to the flight deck for launching, much like a modern carrier, only on a ship more than twice the size.

Propulsion for the *Habbakuk* was provided by twenty-four electric motors mounted in exterior nacelles along the carrier's side. These engines would be powered by a central power plant, probably multiple battleship-class diesel engines capable of generating the force to propel the ship at a break-neck top speed of 6 knots. Maneuvering the *Habbakuk* would have practically required a calendar to schedule in its ponderous turns. Very few harbors could accommodate a ship with as deep a draft as the *Habbakuk*. Combine these two facts and operating in even deep-water ports would have been a horrific and gruelingly slow experience for its crew. Imagine trying to thread a needle, and if the thread touches the side of the needle, you become frozen in place until you melt.

The *Habbakuk* would have necessarily incorporated the full amenities of a normal carrier on a scale that could bunk, feed, and wash over a thousand men. While no provisions were specifically made for boarding parties or amphibious infantry, the size of the *Habbakuk* makes such a complement of soldiers or marines seem almost a foregone conclusion. They probably could have assigned a cavalry company to the *Habbakuk* without crowding. Spacious accommodations would not have necessarily translated to comfortable accommodations. Even with the thick cork insulation and any surface covering or decking on top of that, temperatures inside the *Habbakuk* would have been fairly unpleasant.

Armament for the *Habbakuk* was not fixed at the time when the project was canceled, but would have likely consisted of a wide array of antiaircraft weaponry as well as larger guns for engaging surface vessels. British 4.5-inch dual-purpose guns were sketched into some diagrams mounted on gun nests on the periphery of the upper deck. This armament is purely speculation, but is probably not far from the mark; the *Habbakuk* was an aircraft carrier first and foremost. At 610 meters long and nearly 91 wide, the *Habbakuk* provided a sufficient landing area to accommodate noncarrier aircraft, including all but the largest bombers in the Allied arsenal.

With seaborne replenishment of expendable supplies, the *Habbakuk* could remain at sea almost indefinitely, or so the experts say. The ingenious refrigeration and the expansive insulation cannot conceal the fact that pykrete still melts almost nearly as fast as normal ice does. The wood pulp contents of the ice act as additional insulation, but Pyke's speculation that the ship could remain functional for "several years" seems overly optimistic.

The real advantage of using pykrete over plain ice was the reliable load-bearing capability and resiliency of pykrete. Normal ice has a very unpredictable stress fracture threshold, whereas pykrete has a uniform mechanical strength of 70 kilograms per square meter. It would hold weight, and just as importantly, it could withstand much more damage. The *Habbakuk*'s 12-meter-thick exterior hull would have to be struck several times in the same spot with cannon fire or torpedoes before suffering any lasting damage. Superficial damage could be repaired with a hose and some sawdust while the Habbakuk was still moving. Sort of moving, anyway.

Variants

Any type of vessel could have been constructed out of pykrete, and any type of vessel constructed out of pykrete would have been inordinately expensive, oversized, clumsy, and slow. Pykrete ships were basically the hulking retardate cousins of their more conventional counterparts, with a shorter life expectancy. Also like the retarded, you would have to keep a close eye on them or they would start sliding their hand down the waistband of their sweatpants to play with themselves in the middle of the grocery store. I'm sorry, go ahead and replace most of that last sentence with the word *melt*.

Analysis

The HMS *Habbakuk* was initially proposed as a cost-effective means of addressing the problem of lethal submarine warfare being waged against the Allies. By the end of the project in 1943, costs had spiraled out of control to an estimated budget of $100 million (over $1.2 billion in 2006 when adjusted for inflation), proving that even ice is not cheap. By that point, existing antisubmarine technologies and strategies had become increasingly effective, rendering the *Habbakuk* a curiosity rather than anything really necessary for the war effort. In fact, the huge supplies of raw materials necessary to construct the vessel would have placed a strain on even American stockpiles. Forty thousand tons is a lot of cork, and you can't exactly cruise over to Home Depot and ask for 280,000 tons of sawdust. The damage just the abortive *Habbakuk* project inflicted on the Allied war effort will probably never be fully calculated. An effort to construct the full-sized ship would have been disastrous.

Hypothetical Deployment History

Construction began on the HMS *Habbakuk* in August 1943 under the supervision of the United States with the assistance of Canada and Britain. The deep-water port of Halifax, Nova Scotia, was selected for its cool climate, and the Habbakuk project was conducted semisecretly under the name Project Cyclone. Work was completed on the immense floating construction platform in November 1943, and as the *Habbakuk* grew, the platform gradually disappeared into its mass. Construction had to be halted several times because of logistical problems that led to a dangerous shortage of refrigerants and uneven surface melting during particularly hot summer weather in June 1944. Tens of thousands of workers were involved in the construction and millions of tons of resources disappeared into the project.

Critical shortfalls in supplies continued to plague the slowly growing *Habbakuk*, delaying its projected launch from the original January 1945 date. Resources that could have been used in the construction of conventional ships were being poured into the Habbakuk project. The most notable project to suffer was the U.S. effort to construct a fleet of destroyers to protect each and every transatlantic convoy from German U-boats. The shipping losses mounted, and the Royal Navy was forced to divert ever larger portions of its fleet to submarine interdiction, even after the D day landings. Lord Mountbatten continued to assure an increasingly furious Churchill and Franklin D. Roosevelt that the *Habbakuk* would pay off. The damage being dealt to Soviet Lend-Lease shipments was such that the Allies agreed to inform Joseph Stalin of the project during the Yalta Conference. Churchill later quipped in his memoirs that when Roosevelt informed "Uncle Joe" of the *Habbakuk*, he thought that Stalin would "pitch poor old Roosevelt through a window."

Defenestration notwithstanding, the project procceded, and the Americans christened the *Habbakuk* the USS *Avenger* in April 1945. The *Avenger* set sail on April 19, bound for Scapa Flow, where it was to rendezvous with a British fleet and serve as the keystone of an anti-submarine taskforce. The war in Europe ended long before the sluggish supership reached its destination. While en route to Scapa Flow, the *Avenger* was able to launch aircraft against an enemy submarine once. The unidentified U-boat fired torpedoes at the *Avenger* to no effect and then escaped below the surface. Naval bombers swept the area for several hours and, after dropping depth charges, declared the submarine killed when oil was spotted on the surface. After the war, confiscated Kriegsmarine logs showed that no German U-boat went missing in the vicinity of the *Avenger*.

Harry S Truman briefly discussed sending the *Avenger* to the Pacific, but naval planners informed the president that it would require several months to reposition the ice ship. The war in Japan was projected to reach a satisfactory conclusion well before the ship could arrive. The *Avenger* ended the war with a tour of liberated European ports. It was already beginning to diminish in size slightly when it limped back to the United States. The *Avenger* was permanently anchored at the naval station in Newport, Rhode Island, and melted in Narragansett Bay over the course of two years.

What Fight Have Been

9:47 A.M., December 29, 1943
Aboard the Harbor Tug *Lil' Johnny*
Halifax Harbor, Halifax, Nova Scotia

R. E. Lincoln blamed the fog. He could have blamed the ocean. He could have blamed the horrible boiled eggs he had for breakfast. He could have blamed Lars, the giant Viking captain of the habor tug *Lil' Johnny*. He wiped the vomit from the corners of his mouth and looked up again at the dense white fog that clung to the surface of Halifax Harbor. No, the fog was to blame for all his woes. That damnable fog had reduced visibility to near zero and made it so the sky was just the two or three inches above the water before the fog started. R.E. felt strangled by it, and this was the third day it had put in its stifling appearance.

Lars whistled, and that meant they were close. He never spoke a word, but R.E. had learned to communicate with him nonverbally, much the same way he communicated with Brassy, his bluetick coonhound. He didn't love Lars like he loved that dog, but Lars seemed to have the same simple motivations. Give him some money and a gift, and he would sniff out the trail and lead R.E. to his latest big game.

Project Cyclone was secret game that was way too big to stay secret. Too much wood, copper, steel, and cork was being hauled crosscountry and across the ocean to Nova Scotia. He would find it, and he would document it. He knew it was in the area from talking to barge pilots running sawdust out to McNabs Island. They delivered to a newly constructed miniature port on the island, and they said on the good days they could see a floating house.

Today was not a good day. R.E. considered it lucky that he could look down and see his shoes through the fog, let alone a floating house thirty feet away. Lars clucked and whistled louder. R.E. looked back up from his shoes and out past the netted prow of the harbor tug. There was a rumbling engine noise approaching through the fog, but beneath that, further in the distance, he could hear the buzzing and hammering of construction.

His hopes of seeing Project Cyclone were dashed as an armed harbor patrol boat thrashed its way through the fog at dangerously high speed. Beneath the rippling Canadian flag stood a phalanx of armed sailors with fur-lined jackets and shiny new carbines.

"Prepare to be boarded." The message from the bullhorn was to the point.

The patrol boat thumped and grappled with *Lil' Johnny*. Lars just stared at the sailors as they clambered aboard, his impassive angular face reminiscent of a dime store's wooden Indian. The boarding party wasn't rough, but they didn't mince words. They searched *Lil' Johnny*, Lars, and R.E. from stem to stern. Despite the Canadian standard on the patrol boat, it was readily apparent that the actual men were about as Canadian as a taco. Two of them had instantly recognizable Texan accents and the man in charge—a big mustachioed bruiser named Petty Officer Clark—talked like a New Jersey longshoreman.

"I dunno what you think you're doing out here, Mister Lincoln," Clark said when he handed R.E. his passport. "Didn't you see the warning buoys?"

"Might have missed them," he gestured to the fog enclosing their conjoined vessels.

Clark looked around as though just noticing the impenetrable wall of white.

"Might have missed them." Clark smiled and shook his head. "I ain't no palooka. A fancy pants reporter from the Big Apple don't just get lost in no fog bank in the middle of winter in Canada."

"I suppose it isn't the holiday season."

"Yeah, Santa came and went, and unless you're—" Clark snapped his fingers and looked to the other sailors. "What was that reindeer with the nose?"

The nearest sailor shrugged.

"Rudolph," Lars said.

Everyone stared at the Viking and the man reddened and turned back to some vague task behind the helm.

"Look," R.E. began, "I am here to follow up on a story about American steel exports to Canada. Whatever you guys are building is using almost nineteen percent of the country's steel."

It was less than 1 percent, but he figured it wouldn't hurt his case to embellish.

"Mister Lincoln, I don't—"

"Why has Admiral Tenant relocated his HQ to Canada?"

As far as R.E. was aware, there was no such man as Admiral Tenant.

"Mister Lincoln, you need to tur—"

"Why did I run into Geoffrey Pyke buying crab legs yesterday?"

His risky trump card was played. He had not actually run into Pyke, but Nancy Starling of Sid and Nancy's Seaside Delights had met him three weeks earlier. Pyke had boasted that he was "the man behind the house on the lake," apparently unaware that it was on the Atlantic seaboard.

Petty Officer Clark remained silent for several moments, frozen in midretort, and then he sighed loudly.

"Get Cook on the radio," Clark said. "Tell him we've got a snooper here who knows a bit too much for his own good."

Clark looked back to R.E.

"Mister Lincoln, you probably just bought yourself and your big friend here a nice long interview with some men in overcoats and hats."

He had, in fact, bought himself a four-hour-long interrogation by men who could only be from the Office of Strategic Services. After they had pried every shred of knowledge out of his head, they forced him to sign extremely dense legal documents. These documents stated that if R.E. so much as mentioned Project Cyclone to a garbage man in passing, he could be found guilty of treason and hanged. The kicker came after the interrogation and the signing of documents. The OSS men bundled him into a car outside their little city of heated Quonset huts and through the car's window he could see all of Project Cyclone.

A house-like wooden frame the size of a football field and then some was floating next to McNabs Island. It had a massive slatted roof of cheap plywood, but beneath it was an astonishingly complex frame of wooden and steel supports, pipes, and bundles of electrical cables. Around the oddly curved edges of the structure were several tapered cylinders ending in propellers. More of these were suspended beneath two five-story-high floating cranes. The whole structure appeared to be floating atop a giant discolored ice cube. Hundreds of men swarmed over the thing, hammering in new cross-beams and pumping a pulpy liquid down preformed channels. With a start, R.E. realized that the tapered cylinders were individual engines and the whole thing was some sort of massive ship. A massive ship made out of ice.

"Ice?" he couldn't help but wonder aloud.

"Amazing isn't it?" the OSS man on his left smiled.

"Too bad you can never say a word about it," the OSS man on his right smiled as well.

"That shouldn't be too hard," R.E. said with a voice full of awe. "For once, I am at a loss for words."

The grins on the faces of the OSS men broadened.

"That is the goddamn stupidest thing in all of God's creation."

The grins disappeared, and the car was silent for the remainder of the ride to Dartmouth.

Chapter 18

Project Loedinge: Seeteufel

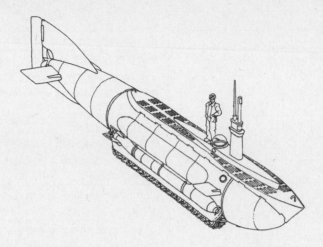

Overview

Amphibious vehicles were developed by nearly every military power in World War II and ranged from light amphibious landing vehicles to snorkel-capable tanks. Generally, these vehicles were intended to serve as part of an amphibious assault force that would need armor and mobility before landing facilities could be secured. In the case of snorkeling tanks, such modifications were usually developed to achieve river crossings when bridges were blown or otherwise impassable. Among these amphibious vehicles, both effective and ineffective, the German Seeteufel (Sea Devil) was a complete anomaly.

The Seeteufel was at its heart a really bad miniature submarine with dismal range, poor speed, and minimal armament. Designers took this award-winning combination and applied tank treads to it, so that it could drive into and out of the water and theoretically along the bottoms of lakes or rivers. The reasoning behind this was that deploying miniature submarines normally required full port facilities or naval craft specially modified to the purpose. The Seeteufel could follow behind an advancing armored force on its tank treads and then go for a dip in a nearby lake to put torpedoes into geese or trout or something.

Category:	Tracked submarine oddity
Phase of Development:	Completed prototype
Development Start:	Unknown, prototype completed in June 1944
Development Team:	Alois Loedinge and the development division of the Kiel Torpedo Laboratory
Crew:	2
Weight:	20 tons
Propulsion:	80 hp Opel truck engine for testing 250 hp marine diesel and 100 hp marine electric engine for production model
Speed:	10 kt surfaced 8 kt submerged with snorkel 6 kt submerged electric power 30 kph on land
Range:	30 hours maximum speed diesel operation
	10 hours maximum speed electric operation
Maximum Depth:	50 m (20 m proven)
Length:	13.5 m
Width:	2.0 m
Height:	2.9 m (5.5 m with snorkel)
Armament:	1 × MG34 machine gun 2 × 53.3cm torpedoes OR 2 × naval mines

Obviously, it could also function as a river-fording vehicle, but the usefulness of this is also questionable because it was lightly armored and outfitted with only a machine gun.

In the few inland lakes where the Germans might have encountered significant naval forces, the Seeteufel would have been of some limited usefulness. Imagine a freighter captain's surprise when he was torpedoed by a submarine in the middle of an inland lake. He probably would have laughed at the absurdity of it up until the exact moment when a torpedo tore his ship in half. The idea of driving the Seeteufel along the bottom of a lakebed covered with debris is pretty preposterous. It's much more likely that the Seeteufel would have floated beneath the water as any normal submarine and only engaged its treads when driving up onto land or into the water.

Development History

Like a fanciful legend about mighty dragons, the origin of the Seeteufel is shrouded in mystery. It is known to be the brainchild of Director of Engineering Alois Loedinge of the Kiel Torpedo Laboratory. Apparently, inspired by staring at the sun too long, Loedinge believed that applying caterpillar treads to a miniature submarine would dramatically improve its flexibility as a military asset. Loedinge's bizarre dream became known as Project Loedinge, perhaps because no other engineer would put his name to it. The experimental designs were originally known as the "Elefant," but this was discarded in favor of "Seeteufel."

Most of the parts for the prototype Seeteufel were manufactured at the Kiel facility, and the vehicle was completed, but engineless, by May 1944. Delays in both the diesel and the electric production engines for the Seeteufel precluded a fully completed trial run. In lieu of these two engines, an 80-horsepower Opel gasoline-burning truck engine was installed in the prototype, along with a 30-horsepower electric engine. Though obviously underpowered, the Seeteufel managed to achieve speeds approaching its projected baselines during this trial run. A submerged depth of 20 meters was successfully attempted, and the vehicle proved capable of entering and exiting the water under its own power.

Unfortunately, the treads used were far too narrow for a vehicle of the Seeteufel's weight and size. Maneuvering on land had to be conducted very carefully, and the small surface area of the treads made them prone to being thrown, as well as likely to damage paved surfaces. A redesign before production was likely. Despite the relative successes of the Seeteufel during testing, the vehicle was given a very low development priority. A production order was placed with a car manufacturer in Bremen, but production never actually started.

The prototype Seeteufel was destroyed in 1945 at a training camp near Lübeck, to prevent it from falling into the hands of the nefarious British.

Technical Mumbo Jumbo

The 250-horsepower marine diesel and 100-horsepower electric motor for the Seeteufel were certainly within the realm of feasibility, even if they were not readily available when the prototype was produced. They did not give the small submarine impressive speed performance, but the Seeteufel had proved to be very maneuverable in the water. With the production engines, it would have at least functioned as an adequate U-boat.

Armed with a pair of underslung 53.3cm torpedoes, the Seeteufel would have certainly been able to sink an enemy vessel if it managed to achieve surprise. These torpedoes would have most likely been the T2 rather than more advanced types that required a submarine to fire and then dive to depths beyond the capabilities of the Seeteufel. The torpedoes could be replaced with naval mines for mine-laying operations, although with only two, this would be a bit like an astronaut throwing a rock and hoping to hit Jupiter.

One interesting feature of the Seeteufel's construction was the inclusion of a Perspex dome for the driver to use when operating at snorkel depth. In this way, the submarine could be piloted much as a surface vessel by a single driver. The driver communicated by intercom with the machinist in the cramped engine closet. Air filtration was provided by the Dräger air filtration system.

The exact cargo capability of the Seeteufel is not known, but estimated at four people in addition to the crew or roughly 400 kilograms of cargo. Because of the vessel's already diminutive size (for a submarine), the few amenities included during normal operations would have to be ditched to accommodate passengers or cargo. Say hello to a few commandos and say good-bye to fun things like escape equipment, fire extinguishers, food, fresh water, and room to move your arms.

Analysis

The Seeteufel was ridiculous. Its tank treads were far too narrow to make it an effective tracked vehicle on the land, and its performance as a submarine was only slightly better. While driving, it would have been a gigantic target for anything more suited to terrestrial combat, such as a car or a baby with a rock. Just picture for a moment the sheer joy of driving something that is almost 14 meters in length and as slow as a bicycle when the sky is swarming with hostile aircraft. With a single machine gun as its armament, the poorly maneuverable Seeteufel would have likely fallen victim to a lone infantryman with one hand grenade.

When the Seeteufel took to the water, it was barely better. Able to operate for less than two days, incapable of delivering any significant commando or raiding force, and armed with only two mines or two torpedoes, it would have probably had a very short and violent life. The surprise achieved by being able to deploy it anywhere would have been negated by the aircraft that would have almost certainly spotted a 13.5-meter-long submarine driving toward the coast. Even if it managed to achieve the surprise for which it was intended, it would have been little better than a suicide vehicle. Torpedoes fired and presence revealed, almost any military vessel could have sunk the poor Seeteufel, and aircraft would have ruined its day even more quickly.

Exacerbating all these problems even further, the Seeteufel would have been a very inappropriately expensive vehicle to produce. It was large, required specialty engines for the production model, and assembly of virtually all its components would have to be custom. With most German naval industry devoted to U-boats and small surface vessels, by the point the Seeteufel would have entered service, the changeover in production would have just robbed production from some much more worthy project. On the positive side, the Seeteufel only required two crewmen, so that might have at least kept casualties down.

Hypothetical Deployment History

Five Seeteufel boats entered production in August 1944. Three were completed in October of that year, and the remaining two were completed in November. Bad weather and frequent Allied bombing prevented their deployment until February 1945. The miniature submarines were transferred west using the Kaiser-Wilhelm-Kanal and on February 6 all five boats were deployed in the North Sea. Four of the boats attempted an attack on an Allied convoy near Holland. While they managed to cripple the British light cruiser HMS *Gauntlet*, all four Seeteufel boats were subsequently sunk by destroyers operating in the area.

The fifth Seeteufel boat, U-768 *Schildkroete*, experienced electrical motor failure less than an hour out to sea and was forced to return to land for repairs. On February 9, it was put back to sea and was almost immediately sighted by a British spotter aircraft. Dogged by naval bombers and Allied surface vessels, the *Schildkroete* was unable to mount an effective attack run on any enemy ships. It returned to land in the cover of darkness on the night of February 10 and managed to make contact with a retreating force of the Waffen-SS.

The *Schildkroete* was repaired and refueled to the best abilities of the failing logistics of the Reich. After conferring with High Command, it was decided on February 18 that it would be used to deliver a team of commandos behind enemy lines. Only four passengers could be crammed inside the *Schildkroete*, and these commandos were tasked with assassinating a German mayor who was assisting the Americans in occupied western Germany.

Schildkroete put out to sea on the evening of February 22, but the seas were too rough, and it was taking on water. It returned to land and was repaired by February 24. It entered the North Sea that night and managed to make fair progress at snorkel depth. At dawn, it was spotted by an American convoy, and an hour later *Schildkroete* was forced to dive to avoid enemy aircraft and Canadian torpedo boats.

In the late afternoon, *Schildkroete* took advantage of a seeming lull in Allied air patrols and drove into the Rhine for shelter. That night, the *Schildkroete*'s pilot, Hans Neumann, made the disastrous decision to move overland under cover of dark. Moving southwest, the vehicle ran directly into the northern flank of Canadian forces participating in Operation Blockbuster. *Schildkroete* almost immediately came under small arms fire from a Canadian police unit, although it managed to repulse this attack with its machine gun and assistance from the four commandos.

The commandos attempted to disperse, but were caught hours later. Allied armored vehicles made an effort to encircle the *Schildkroete* and capture it intact, but as the vehicle attempted to trundle away, an overeager Firefly gunner hit the Seeteufel with an antitank round. Both crewmen were killed, and the vehicle was gutted by fire.

What Fight Have Been

6:12 A.M., February 26, 1945
Operation Blockbuster, Lincoln and Welland Regiment, First Battalion
6 Kilometers Northwest of the Hochwald Gap

"Poking around Project Cyclone," said the American in a First Infantry Division lieutenant's dress uniform as he tossed a folder onto the dining room table.

"Shouldn't you be with your division?" R.E. Lincoln said with a grin and reached for his pipe, then realized they had confiscated it along with his notebooks.

"Spelunking at the London Gun site," the man tossed another folder onto the table. "That got you sent up to Patton. I believe he threatened to shoot you before sending you back toward the Channel coast."

"That incident was blown totally out of proportion."

"We thought we were rid of you when we shipped you back to England," another folder joined the growing pile, "but you went on that little sight-seeing flight with the RAF and your plane had to put down . . . where was it?"

"Tantoville."

"Tantoville." The faux-lieutenant opened the final folder. "That was three goddamn days ago. How did you get mixed up with the Canadians that fast?"

"A reporter never reveals his methods." R.E. sipped at the tepid cup of tea his host had so generously provided.

"That's a magician." The man flipped the last folder closed and tossed it onto the pile. "Hell, maybe the OSS should hire you."

"Is the pay good?" The question prompted the otherwise unflappable lieutenant to furrow his brow.

"The question now," the man leaned in, "is what does the United States government do with a bear that keeps getting caught with his paw in the beehive?"

"You could always frog march me in front of a wall and be done with me."

"Cute." The man pulled his glasses from his face and pinched the bridge of his nose. "Unfortunately for my sanity, the United States government does not employ Gestapo methods, even on pests as persistent as you."

"What then?"

"What then?" the man echoed the question. "Ground transport has been arranged for you right back to Tantoville. From there, it's Scotland and a nice long voyage on a passenger liner."

"That's all, then?"

"Your war is over, Mister Lincoln." The man finally smiled. "A very uncomfortable truck will be arriving in about six hours to take you out of this theater. Who knows, maybe you'll find your way to the Pacific and make trouble for some poor s—"

There was a sudden rattle of gunfire outside the house that the not-lieutenant had turned into his interrogation room.

"Stay here," the man said as he drew his sidearm and disappeared out the door.

R.E. had absolutely no intention of staying "here." He snatched up the satchel containing his confiscated possessions and followed his captor out the back door of the house. He emerged into chaos. Bullets were shivering the snow-dusted pines near the outskirts of the village, and he could hear the creaking of tank treads. The erratic crackle of Canadian carbines was overwhelmed by a canvas-ripping burst from a German machine gun.

R.E. ducked around the side of the house. The Canadian military police attached to the Lincoln and Welland Regiment were ducking behind what cover they could find. They looked like armed beekeepers in their bulky white winter gear with snow-cloths draped over their doughboy helmets. There was a snap of timbers and the enemy tank burst into the main thoroughfare, such as it was. R.E.'s fear of being confronted by a roaring Panzer was replaced by total bewilderment as a German submarine smashed through the last of the pines and onto the dirt road. It would have been laughable, but he watched as a Canadian with a PIAT to his shoulder was cut down by machine gun fire. The blood bloomed on the poor man's white uniform as he staggered back and then toppled over. A grenade popped and shrapnel sparked off the curved flank of the bizarre machine.

"Goddammit, Lincoln!" The not-lieutenant grabbed Lincoln from behind and yanked him around the corner and back into the house.

"What the Christ almighty was that?"

"The ah, Panzer Eight." The man cranked a field telephone, "HQ, HQ. This is station nine, enemy tanks advancing on our position from the northeast. Requesting armor support."

Two Canadians stomped through the back door carrying a Browning machine gun and boxes of ammunition. They nodded deferentially to the not-lieutenant as they trundled past him toward the other side of the house. The submarine-tank's machine gun fired once again, shattering glass and tearing ragged holes through the walls of the dining room. R.E. felt a tug on his hip and fell to the floor.

"I'm shot!" he yelled and rolled onto his other side trying to get a look at the bullet hole.

There was a neat hole blasted through the rucksack hanging over his shoulder. He opened the sack and peered inside. His pipe was shattered.

"My pipe is shot!" he yelled, even more upset than before.

"Keep your head down, you idiot." The not-lieutenant was flattened on the floor.

"It took me fifteen years to season that pipe."

Another burst of gunfire tore through the walls and was answered by the deafening roar of the Browning firing from within the house.

Chapter 19

Submarine-Launched Rockets

Overview

Nazi Germany equipped with a functional atomic weapon is a scary thing. The concept is so scary that it has appeared in several really bad time-travel movies and probably ten times as many pulp-action novels. I am fairly certain that I have even seen a quilt depicting the Nazis with an atomic weapon. However, getting the bomb was only half of the proverbial battle. The Germans still had the problem of getting the bomb to go somewhere that was useful before it exploded. They did not possess a strategic bomber capable of carrying an atomic bomb even half the size of the American Fat Man implosion bomb.

A suicide aircraft could have conceivably been rigged to carry the bomb strapped beneath it to London or perhaps Moscow, but atomic

	Super V-2	Prüfstand XII
Category:	Modified V-2 rocket	Towed submersible rocket barge
Phase of Development:	Theoretical—based on immediate postwar V-2 and A9 developments	Prototype testing
Development Start:	n/a	1944
Development Team:	Wernher von Braun	Vulkanwerft Stettin Facility
Payload:	2,000 km Diebner atomic device	One V-2 or modified V-2 rocket
Fuel:	Nitric acid/kerosene	Unpowered
Length:	14.5 m	
Wingspan:	3.6 m	
Weight:	21,000 kg	500 metric tons (displacement)
Thrust:	55,000 kg of thrust	n/a
Range:	100 km	Limited only by submarine range

bombs are notoriously fragile devices and the Diebner atomic device might not have taken a liking to being wedged under a giant seaplane. Such a suicide weapon is too far outside the realm of fact to really devote much time to in this book. If you would like to, you can put this book down for a moment, close your eyes, and envision such an attack using the limitless book titled *Your Imagination*.

The real juicy target for Germany—the target it had created all manner of fanciful bombing maps and unusual prototype aircraft to attack—was New York City. Its plans mostly hinged on aircraft and weapons that could be produced in a series and sent in large formations to inflict significant damage. With an atomic bomb, the Nazis only required a single delivery mechanism.

The simplest means of attacking the United States was to load the atomic bomb onto a disguised merchant vessel and sail it to New York City. In Albert Einstein's famous letter to President Franklin D. Roosevelt about the feasibility of an atomic weapon, he suggested such a method for the United States to deliver an atomic bomb to a port city. Although this plot would involve no additional technical innovation, it was also quite risky. It required traversing thousands of kilometers of ocean and hoping that the ship was not intercepted and boarded by the British or Americans. This method was also a guaranteed death sentence for the crew of the transport vessel. Although the Germans were not actually averse to suicide weapons, they liked to tell themselves that they were.

Another means for attacking the U.S. eastern seaboard existed in a scheme cooked up by a German politician and circulated among rocket scientists at Peenemünde. This plan called for a V-2 rocket to be placed inside a water-tight container and towed by submarine to within range of New York City. This plan ran into technical problems and was temporarily halted. Months later, for unknown reasons, the plan was adopted as a fully operational development project. Did the Germans believe they were close enough to developing an atomic bomb that such a project should be given a second life, or had they simply run out of ideas? No, I'm asking you.

Another obstacle remained in the path of the Germans, even if their missile-in-a-bottle design had worked: the V-2 was not capable of mounting a roughly 2-ton warhead. The solution to this problem can be found wedged in between Wernher von Braun's A9 (covered in chapter 10) and the V-2, but it was not developed until after World War II, and it was developed by *France*.

Development History

The Super V-2

The three greatest deficiencies of Braun's V-2 ballistic missiles were their poor accuracy, their volatile fuels, and their poor range. The V-2 was guided either by an internal analog computation device or a radio guidance beam. Neither method produced reliable accuracy greater than a circular error probable (CEP) of 6 kilometers. That means that on average, half the V-2 rockets fired would land within a 6-kilometer circle around their intended targets. By comparison, modern strategic missiles have a CEP measured in single-digit meters around a target with ranges thirty times that of the V-2 rocket. A major contributing factor to the V-2's poor accuracy was the instability of the rocket itself. The CEP of a weapon tends to go down dramatically when 10 to 20 percent of your missiles explode or crash within sight of the launch pad. Despite worsening conditions in Germany during the closing years of the war, the accuracy of the V-2 climbed slowly as the myriad technical flaws were worked out of the production models in service.

Making the V-2 more stable required a switch to a less volatile fuel and an increase in the quality control during the manufacturing process. The former could be achieved, but the rockets were being constructed largely by slave laborers working in mountainside bunkers. You can only threaten slave laborers with horrible death so many times before their quality level stops rising. The Germans had also developed a number of cutting-edge guidance systems that might have improved the accuracy of the V-2. Unfortunately, most of these developments were intended for weapons that required a constant line of sight on the target. Adapting the remaining systems, such as wire-guidance and weapon-mounted cameras, was nearly impossible for a weapon with a ballistic trajectory. The solution to this problem involved a number of technical advancements unavailable to the Germans at the time, including electronic computers, laser guidance, and satellite guidance systems.

The standard V-2 had a maximum range of approximately 320 kilometers. Braun worked on a number of ways to extend the range and fuel capacity of the rocket, including the use of multiple stages. Braun explored this concept with the A9/A10 two-stage rocket, as well as the even more complex rocket covered in chapter 10. The only effective way for a rocket to achieve the range needed to become truly intercontinental is to leave the earth's atmosphere. Germany's development of a submarine rocket launcher was an attempt to address this issue without the need to dramatically increase the cost and complexity of the rocket. Unfortunately, one of the obstacles facing this effort was the volatility of the V-2's primary fuels.

The V-2 was fueled by A-Stoff, which was a mixture of 75 percent ethanol and 25 percent water, and B-Stoff, which was liquid oxygen that had to be stored at minus 183 degrees Celsius. The liquid oxygen required careful storage and high-energy refrigeration. Fuel trucks loaded with A-Stoff were veritable bombs and would lose hundreds of liters of fuel to evaporation during the fueling process. A fueled V-2 rocket could remain ready to fire for a matter of a few hours, not the days and weeks that would be required to transport the rocket by submarine to the United States.

A project was already well into development at Peenemünde that could provide the technological solution for the fuel storage question. In 1943, Walter Thiel, who had played a major role in designing the V-2 rocket engine, was tasked with designing the engine for a new antiaircraft rocket called the "Wasserfall." Thiel was killed during a bombing raid in August 1943, but he managed to cook up an engine that used vinyl isobutyl ether (Visol) and SV-Stoff, which was a mixture of 90 percent nitric acid and 10 percent sulfuric acid. That may sound just as bad as the V-2's rocket fuel, but as long as the two fuels were kept separated within the rocket's two fuel tanks, they could remain stable for months on end. The Wasserfall also incorporated a number of safety features that would prevent explosions on the launch pad and premature fuel mixing. The missile entered prototype launch testing in 1944 and by January 1945, the Wasserfall had reached the final preproduction phase.

The technology developed in the Wasserfall could be scaled up with only moderate difficulty to be used with a larger rocket like the V-2. Postwar rockets such as France's Super V-2 incorporated very similar fuel systems on a scale commensurate with the V-2. The French Super V-2 utilized a mixture of nitric acid and kerosene (jet fuel), was very similar in size and appearance to the V-2, had a range of over 1,000 kilometers, and could mount warheads roughly 25 percent larger than the V-2.

A final issue faced the designers of a rocket being created specifically to mount an atomic warhead. Based on Kurt Diebner's design and the technology available at the time, it would have been possible to develop an atomic bomb weighing approximately 2 metric tons. This was more than twice the payload capacity of a V-2 rocket and exactly twice that of the Super V-2 developed by France following the war.

Doubling the payload capacity of a rocket of similar size to the V-2 would have involved scaling up the rocket motor within the missile, not a particularly easy task, and reducing the fuel capacity. It would not be possible to double the thrust of a missile without enlarging it dramatically. A V-2–sized rocket would have a reduced velocity and, as a direct result, a reduced range. Based on similar rockets, I estimate a maximum 100-kilometer range for a V-2 with the aforementioned modifications and a 2-ton atomic warhead. I am not some sort of physics genius or rocket brainiac, so please do not cite this figure as authoritative.

Prüfstand XII

From 1943 through to the end of the war, Peenemünde was involved in developing submarine-launched rockets. This involvement of high-level rocketry experts began after a successful test firing in May 1942 of 21-centimeter artillery rockets launched from the deck of a submarine. Though inelegant, this experiment proved that rockets fired from beneath the surface of the water did not suffer a noticeable degradation in performance.

The immediate result of this was a project codenamed Ursel to design a torpedo tube–launched missile for antiship purposes. This project was headed by Ernst Steinhoff, a Kriegsmarine expert, and underwent extensive tests on Lake Toplitz throughout 1944. The Ursel weapon underwent many design changes, and by early 1945 one of the new Type XXI U-boats had been fitted with a modified torpedo tube designed specifically for firing the missile. The weapon never went into service, primarily because the accuracy required to hit a vessel on the surface from 3,000 meters exceeded the available technology, but also because the rockets had a bad habit of exploding immediately after being launched.

In 1943, Director Otto Lafferenez of the German Labor Front cooked up his own scheme in which a V-2 rocket would be placed inside a water-tight vessel of similar shape and towed behind a submarine to a launch location. Based on this suggestion, the SS military commander at Peenemünde put the scientists to work developing the idea.

The barges they designed consisted of a large hollow chamber containing the missile and a fairly elaborate exhaust redirection system. Beneath this was a small chamber for missile control and ballast tanks that could be used to trim the barge for either vertical or horizontal positioning. It would be towed horizontally and then the tanks would be flooded and the barge would trim to a vertical firing position. Hatches would open at the top, the rocket would be launched, and the unfortunate officer in charge of launching the rocket would (hopefully) survive the process, thanks to the exhaust venting.

Development of the barge ceased early in 1944 and then resumed for unknown reasons near the end of the same year. The cessation was probably a result of complications with the fuel source of the V-2 and the inevitable conclusion that the rocket's short shelf life meant towing one across the Atlantic was unfeasible. Development of the barge resumed in late 1944. Some historians believe this was a result of a change in target from New York to England, but I do not share that opinion. V-2 rockets fell on England almost until the very last days of the war without the need for a submarine-launch platform. My belief is that development with the Wasserfall held the promise of a rocket motor for the V-2 that could be stored for long periods. If recent revelations about Germany's atomic bomb program are proven out, then this may have also given the Germans an incentive to continue the project.

Whatever the real motivation, a contract was granted to Vulkanwerft Shipyard in Stettin (now Szczecin in Poland) to complete the designs and consult with rocket experts at Peenemünde. Construction of the test beds began in late 1944, with tests following in early 1945. One, full-scale prototype was completed and tested, although these tests did not include a test firing of the rocket. These prototypes and plans for the barge fell into the hands of the Soviet Union. The Russians went on to develop this design into the Golem submarine-towed launcher, with the assistance of some of the experts originally participating in the German project.

Technical Mumbo Jumbo

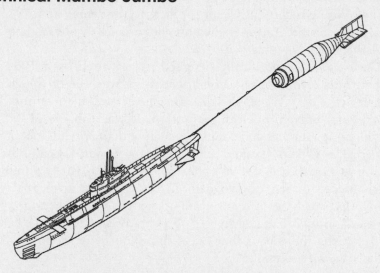

A Super V-2 rocket equipped with the Diebner bomb prepares for launch from a Prüfstand XII rocket cylinder.

The hypothetical German Super V-2 utilized an engine functionally identical to the Wasserfall, but scaled up to provide thrust for a missile with a total weight of 21 metric tons. The internal tanks of SV-Stoff and Visol had a reduced storage capacity and resulted in a matching reduction in the range of the rocket to roughly 100 kilometers. The 2,000-kilogram Diebner implosion fusion/fission bomb was mounted in place of a conventional charge behind a nosecone containing a simple radar altimeter. The altimeter would trigger a detonation of the Diebner bomb at a preset altitude, reducing the chances of a fizzle and increasing the damage potential.

The Prüfstand XII barge displaced 500 metric tons and was constructed as a large pressure hull approximately 25 meters in length. The barge's primary chamber contained the rocket and its launching equipment and was topped by a split hatch that could be electrically opened. A thick bulkhead separated the rocket chamber from the launch crew's control chamber, and exhaust systems in the primary chamber were positioned to redirect exhaust to emerge out of the open hatch. Beneath the control chamber was the ballast system used to achieve neutral buoyancy during horizontal travel and then flooded to rotate the barge into an upright firing position.

Diagrams of the design indicate that it was meant to be fired at the surface. Ursel tests conducted at Lake Toplitz demonstrated the practicality of firing rockets using similar methods at depths up to 100 meters. Modern submarine-launched missiles are nearly always launched while the vessel is submerged.

The barge was specifically designed to be towed by a Type XXI U-boat. This revolutionary submarine design was one of the greatest achievements of naval engineering during the twentieth century, perhaps second only to nuclear propulsion. It was capable of extreme long-distance journeys and could travel more than 350 kilometers submerged. The Type XXI could remain submerged for days and did not have to surface to recharge its batteries, making it virtually immune to attack aircraft during long voyages. It was also deep-dive capable, although this was of less use for evading enemy vessels when the rocket barge was in tow. The first Type XXI U-boats entered service early in 1945, and by the end of the war, a thousand more were in various stages of construction.

Variants

The obvious variant would be to use a conventional V-2 rocket in place of the hypothetical German-built Super V-2. Such a rocket could be equipped either with a normal payload or a chemical warhead. Some evidence exists that the Germans were in the process of creating a "doomsday stockpile" of chemical-equipped V-2 rockets at a munitions factory in Espelkamp. Though many rockets were found at this facility—a facility known to produce chemical artillery shells—no V-2s had been loaded with chemical agents.

Analysis

This chapter is fairly speculative compared to the other chapters in this book. It takes for granted recent revelations about the German atomic bomb, and it projects a refined version of the V-2 that was not actually under development. The creation of the Super V-2 would have represented a project nearly as expensive and time consuming as any other major offshoot of V-2 development. It would take the type of effort that went into the Wasserfall rocket, only compounded by the necessities of preparing it for sea-launch. The rocket would not have been more accurate than the V-2 (if anything, it would have been somewhat less accurate), although this was obviously offset by the sheer destructive force of its atomic payload. The process of combining something elaborate and complex such as an early ballistic missile with something even more complex such as a prototype atomic weapon would have been a logistical and technical nightmare.

Getting the weapon into firing range of New York City was another daunting undertaking for the Germans. The Type XXI might have been adept at evading incidental sightings, but the mission required the submarine to get within range of well-traveled shipping lanes and active coastal patrol areas. By early 1945, the United States was confident in victory over Germany, but still very wary of a rocket attack on the East Coast. The Germans had spent much of 1944 playing to this fear by mentioning the use of V-1 rockets against distant enemies in various propaganda broadcasts. In this environment of heightened alert, the submarine would have to move to within 100 kilometers of New York City, one of the most defended ports in the United States.

The detonation of the 1 kiloton Diebner device in or near New York City would have been a disaster unparalleled in U.S. history. Tens of thousands would be killed almost immediately and well over a hundred thousand would likely expire in the first day from radiation. If the bomb detonated above Washington Square Park in New York City, it would destroy virtually everything within a kilometer radius. That means everything south of Twenty-third Street, west all the way to the Hudson, north of Canal Street, and all the way to the edge of the Lower East Side would be in ruins.

Large buildings would be toppled and gutted, smaller buildings would be in ruins or gone entirely. Lesser damage from the blast would reach all the way north to Central Park and east to Queens. Fires would rage out of control as far away as New Jersey and those trapped on Manhattan Island would die by the thousands from their injuries and radiation poisoning. A plume of radioactive fallout would stretch dozens of kilometers across the East River and cancer would afflict hundreds of thousands in the following years.

Perhaps worst of all, the submarine responsible would likely be able to escape in the aftermath of a successful attack, making its way either back to Germany or to a neutral port in South America. Although the blow dealt to the United States would have a terrible impact on the nation, it would hardly result in the victory of Germany. The earliest conceivable period during which the submarine might depart would have been March 1945. By the time the attack was launched, it would have been well into April, and Adolf Hitler might very well have been dead by his own hand.

Hypothetical Deployment History

Kurt Diebner's Research Center E produced two functional atomic weapons by the end of February 1945. The Vulkanwerft facilities in Stettin constructed and fitted a single launch barge to a Type XXI U-boat (U-2526) in mid-February 1945 and transferred this vessel to Kiel at the end of February. One atomic device, designated Sigurd after the dragon slayer who offed Fafnir in *Beowulf* and other ancient texts, was relocated to Kiel for mounting within the rocket. The Super V-2 rocket, however, was delayed by U.S. advances and had to be smuggled to Kiel in early March by a daring operation using stolen American transport trucks.

With the situation rapidly deteriorating in Germany, the U-boat set sail for New York City in mid-March. The crew was under strict orders to maintain radio silence and not attempt to contact Berlin. This was a Fuehrer order given specifically to prevent a cancellation of the attack, in the event that Berlin fell before it arrived at its destination. On April 23—just days before Hitler would die by his own hand—U-2526 surfaced less than 100 kilometers from Manhattan Island. A passing passenger vessel's crew spotted the U-boat almost immediately, but their ship was unarmed, and they could do little other than radio the sighting to the harbor. Nearby naval vessels began to make their way to the U-boat's location, but they were still many kilometers away when the Super V-2 was launched.

The world entered the nuclear age at 9:54 A.M. on April 23, when the Diebner atomic device detonated 300 meters above ground over New York City. It was a near-perfect hit, considering the poor accuracy of the rocket, and it devastated the city. The immediate death toll was estimated at 58,000 and more than 120,000 died in the following 48 hours. Bridges and harbor facilities were in ruins and fire brigades struggled to control the conflagration raging on the mainland. The navy was forced to evacuate the survivors from the island using a fleet of commandeered vessels that would come to be compared to the fleet used by the British to evacuate Dunkirk.

The U-2526 escaped the immediate aftermath of the attack, but was pursued mercilessly by American aircraft and destroyers. It was struck hard by aerial depth charges on April 26 and was ultimately scuttled by its crew. The survivors of the sinking were picked up within hours by the U.S. Navy. They were put on trial and executed by hanging two days later. The offices of the *New York Times*, relocated to Albany temporarily, ran a front-page photograph of the captain hanging along with the headline: REVENGE! Despite vociferous disagreement from his military advisors, President Franklin D. Roosevelt insisted on reserving America's own atomic bomb for use against Japan.

Germany had one final surprise for the world. On April 30, 1945, the second of Diebner's atomic devices was detonated at ground level above the Fuehrerbunker. The German history books would mark it as Hitler's final betrayal of the German people. Thousands of German soldiers and civilians and over 15,000 Soviet soldiers perished.

What Fight Have Been

9:47 A.M., April 23, 1945
Aboard the Passenger Liner *Magnanimous*
102 Kilometers Northeast of New York City

R. E. Lincoln tapped his new and inferior pipe out over the rail and watched the charred tobacco remnants cascade down into the smooth surface of the Atlantic. It was a beautiful day, perhaps the finest since they had set sail from England, and if the captain's bulletin was to be believed, he would be walking the streets of Manhattan that afternoon. He looked back from the foredeck at the length of the ship. The twin stacks were chugging out white smoke into the crisp morning air, and he could make out the bustling afterdeck. He preferred to enjoy a good smoke and a cup of coffee up at the front. Just a few busy crewmen to keep him company, but he liked the crew, and he liked the ship. The accommodations were far nicer than freezing his stones off aboard a glorified iceberg.

"Fine day," one of the deck hands commented absently as he coiled rope around his elbow and hand.

R.E. smiled and nodded in the deck hand's direction, then turned his attention back out to the Atlantic. He sipped his coffee and savored the way it warmed his stomach. The nip of whiskey in it didn't hurt either. He was about to turn back and head for his cabin when he spotted a strange wave breaking to the southwest. It seemed to keep breaking in the same place and then, after a few moments' observation, it took on an unusual cylindrical shape.

"Come have a look at this," he said as he gestured out to sea. The deck hand joined him at the rail.

"That's just a—" the words froze in the crewman's mouth.

"That's a goddamn submarine!" R.E. finished as he watched the shape of the conning tower became apparent.

"Submarine!" The crewman shouted with all his lungs and dashed toward the superstructure.

The shout became a chorus as the cry spread among the crewmen on the vessel. R.E. simply watched from his position at the rail as more and more of the submarine became visible. A second and more unusual shape appeared in the water a hundred or so meters behind the submarine. It looked at first like a great sewer lid had been set into the ocean, but as they neared and then passed the stationary submarine, it began to open. Two huge hinged doors swung open and rained water down into the waves lapping at their base. Crewmen of the U-boat appeared at the conning tower. A few waved or saluted the ship. What little fear R.E. still had of dying gradually faded.

By then, passengers had gathered all along the rail and were surrounding R.E. and jostling one another for a better view.

"Probably going to surrender," a British man in a sharp suit commented. "Jerry's finished."

"What's that about?" A woman pointed to the peculiar doors that finally banged all the way open with the help of gravity.

Theories were the topic of gossip among the passengers as the German submarine began to recede in the distance. Abruptly, and within absolute certainty, R.E. knew what it was.

"A missile," he whispered to himself, recalling his own look at a captured German rocket in France.

"What's that then?" the British gentleman asked.

"Oh God, New York." R.E. began to shove toward the crew entryway. "A missile! It's going to launch a missile!"

His conclusion was proven out a moment later when a deep vibrating rumble could be heard and felt. With seeming slowness, the terrible rocket was birthed out of the sea and into the air atop a thick column of smoke and fire. It lifted higher, curving almost imperceptibly toward the west. The higher it flew, the more apparent its arc became. By then, the passengers were shrieking with horror. Some were fearful that the rocket might crash down on *Magnanimous*, others rightly realized that it was bound for New York City.

They followed its path down, after the rocket had gone silent but still trailed out smoke. By then, New York was faintly visible in the distance, not seen in detail, but a presence at the very curve of the horizon. It disappeared into that faint shape.

"Well that's it then," someone said near R.E. "Sad business."

A light appeared, at first like a bright spotlight and then it grew, terribly fast, in both size and intensity. Some stared directly into the light, others turned away in fear or pain. A ball of fire spread out on the horizon, and as it began to rise into the sky it took on the roiling shape of a mushroom. R.E. knew it must be taller than the Empire State Building to be seen so clearly. A wave radiated from New York City across the surface of the ocean, visible as a white spray racing toward them. It faded out long before it reached *Magnanimous*, but he saw enough to recognize an immense wave of pressure from the blast. Then came the sound, a crack, terribly loud, followed by a hideous freight-train rumble. Chaos erupted among the dumbstruck passengers as the rumble engulfed them for many seconds. Finally, it dulled to a roar and men, barely composed themselves, began to comfort sobbing women and hysterical children.

After some time, with the terrible cloud beginning to fold in on itself and come apart, R.E. found an isolated patch of railing. He packed his pipe and took a pad of paper and the last stub of a pencil from his jacket. With a detached eye, he began to make a careful record of what he saw.

Epilogue

8:58 A.M., January 2, 1946
Ames Aeronautical Laboratory
Sunnyvale, California

Major General Vernon Reese was a slightly paunchy man in his late fifties with a nebbish look and a nervous smile that would break out spontaneously at the end of a sentence. He did not seem the sort of man the U.S. Army would pick to hold a press conference. He looked pitifully small standing on the lectern at the rear of the hangar, and the eye was naturally drawn away from him to the sleek American fighter planes on display just behind him.

"Thank you all for coming out today." Reese looked up from his notes and grinned, then quickly looked back down at the lectern. "The National Advisory Committee for Aeronautics has set two major goals for the coming decade. We believe both of these goals to be within the reach of the greatest and most prosperous nation on earth. Our first and most important goal is the development of a rocket vehicle capable of carrying a man into space. Our experts will have the full cooperation of a number of experienced European scientists as we move toward this goal."

Major General Reese looked up and grinned again. Then he continued to read from the cards, but his words were drowned out by the applause echoing in the hangar. Reese seemed baffled that he was receiving the applause.

"Our second goal is to establish a permanent base in orbit around the earth. This will be a place for our space explorers to conduct experiments and explore the outer reaches of our solar system. One day, Americans will venture far beyond the earth to the moon, Mars, and the edge of known space."

Reese was met with more applause. R. E. Lincoln yawned and stretched in his chair somewhere near the back of the press seating. For R.E., writing a story about a staged event like this would be akin to a photographer taking a picture of someone's painting. The NACA had written this story, and his paper had sent him to copy it.

Reese droned on about "grand visions" and "new and exciting technologies" for nearly half an hour before getting to the gathered panel of experts. R.E. was a bit surprised when the floor was immediately opened to questions, but as soon as the panel was introduced, he knew he had something to ask. None other than Wernher von Braun was sitting on that panel. If the rumors about Germany's rocket program were true, R.E. had a prime opportunity to turn a nonstory into a real story. At the very least, he'd get a chance to embarrass Braun's military handlers.

The reporters with the big names and the impeccable government relationships were in the front rows. They were called on first.

"What dangers might confront a space explorer?" one reporter asked.

"Do you think we will encounter creatures from outer space?" another piped in when his name was called.

R.E. chuckled quietly. Those were two of the best questions; the rest ran the gamut from utterly inane to pointlessly esoteric. By the time Reese got around to acknowledging R.E.'s raised hand, the entire panel was looking a bit drained.

"Ah, yeah, my question is for Doctor Braun." Most were. "Doctor, I am sure everyone here is aware that Germany attempted to launch manned rockets into space during the war under the auspices of something called Project Valkyrie. It mentions in your biographical material that was handed out that this was the 'failed attempt' to put Germans into space. I was wondering, Doctor Braun, what exactly happened to Unterscharfuhrer Karl Matzig?"

Reese immediately covered Braun's microphone and leaned in to his ear to whisper. After several seconds, he uncovered the microphone and leaned forward.

"Herr Matzig was killed in our failed attempt to launch him into space," Braun said. "It was very tragic."

"I have seen photographs of him in—"

"Those have all been denounced as forgeries," Reese cut in. "Remember, please, that the magazine of which you speak was published by the German Propaganda Ministry. Next question."

"Oh, if I may ask one last follow-up."

"Be quick," Reese seethed.

"Doctor Braun, are you aware that the radar tracking and radio facilities at Kummersdorf kept extensive logs of all communications fr—"

"Forgeries," Reese cut in. "Thank you again to everyone for coming out today. The tours of our facility will begin in fifteen minutes. Help yourself to something to eat and drink."

Reese glared murder down at R.E. and then ushered the experts out as quickly as possible.

The journalists and visiting officials were broken down into manageable groups by the tour guides and told to leave their drinks on the tables in the hangar. Ames was a sprawling complex, and the tour was boring despite the surprising level of access given to the visitors. However, in the radio and telemetry center the guide hurried them past a door with a sign that read: RESTRICTED—TOP SECRET AND ABOVE ONLY. A few journalists joked about the door, so the tour guide explained that it was where they kept all the Russian space explorers. R.E. feigned disinterest.

As they were nearing the exit for the radio and telemetry center, R.E. whispered to the guide that he desperately had to go to the restroom. The guide pointed back the way they had come and gave him simple instructions to the restroom. She smiled and told him that they would wait for him to catch up.

The moment R.E. was out of sight, he took a right when he was told to take a left. Another right brought him to the long hallway that included the seemingly only off-limits room in the entire tour. He smiled and whistled as a pair of men in suits bustled past him. When he reached the door, he opened it without hesitation. The room inside was small and nearly empty. A folding table was set against the wall opposite the door. There were no chairs. Sitting on the table was a simple microphone and a radio receiver that appeared to be connected to a magnetic tape recorder. The reels of the recorder were turning, but there was no sound coming from the radio receiver.

R.E. stepped closer and inspected the radio. A simple toggle alternated between the tape recorder and the speaker of the radio receiver. He flipped the toggle.

"—ifteen days since you have contacted me." The voice was in German, wracked with emotion. "I am nearly out of water filtration chemicals. Please, you have promised me help."

There was a sigh followed by a long pause. Then came a strange squeaking noise distorted by the radio waves. It took several seconds for R.E. to realize the man was sobbing.

"I think I am going mad. I think I need to throw myself out into space, but I am a coward."

R.E. tentatively reached a finger out to the transmit button on the microphone stand.

"I wonder where Magda has gone. You say she is not to be found, but I cannot give up the hope that she is still alive. I dream—"

"Hello," R.E. spoke into the microphone. "Who am I talking to?"

"—she holds me in her arms. I . . . I didn't bring a photograph. I don't know if the face I remember is hers or—"

R.E. heard his "hello" echo over the radio and then silence for several seconds.

"Is this Franklin!? Doctor Peterson!?" The voice replied so happily that it seemed more pitiful than the man's despair.

"No, my name is R. E. Lincoln. I am a reporter in New York City. Are you Oberststurmfuhrer Matzig?"

For several seconds the radio crackled without a reply.

"No, Oberststurmführer Matzig died more than a month ago. My name is Manfred Schafer. I am—was—an Unterscharführer. That does not matter anymore. You can call me Manny. That is what Franklin calls me."

"Hello, Manny."

Another pause.

"Hello, Arty Lincoln. You say you are from New York? I am so sorry about New York. I always thought America was a good country."

"It's okay, Manny." R.E. flashed on a memory of Pforzheim utterly consumed by fire. "You guys started the darn thing, but I reckon we had something coming our way for some of the stuff we did."

Silence.

"Well, I am very glad there is peace now. Are you going to write a story about me?"

R.E. closed his eyes and paused to reflect on the question.

"Yes, Manny," he finally answered. "Yes, I am going to write a story about you."

A long pause.

"This is great, Arty Lincoln!"

Published Sources *(Selected)*

Bean, T., and W. Fowler. *Russian Tanks of World War II*. St. Paul, MN: MBI, 2002.

Beevor, A. *Stalingrad*. New York: Penguin, 1999.

Beevor, A. *The Fall of Berlin 1945*. New York: Penguin, 2003.

Breuer, W. B. *Secret Weapons of World War II*. New York: John Wiley & Sons, 2000.

Chamberlain, P., H. Doyle, and T. Jents. *Encyclopedia of German Tanks of World War II*. London: Arms and Armour Press, 1993.

Doyle, H., and T. Jentz. *Panther Variants*. Oxford, UK: Osprey, 1997.

Georg, F. *Hitler's Miracle Weapons*. Solihull, UK: Helion, 2003.

Griehl, M. *Jet Planes of the Third Reich*. Sturbridge, MA: Monogram Aviation Publications, 1998.

Griehl, M. *Luftwaffe over America*. London: Greenhill Books, 2004.

Herwig, D., and H. Rode. *Luftwaffe Secret Projects: Strategic Bombers, 1935–1945*. Midland Leicester: Midland, 2000.

Lucas, J. *Das Reich: The Military Role of the Second SS Division.* London: Cassell, 1991.

Perrett, B. *German Light Panzers.* Oxford, UK: Osprey, 1998.

Perrett, B. *Panzerkampfwagen III.* Oxford, UK: Osprey, 1999.

Schick, W., and I. Meyer. *Luftwaffe Secret Projects: Fighters, 1939–1945.* Hinckley, UK: Midland, 2004.

Senich, P. R. *The German Assault Rifle, 1935–1945.* Boulder, CO: Paladin Press, 1987.

Acknowledgments

The Internet was the single most valuable tool in my research for this book, as I would guess it is for many other authors. I can't be sure, since they're not returning my calls. However, the Internet is a minefield of mistruths and rumors that often wasted as much of my time following false leads as was spent on good information. An interesting falsehood on the Internet will not receive the same scrutiny as something in print, and because of the speed of the medium, it will be reproduced again and again. This can give the impression of a number of independent sources, when all of these seemingly independent sources were using a few lines from a blog about pickles as their key source.

I stand on the shoulders of those authors and those researchers who went to military archives, translated internal memorandums, interviewed survivors, and examined the artifacts in person. I read their books, collected their facts, and tried to make them more interesting and exciting. I'm not apologizing, but I want the readers to understand that all the historians in the bibliography dealt with jet lag and Russian archival bureaucracy, and I dealt with e-mails, interlibrary loan, Amazon, and Google. When you're done reading this book, I highly recommend you check out some of the other books listed in the bibliography.

I owe an immense debt of gratitude to the people who have helped make this book possible. First and foremost, Mike Doscher and Josh Hass, who have turned an okay book into what I think is an amazing book with their incredible illustrations. Mike knew the material almost as well as I did, and he had a great eye for details and taking my text and turning it into an illustration. Josh simply stunned me with each and every one of his color illustrations. Both guys were a real pleasure to work with.

Jim Boswell was brought in to work with Josh Hass on the design of the front and back cover of this book, and they made a great team. Suji Allen helped design the interior layout. Jeremie Ruby-Strauss, my editor at Kensington, has been a great person to work with and very helpful throughout the process.

I also have to give a huge thanks to all the people out there on the Internet who run Web sites devoted to this sort of material. Dan Johnson from Luft '46 (www.luft46.com) maintains an immense archive of material on experimental German aircraft of World War II. The Axis History Factbook (www.axishistory.com), created by Marcus Wendel, is an amazing catalog of reference material on units, uniforms, and equipment of Axis forces. Information on the German navy at www.german-navy.de/ and www.u-boat.net was invaluable in writing this book. Web sites devoted to German armor like www.panzer-schreck.de/ and George Prada's www.achtungpanzer.com/ were great resources and a real inspiration for further research.

Information was sometimes found in the most unexpected places. M. Hofbauer's Geocities site about the X-7 Rotkäppchen had the most accurate and detailed information on the subject available on the Internet. The Web site of the International Hydrofoil Society (www.foils.org/), though not particularly easy on the eyes, was probably the single most reliable source for information when writing chapter 15 on the VS8 hydrofoil.

Finally, and most of all, I would like to thank dear Richard. Rich "Lowtax" Kyanka gave me the chance to write for Something Awful way back in 2001. Without that opportunity and his constant support and friendship, I doubt I would be where I am right now. Oh God, I don't know where I am right now! It's pitch black in here and it smells horrible! Why, Rich? Why did you put me in here!?

Index